My Wife
Her Shining Life

Dr. Jim Rosscup

SOJOURNER
PRESS

Contents

The Writer's Preface

THIS BOOK IS A tribute to God for what He can do in a life that yields to Him to do His will. The life surrendered is that of Mildred Currey Rosscup. In every stage of her life since receiving Christ in early girlhood, her testimony was a radiant light. As her husband, who knew her best, I dedicate this "labor of love" in memory of her extraordinary life. And since we were "one," helping each other in the many ways that we served the Lord, it is necessary to tell of both to make her story reasonably complete.

No account of a lifetime can recall every detail. Besides, the myriad facets would fill many books. Here the accent is on main "windows" into the life of Mildred and of myself. We were for more than half a century "heirs together of the grace of life" (1 Pet. 3:7). God drew us in our youth to Himself, guided us to one another, bonded our hearts in love, outfitted us to serve Him, and led us through nearly 54 years. He blessed our marriage with a ministry in which He influenced hundreds of His servants. Scores of these have gone to various countries to live for Christ and hold forth the Word of life.

My aim, in writing personally, is not at all to glorify myself. It is to honor the Lord and His servant, Mildred. In all candor, she lived a very exemplary life. Her triumph is that of a young girl, a young lady, then a mature woman. It exalts God for what He can do even when He entrusts a life with much suffering. May it encourage others to offer their lives unreservedly to Him, even if the path leads through difficult trials as Mildred's and mine did. Such a life fulfills its goal with fruit that is eternal (John 15:16).

I offer the tribute with an insistence to tell it in truth as it was, and give all the glory to Christ. For anything in us that magnified Him, we owe it all to Him (cf. the last chapter). What do we have but what we received, as God gave (1 Cor. 4:7)? God made Mildred a light shining in our home and a model of things beautiful to all who knew her. Her story cries to be told. I can share what I witnessed, Mildred's being an extraordinary example of Paul's words, "to me to live is Christ, and to die is gain" (Phil. 1:21).

Within hours of God taking my dear one home April 15, 2008, I felt Him draw me as by a powerful magnet to 2 Corinthians 5:14-15. Those words fixed their grip afresh upon my heart. God gave me a new focus on Christ's love. May that love control us!

Many lives are faithful to God in a great variety of trials. These also could fill books. I can truthfully say that Mildred's example stood out. A life so true is potent to give one new focus so also to live. And some day we whom Christ is transforming shall gaze on Him who can make people count as He helped this lady to be faithful (1 Cor. 4:2).

> Dr. Jim Rosscup
> Long-time Professor of Bible
> The Master's Seminary, November, 2009

The Writer's Credits for this Tribute

THIS WORK REPRESENTS AN all-out effort to keep integrity by being historically accurate in telling the story. It has received assists from several sources.

One is in things Mildred shared by word of lip during our marriage before God took her to Himself. Another is files in which she faithfully kept various records and papers. For example I found a treasury with such items as her earliest church's Sunday bulletin, and the pastor's wife's memories of her husband. There were Mildred's high school commencement program, and a copy of the special theme song at the Arizona Bible Institute where she graduated ("that in all things He might have the preeminence," Col. 1:18). Other helps were a printed biography of Mildred's most impacting Bible school teacher, the beloved Dr. John Hubbard, birth and baptism records, and newspaper clippings at certain times during Mildred's life.

A further, great contribution came from Mildred's early picture albums, which she meticulously kept. These supplied faces, events, places, dates, and such details. Along with these were incredible records that her family had passed on to Mildred's brother Bob. He graciously spent many hours bringing together documents and showing them to me. He had receipts even of vehicles their father bought, where, the date, the price, and exact data on details about each of the three farms. Computer sources supplied some information, or confirmed details.

Mildred's friends from various stages of her life had vivid memories on points I did not know or could not recall. Examples appear in chapters 28-32 in ladies' tributes. I myself had kept several thick pictorial albums of Mildred and my family. These supply exact details. For my own life, I had kept picture albums with identifications of these, news clippings, family records, etc.

Other sources are letters, cards, filed documents, yearbooks of high school, colleges, and seminaries of Dallas and Talbot. I even found in Mildred's folders stenciled newspapers of which she was the associate editor at her Bible school.

My thanks goes to proof-readers who helped: Mildred's brother Bob, my daughter Carolyn Long, and Mildred's and my friend Jackie Jenkins, who also wrote one of the tributes in the closing chapters. These pointed out many corrections.

God deserves the main credit. He supplied the fervency to honor His Name and His faithful servant Mildred. He watched over us to give us such details of history. And He led my mind to check the various kinds of sources, or used others to suggest trying those veins of information. So, above all, <u>to God be the glory!</u>

Foreword

THERE ARE FEW MEN I respect more than Dr. James Rosscup. Yet, it is impossible to fully appreciate his ministry without understanding his deep affection and profound love for his wife, Mildred.

I first met Jim when I was a seminary student. Even then I was impacted by his contagious love for Christ and his sacrificial care for others. His profound prayer life was an encouragement and a conviction to all who knew him. He would often ask his students if he could pray for us. And we knew that he meant it, because he would follow up and ask us for updates, sometimes even weeks later!

Needless to say, his godly example left a lifelong impression on my heart. So, when the opportunity came to hire him at The Master's Seminary, we were eager to do so. And I am so glad we did. Generations of students from our seminary have been blessed by Jim—through both his ministry of teaching and his ministry of prayer.

Of course, Jim's humility did not just exhibit itself in the classroom. His dedication as a father and husband stands out as nothing short of exceptional. Despite Mildred 's ailing health—as she found herself in the hospital some 20 times—Jim never stopped serving and caring for her. His faithfulness to her reflected the very example of Christ. As Paul told the believers in Ephesus, "Husbands, love your wives just as Christ loved the church." Jim and Mildred's marriage certainly reflected the gospel that empowered it.

By Jim's own account, Mildred was a remarkable woman. She exemplified the grace of God in the midst of her suffering and modeled "to live is Christ" (Phil. 1:21). She selflessly supported her husband's call to ministry and resolutely embraced the Lord's will for her life. Jim's own effectiveness would have been greatly hindered were in not for her sacrificial efforts behind the scenes.

The book of Proverbs tells us that the family of an excellent wife "will rise up and call her blessed" as her husband "praises her" (Prov. 31:28). The pages that follow give wonderful testimony to Jim's thankfulness to God for the excellent wife with whom he was blessed. I trust that you will be similarly blessed as you read this Christ-exalting tribute to Mildred Rosscup.

Dr. John MacArthur
President, The Master's Seminary
Pastor, Grace Community Church, Sun Valley, CA

1

Mildred—Her Earliest Years

GOD FASHIONED HER TO be the woman He wanted her to be. He made a shining light that passed through this world and brightened those who lived in its rays.

In His eternal counsels He planned for her. He chose her to be His very own, and gave her grace that was glowing like the sparkle of a star in her. And on this earth when He made the way for her, here is how He did it. First He skillfully wrought her in her mother's womb, fashioning in secret her inward parts as one "fearfully and wonderfully made" (Ps. 139:14). And His eyes saw her before her birth; in His book He wrote the days ordained for her when as yet there was not one of them (v. 16). Now she has completed the days God had ordained for her (Ps. 139:16).

Mildred Louise Currey came into this world February 4, 1932 in Poughkeepsie, New York, the second of three children and the only daughter of William and Harriet Currey. Richard, a brother, had preceded her in 1929, and Robert was to follow in 1934.

The girl's arrival was in the Vassar Brothers' Hospital, Poughkeepsie, at 11:35 p.m.

Mildred herself told me of an unusual predicament the night she came into this world. Her father helped her mother, who felt birth pangs, into the Willy's Knight car to rush from the farm to a doctor 20 miles away at the hospital. Along the way, fast pelting snow halted the couple's progress. The vehicle was stuck on a hill. Her dad furiously shoveled snow to clear a way free, got the Knight moving again, and sloshed on to the hospital. There Harriet gave her young son Richard a baby sister, Mildred.

The Curreys before they had children had run a tea room in New York City in the early and mid-1920's to which some of the famous Rockefellers came. The restaurant was at 1277 Madison Avenue, near Central Park. The younger son, Bob, still has one of the tables and its chair that the couple kept from this popular haven. The tables were black with an orange band around them just below the table top, and the chairs were likewise black with the orange stripe around the top of each leg.

William had been born October 12, 1896, at Grahamsville, New York, of Scottish stock in the "McDonald" clan. An ancestor, Richard Currey, had migrated from Bonnie Scotland to settle in the town of East Chester, West Chester County, New York in 1690. Several generations later, William's father George was the caretaker of a New York estate near Grahamsville, with three lakes to which tourists resorted. George also was city supervisor of Grahamsville, and later the manager of two lumber yards, one in Liberty and the other in Livingston Manor. He had been born November 29, 1870, and at the age of 85 finally put his trust in Christ in 1956. A "Certificate of Baptism" at the Unadilla, New York, Methodist Church reads that he turned from his sin and put his trust in Christ, shortly before his life ticked to the midnight hour. He would pass away three years later.

Theda Grant was born in Grahamsville April 24, 1873, grew up to marry George February 28, 1895, and these Curreys resided most of their married life at Liberty, New York. The three Currey children would make many happy trips to visit these beloved grandparents. Later, Mildred would be away from home going to Bible school in Phoenix when her beloved "grammy" would die at Unadilla in February, 1952. She also was away with me in December, 1959 at Dallas Theological Seminary when her "granddad" would pass away at Unadilla.

Two other children besides William were born to George and Theda, but neither of them lived long. Ralph died at seven months, and Paul passed away at 16 following a day's illness.

In his teen years William was a chauffeur for a Mr. "Roof," the owner of the estate where his father George was caretaker. Still young, "Will" sorted mail into bags to drop off at various stops as he rode a train from New York City to Binghamton, New York. Then he rested overnight before sorting mail along a return route. Later he graduated in engineering at Lima College in Lima, New York, near Buffalo, and enlisted in the Army in May, 1917, for officer training. He served during World War I in Panama, and also at Fort Slocum, New York, as well as in Georgia, rising to the rank of First Lieutenant.

A special passion to study and to teach would stand William in good stead in many years to come when he would lead church Bible classes.

The love bug bit and Will married Chima Munroe of Kerhonkson, also in New York, August 31, 1918. The couple's wedding was in Haefen, Georgia. Heartbreak cast its mournful shadow on the marriage when, just 15 months after the tinkle of wedding bells, Chima died of pneumonia November 27, 1919. William had to go on alone, for the pair had borne no children. Yet the surviving husband was not alone, for he had come to know Christ early in life, and was up to making the most of things in strength his Lord gave (Phil. 4:13).

Then God led Will to Harriet Clark Misner of Fallsburgh, New York, who had entered this world September 27, 1896. She, too, was a devoted Christian. The two married in 1921. Harriet was a daughter of farmers Milan and Carrie Misner of an ancestry on the border of Dutch/German lands. Misner ancestry migrating to New York can be traced to 1740. Harriet had gone to a Wesleyan college in New York to prepare to teach, and had become adept at playing the organ and the piano. Soon after the wedding, the couple opened the tea room in the heart of bustling New York City. To this delightful place where Harriet was a gracious and sparkling hostess, as mentioned above, some of the Rockefellers came to enjoy morning tea.

Like a magnet, the shop attracted patrons. They called it "Harriet Clark's Tea Room," the name derived from Harriet and a Clark in the family history. The hostess was short, stout, and charmingly graceful, elegant, meeting customers with twinkling eyes, a brightening smile, a pleasing chuckle, and expertise as an engaging, considerate conversationalist. She was quick to spot any way she could put people at ease, help them enjoy coming in, and prompt them to return. And she trained her waitresses, who were in neat, tidy outfits, to extend sunny welcomes, serve winsomely, and keep things first class. William was tall, arresting in smile, and versatile to converse with visitors about subjects in *The New York Times* and life. People might come in heavy of heart, but go away brightened to face their day.

The Curreys and their workers arose extremely early, long before a rooster would crow in the country, to get to the tea room. They allowed a cushion of time for their crew to bake or receive deliveries of dainties such as mouth-watering breakfast rolls, bon bons, donuts, cookies, brownies, pies, and cakes. They and their staff were ready to serve full breakfasts or sweets, jellies, hot coffee or tea, milk, and juices, all to the melody of upbeat, soothing music. Later in the day they featured various sandwiches, salads, soups, and soft drinks. The enterprise's hospitality and foods drew folk as nectar lures bees to flowers. Harriet later shared with Mildred how the customers bragged about the soups the shop featured.

For a while the Curreys commuted to their business from 23 Colfax Avenue in Roshell Park, New Jersey. But later the "wear and tear" convinced them to move to an apartment just a block from their shop.

Today, other businesses occupy not only the much frequented tea room site but surrounding spaces close by on Madison Avenue—Citibank, Penny Whistle Toys, Milton Cleaners, Marco Polo Pizzeria, and the Hotel Wales.

A burning desire set the hearts of William and Harriet on farming. They yearned for a simpler life in the wide open spaces close to the soil. For both had known this earlier, and longed to start a family. The tea room had built up profit to reach for their dream. So William made a trial trip to scout out a place, and chose a farm of 194 acres about two miles from Clinton Corners. This was in southeast "upstate" New

York, not far away from the big city, but any place north of New York City which is in lower, southern New York State, is "upstate" from there. Other towns within two to three miles of Clinton Corners were Stanfordville, also called Stanford, and Schultzville. And the family could drive to the larger Poughkeepsie every month or so to stock up on supplies.

William had signed to buy the farm on November 10, 1927 for $6,000. But he and Harriet continued to run the tea shop until the next April. He bought a half-ton Chevrolet National pickup for $619 April 23, 1928 on Broadway and 57th Street in New York to move their things. So in that month the couple closed the shop, loaded high their new vehicle, and drove all they chose to keep to their country home and happy days there.

Here the Curreys, as in New York City, had electricity and running water.

They soon built their family, and William's heartbreak in his first wife's sudden death was a sorrow fading into the past. A son, Richard, joined the couple in 1929, a daughter Mildred in 1932, and a second son, Bob, in 1934.

They had a three-story home, a barn with two silos, a large wood shed, a chicken house, a pen for a few hogs, a car garage, and a manual gas pump in the yard with an underground tank. William would rotate crops of corn, oats, alfalfa, timothy, and clover on the place which featured low, rolling hilly woods of evergreen, ash, maple, oak, and lush pasture land. There he would eventually have about 15 dairy cows, a mule, and a work horse.

Pastor David Freer, a Moody Bible Institute graduate, led the Congregational Church (1932–1947) about a quarter of a mile up the road from Schultzville with its grocery store and about four houses. The house of God was about two miles from the Currey farm. Freer nourished the family in the knowledge of Christ. This man of God from Blue Earth, Minnesota soon came to have great respect for "Will" and Harriet as earnest Christians who were willing to stand up and be counted. The couple steadfastly served the Lord, and always on Sundays attended the church that was painted white both outside and inside, just as it is today as the Christian Alliance Church.

In the Sunday bulletin of April 18, 1941 when Mildred was nine, Freer wrote an attention-getter in his burden for his flock, "Are you sure, beloved, that your life is cleansed from sin? Are you very sure that Jesus is within? How is it, beloved?"

Pastor Freer became dear to his people for several reasons. He preached the Word faithfully; led the way in love; was a sterling example of all-around godliness; and made himself a servant to all. For example he did all the milking for one member who had an extended illness, and worked out in the field for another who was laid up for a few days. He also was on hand to drive his people places when they had special needs. The Curreys and others picked up on such a servant spirit, of which Jesus was a spectacular example when He washed His disciples' feet (John 13).

Will Currey gained strength for grueling tasks from a God given six two frame and lean, tough, muscular body of 195 pounds. His vigor would last all his days, with little change, until he died at 84 (1981). God also had gifted him with a mind and resourcefulness to figure out how to repair his tractor and fix other farm equipment. And a resolute work ethic ignited him. But when he would come in from the barn or field, he often became engrossed in God's Word. On the farm he had the help of a hired hand, Eddie Good, a black man who lived in a hill house an eighth of a mile away with his wife and two children.

The farmer's faith was tested in 1937 when the children were young. A hurricane ripped the barn into rubble. God kept the house and the Curreys nearby safe. After the storm wreaked its devastation, Will hired a carpenter to build a new barn, which went up in 1937-38. Meanwhile, Will, his sons, and sometimes Mildred, had to milk his dairy cows in a corral and "make do" until the new barn was ready. Will met the test with resolute trust in God and strength that He gave (Ps. 138:3). His family saw him face the disaster without flinching as he lived in the peace that his Bible counseled (Isa. 26:3; Phil. 4:7; 1 Pet. 5:7).

Sometime in the mid-1930's, Will was selected to be Justice of the Peace for Clinton Corners, in addition to his farming. When visitors would arrive at the farm to transact business in the living room, the children Richard, Mildred, and Bob had to scurry upstairs or into the farm yard to allow privacy to their father's clients.

The Curreys absorbed God's riches not only from the Bible but from several magazines in the home—*The Sunday School Times, The Moody Monthly, The Bible Illustrator* which Will devoured, and in later years at Unadilla, Billy Graham's *Decision* magazine. Harriet spent much time in *The Temperance Magazine* as she was a member of the Women's Christian Temperance Union just as Will's mother Theda was.

Other literature also came to the home and claimed the parents' time, such as *The Farm Journal, The Dairyman's League, The Saturday Evening Post,* and *Reader's Digest.*

Mildred and her brothers read their Sunday School papers from church, and when they were a bit older were drawn to articles in the Christian periodicals as the parents were. In the summers Pastor Freer of the Congregational Church in Schultzville, David Freer, drove his car around the neighborhood, picking up children who packed the vehicle, stood on the "running boards," or sat on the fenders. He drove them to the "Daily Vacation Bible School." In this and in weekly Sunday School lessons Mildred was inspired early with a love for the Word. She later would share it, reaching children for Christ by "flannel graph" board displays and telling the stories with the spiritual gift God gave her.

Times meditating in her Bible were frequent for Mildred. Voracious as a reader, she also enjoyed Martha Finley's series of novels about a girl, Elsie Dinsmore, and many other stories already famous, such as *Bambi, Heidi, Robinson Crusoe,* and later in her growing up, *A Tale of Two Cities, Jane Eyre,* and such writings. The children when young enjoyed comic books or strips such as *Superman, Donald Duck, Dick Tracy, Little Orphan Annie,* etc. When certain radio programs came on, they thrilled to episodes of *Jack Armstrong,* a crime solver, and *Captain Midnight,* a detective. When *The Lone Ranger* and his faithful Indian companion Tonto rode again, the Curreys heard the thundering hoof beats of the great horse Silver and the bark of the ivory-handled six-guns. And they did not want to miss the comedy of *The Great Gildersleeve* or *Henry Aldridge,* or the intrigue of *I Love a Mystery.*

Harriet, when she ironed clothes, sewed, or was making a hook rug, liked to hear Christian music on the radio. One day, the music stopped suddenly. A preacher broke in, saying repeatedly, "What will you have me to do?" She felt she had heard enough repetitions of that phrase, so she turned the radio button to a mystery. The first thing she heard, right on the heels of the preacher's question about what to do, was "Grab your hat and follow me." The abrupt coincidental connection of question and answer touched off a siege of laughing.

The mother was by no means disrespectful of God's Word. But she felt that the preacher had cut off her beloved music sharply. Often the family drove to the then famous "Saddlebag Bible Conference" in the summers to hear some of the country's finest spiritual life speakers. This conference was near Lake Oswego where they went for picnics, and Cooperstown, where the Curreys toured "The Baseball Hall of Fame."

Will rehearsed things of the Bible as he milked his cows or pulled in a load of hay.

Farm life was eventful for Mildred. She sometimes helped milk the cows, fed the Rhode Island Reds (chickens), gathered eggs, carried sticks to heat the wood stove, learned to sew, knit, crochet, tat, make hook rugs, set the table, washed dishes, made beds, helped with washing and drying clothes, picked and helped prepare vegetables, and poked fresh chunks of wood into the stove.

When the Brooklyn Dodgers were playing and on the radio, Bob or "Bub" as Mildred fondly dubbed her brother, would wait anxiously for his "Bums" or "Flatbush" players to score.

Mildred from very early years was drawn to the Bible as by a magnet. She and her mother had chats about it, and so did she and her father. She listened intently to Pastor Freer's messages, drank in the Sunday School lessons, read papers her Sunday School passed out, and articles in *The Sunday School Times.* It was her joy to pick out Bible verses that were especially precious to her. Some would be rich in her mind all her days—God's faithfulness in Lamentations 3:22-23, living for Christ in Philippians 1:21, and being pure of heart and seeing God in Matthew 5:8 She resolved to trust God no matter what, rest in the faithful One, and not doubt His Word.

Her father gave her a light bay pony when she was old enough to ride. She named the pet "Star." That was apt because of the pony's splash of white on the forehead that resembled a star. The young girl would go for rides in the pasture, cut through the woods, or take the road to visit her friend on a nearby farm, Lois Knapp, or another friend, Gertrude.

The three Currey children found games to play. Favorites were "Hide and Seek" and "Kick the Can." Inside in the large Clinton Corners kitchen they devised running the bases in "Three Corner Tag." In their fancy, the bases were the refrigerator at one end of the room, the pantry door at the other end, and a door to the outside. And in the winter they had fun riding in their sleds on a hill near the farm, or ice skating on the pond. Swimming in a creek on the farm was a frolic in summer months.

One day young "Bub" had his eyes closed, counting in hide and seek. Richard and Mildred scrambled to find hiding places. When Bub sought to find them, he searched the barn, woodshed, chicken house, and bushes around the house. He became discouraged, about to give up. He heard teasing heckles above him and saw his brother and sister on the roof three stories up. Then he wanted to go up too, but they had drawn the ladder up behind them. His begging was to no avail as the two high above chuckled at him. So, resourceful as his dad, he went inside, ascended the stairs to a bathroom near the roof, opened the window, and climbed from it to hoist himself to the roof to join Richard and Mildred. His feat surprised them, and he had the last laugh.

Winters could be bitterly cold. So before going to bed, the children would heat flat irons, used for ironing clothes. These they wrapped in cloths and put them at the foot of their blankets to keep their feet warm. Another custom was the mother's. When a child had a cold, she would make a mustard/turpentine "plaster" to cover the chest. Yet a further custom was to store eggs in crocks, preserved in jell something like the substance of today's "cold packs," and keep the eggs in the coldness of the cellar.

Early in the 1930's Will had bought the Willy's Knight, a car that was a product of the Willys Overland Company in Toledo, Ohio. He would have other cars, but one of the favorite pictures in family albums shows this reliable Knight.

The Clinton Corners farm was at a "Y" fork in the road. One road led from Clinton Corners, another up a hill a half mile to the "Bear Market School" close to the road on the left, and a further one down past the Currey land a quarter of a mile away where Mildred's close childhood friend, Lois Knapp, lived on her folks' farm. Another friend, Gertrude, also lived nearby.

One may wonder why the name "Bear Market School." Black <u>bears</u> had stalked through the hills and valleys. Then, too, a country <u>market</u> was a short distance along the same road.

One picture of the school shows 21 students. A pot-bellied stove in the center of the one large room kept the teacher, Harriet, and the pupils warm in winter and spring. Will often delivered to his wife a huge pot of soup she had prepared. She put it on the stove to simmer through the morning, and kept poking more wood in the stove to maintain the fire. The tantalizing aroma of the savory meal reduced children to an agony of hunger pains and longing for time to fly as they suffered the wait for lunch break. When the happy time came, Harriet dipped out a bowl of the well-flavored meat and vegetables for each learner.

After the meal or during other breaks, in winter, the children raced across the road to a frozen pond. Ice skating was their frolic, amid feats of speed and grace, many shouts, giggles, and hard landings. When they came back to the school, any staring out of a window might be met by a cow eyeing them quizzically over a pasture fence.

Richard and Mildred both, in their separate times, finished the first and second grades in a single year. This speeded up their elementary school. Mildred later would graduate from high school at sweet 16.

Some of Mildred's summers at Clinton Corners included special vacation trips to visit her grandparents George and Theda at Liberty, New York. Her two brothers also had visits there. The granddad and grammy had a bicycle waiting for any who came. Grammy Theda won Mildred's heart, and the young girl always longed one day to be a grandmother and be like her own gracious "Grammy." Frequent letters went from Mildred's pen to this beloved one. The girl was also an avid learner in her mother's modeling of household and table etiquette—what was proper—and also cooking, baking, sewing, crocheting, knitting, tatting, making hook rugs in different designs to go under chairs or in doorways, and taking pride in keeping herself and things tidy.

When free, Mildred "mothered" her dolls, or played hop scotch, or hide and seek with her brothers or in winter rode her sled. She did her hair, pored over the Bible or other books, listened to radio programs, enjoyed Christian and classical music, took walks, rode her pony "Star," or went swimming in the creek in the woods.

Recently the family came across Mildred's records on 4-H work at ages 11 and 12. What a stash of prizes, blue ribbons at the Clinton Corners Community Day and the Duchess County Fair in Rhinebeck. Her displays were in sewing, making cookies, laying out luncheon sets, canning, and record book covers. Her gardening featured planting seed, weeding, cultivating and showing her tomatoes, cabbages, egg plants, potatoes, sweet corn, melons, soybeans, and squash.

One picture, earlier, when the girl was about six shows her decked out to go to a Halloween party clad in a tan Indian maiden outfit. This motif was a natural since tribal people such as the Mohawks had roamed to the north.

Bob, Mildred's brother, vividly recalls what Mildred was like in her growing up years. He admired her for her fine qualities. One was her patience to keep on keeping on and not permit her besetting illnesses to "crimp her style." She had a winning spirit. Whenever she had any strength, she rose to the challenge to make the most of things, to find a way, and also brighten others by her contagious spirit. Another trait was her considerate concern to look out for others, and in any time of trouble seek to help work things out peaceably. A further grace was her insistence on what was right and best. Rather than taking some easy short cut that compromised her values, she clung to what was good. Bob also was impressed by her happiness. Her frame of reference was sweet-tempered, a composed tranquility, upbeat, wholesome, bright, and tasteful.

When Mildred was nine, she made a trip to visit her "Cousin May" in Washington, D. C. Carrying her white purse lady-like, she spent a few days with Eleanor (Ella) May Roosa, a cousin on her mother's side. May for many years served as a clerk for the U.S. government. She was a Unitarian, and sharply refused to have anything to do with Mildred's Christ. This broke the heart of the young, believing girl. But Mildred held unswervingly to faith in her Savior despite her cousin's rejection.

About a year before that, Mildred had begun to suffer from frequently serious breathing ordeals. Her mother was troubled by this ailment earlier than her, but not as critically until her late years. When the girl worked in the hay dust helping her father bring in loads for the cattle and put it in the barn loft, the dust she breathed in tickled her air channels and triggered struggles to breathe. With these came severe ordeals of coughing up mucous. She would labor in a desperate fight to get air past the "road blocks" in her breathing channel, and the dilemma would reduce her to a frightful weakness. In the same year as her Washington, D. C. trip, she was bed-ridden for several days in the hospital with her malady.

Doctors appraised her lungs as loaded with mucoid impactions that were "clogs" making her efforts to breathe at times critically awful battles. In various intervals, she would improve and be able to do normal things even if so often at a slowed pace. Then in countless times, new breathing emergencies beset her. How bravely she faced these!

During her growing up she would be hospitalized at least five times, whether in Binghamton or Poughkeepsie, and make numerous other trips for help from the family doctor. At least 15 later stays in hospitals would occur in her life. Bob admits that he would hear her wheezing, rattling, and laboring hard to breathe, and in his childish lack of empathy he would tease her unkindly.

"Why don't you speak up?" he would chide. "Clear your throat so you won't make those weird sounds!"

But how? She would bravely labor to get enough air, but the work was sometimes a fierce effort. Bob humbly recalls to his shame that she was annoyed by his insistence as he failed to understand her trouble. But he says she kept a kind attitude, and just quietly and gamely summoned what energy she did have to cope with her dilemmas.

A frightening calamity to another family member had the Curreys scurrying one day. Richard took the .22 rifle into the woods to hunt rabbits. On one of his attempts to pull the trigger, the gun jammed. He obeyed his father's careful words not to stick the rifle's point into the dust. So, what was left? He stuck the point against a foot while he tried to work out the problem. Suddenly the rifle barked, catching him off-guard, drilling him through that foot. He limped home scared and bleeding, and Will rushed him to a doctor.

The Curreys would farm the Clinton Corners land for 17 years (1928–1945). Then, in March, 1945, Will moved his family around 300 miles to another New York farm, this time 200 acres about six miles northeast of Oneonta, a city with an Indian name. His old farm brought him $11,000, which in those days was a lot of money.

2

The Teenage Years

AT 13, MILDRED HAD a new home nested on a low mountain crest. This would last for nearly three years (1945–1947).

The second farm's location's had a flat-topped, two-story house. Some of the acreage was situated on a broad bench of land. Part of the property was in lush woods, and grazing meadows graced the slopes.

At this farm, the family "made do" without running water, but used a well in the yard with a bucket and rope to crank up water to carry in. They had an outhouse, and for showers used a wooden platform where they stood, and a tank hoisted atop a platform, with a tap at the bottom. They stood inside a circular curtain as they enjoyed the spilling water, especially when the sun heated it.

At Clinton Corners as well as this later place near Oneonta, the children, from early ages into teen years, carried arm loads of wood into the house from a large shed. From this home, Bob went to a grade school, while Richard and Mildred attended Laurens High School in the small, nearby town of Laurens. Two years of Mildred's high schooling were here, and the final two years would come at Unadilla Central High School. Richard received his high school diploma at Laurens.

Richard distinguished himself on the basketball and baseball teams. He was one of the most deadly shots to drill the net in basketball. Later, his brother Bob played on the Unadilla Central hardwood quintet.

While at this Oneonta home, the family went to the Federated Church in Laurens. Will was the Sunday School Superintendent, and Harriet sometimes played the organ.

Will drove Mildred into Oneonta to take piano and organ lessons. She began to develop a skill she would enjoy the rest of her life. In later years, in our marriage, she often would fill the home with music from our baby grand piano and our organ. And when her breathing permitted it, she would sing the words.

Finally, in 1947, Will paid $13,000 for a third farm of 135 acres about two miles outside of Unadilla, a small community which, like Oneonta, had an Indian name. The Susquehanna River flowed through the town. This river began in Otsego Lake, at Cooperstown, New York, a lake where the family went at times for picnics. The river flowed southward out of the state and also drained tributaries of Pennsylvania, surging on into Maryland where it poured into the Chesapeake Bay after its 500-mile course.

The family moved to their latest home that summer.

The Unadilla farm had a two-story home near the highway. Besides this dwelling, the Curreys had a large cattle barn, two attached silos, one wooden and one cement, a chicken house, a milk shed, and a garage for the car. The home was about a half hour west from Oneonta, on land that lay flat just off the highway for nearly a quarter mile, then sloped up a mountain that was a forest of trees—maple, evergreen, ash, occasional cherry trees, and thorny crabapple bushes that had to be uprooted and burned. The cattle pastured in the lowland or up the slope in grassy meadows tucked away, hidden in the timberland.

At each of the Currey farms, and in that part of New York, the fields whether hilly or flat were beautified by lush green clover and timothy. In the summers, in copious displays, purple violets graced the meadows. Yellow dandelions were thick, as were small blue and white "forget me nots" and golden rods. In the woods residents saw "lady slippers" with their flowers shaped like a lady's slippers, and wild milk weed.

Once the family had moved to Unadilla, and in teenage years, they would attend the Federated Church in town, composed of Presbyterians and Baptists. The church's young people would meet on some Sunday evenings with youths at churches of nearby towns such as Sydney and Bainbridge. These communities were west of Unadilla, off the road to Binghamton. On Saturday nights, The New England Fellowship sent rousing speakers to lead young people who attended, and later on Youth for Christ did.

Not long after the Curreys arrived in the Unadilla area, people at the church decided to form two congregations. The Presbyterians and Baptists could not agree on things the church should emphasize, so the Baptists found another site, and called their church Unadilla Baptist. A lay preacher, Archie Benedict, led them for a time, then they secured a permanent pastor, Homer Weatherbee, who came with his wife Pearl and three children. The church's youths continued to have the Saturday and Sunday night meetings of several churches.

Harriet played the organ at the Unadilla church, and taught the women's Sunday School class. Will was an elder and long-time, highly respected Sunday School teacher of the men. His custom at home was to take a break daily after the morning milking to come to the house for his breakfast, and after eating he would spend about an hour poring over the Bible and his lesson booklet. Mildred taught a children's class and also led in several summer Daily Vacation Bible School sessions.

The grandparents on Harriet's side continued to farm. Then her mother, Carrie, died, and later her father Milan came to live with William, Harriet and family. That was still in the years at Clinton Corners. This grandfather, Milan, died in 1942.

In their old age as the grandparents already mentioned, George and Theda came in 1948 to live with Mildred's family. Will and Harriet, shortly after their move near Unadilla in 1947, built a spacious upstairs addition for this couple. Theda died February 25, 1952. While still at home finishing high school, Mildred often would carry her grandparents' food up to them, then sit and visit with them, and share her love of Jesus. They did not know the Lord, and did not receive Him though the girl sought to help them receive the Savior. As far as the family knew, Theda, though a very nice lady, never came to know Christ. George, at 85 in 1956, may have, according to a Unadilla Methodist Church certificate of baptism. Three years later, he too died.

The house had a downstairs bedroom, a front room, a living room, a dining room, kitchen, pantry, and bath. Upstairs were four bedrooms and an attic. In the first two years at the new home, Will put up an addition to the two stories to provide for his aging parents George and Theda. He built a new upstairs bedroom, living room, kitchen, bath, a second attic, and a special stairway to this portion. Once finished, in 1948 he helped his father and mother move into these quarters.

Two years after the Curreys' move to Unadilla, their former Congregational pastor of Schultzville, David Freer, came from Montague, New Jersey, where he had been pastor of a Dutch Reformed Church for a year. Heart trouble had forced him to take a leave of absence from his new ministry. He, his wife Orla and three children stayed with their friends, the Curreys, for a while, then with the Bert Gates family in Unadilla. David hoped that light work a few hours a day might be a relief to his heart, so he helped the Curreys with farm chores.

On June 27, 1949, Pastor Freer, at age 55, climbed down inside the wooden silo to level the silage that was now about six feet deep. Will was using the John Deere tractor to run the corn blower that chopped the stalks and blew the silage up a tube into the wooden and cement silos. He was forking loads into the hopper from a wagon with the help of Bob, who was 14. They were on their last load, near quitting time at 5 p.m. The John Deere, low on gas at this late hour, coughed, gasped for gas and oxygen, and spit out a spark that landed in tinder dry straw, igniting the pile. Wind whipped the fire, which raged rapidly through the straw, blazed up the wooden silo, and snaked around to inflame the barn. In seconds it was obvious that the building would go up in smoke.

Will leaped from his job with a fork, desperate to force his way into the silo. He screamed a loud, frantic warning to Pastor Freer to climb out. When the minister inside did not yell back or emerge, the farmer tried heroically to fight through flames to get in and rescue his brother in the Lord. He banged frantically on the silo to get his friend's attention, hoping the entrapped, beloved preacher would scurry up the ladder and scramble out to safety, even if in the nick of time. Licking flames, shooting up in fierce momentum, made it impossible to reach the minister. To the Curreys' shock, horror, and sorrow, Freer did not get out. He died in the inferno that wiped out the barn and wooden silo, while a cement silo endured the blaze. Will suffered severe burns to his hands, one arm, and an ear.

The farmer dashed to the house to phone firemen, and by the time he rushed back the barn was a sheet of flames. Fire fighters came, but once they had used the water tank they brought, they had to speed away to a creek to fill up with more water. This delayed the battle to douse the blaze. The barn a lost cause, they switched their focus to try to salvage the house, for the wind was lashing fire a hundred yards to assault the roof.

Afterward those probing the ruins found that the pastor had died, lying half covered by silage he had distributed, his body horribly charred. County Coroner C. S. Gould reported an accidental death. The Curreys wondered if in the tumult, smoke and sudden terror, their beloved spiritual brother's weak heart gave way early, and he collapsed, unconscious or in death, before the furnace engulfed him. Since he had made no response to screams of warning, their hope was that he did not die in the flames.

Will, desperate but barred from getting into the silo, had yelled at Bob to get the calves out of the barn. The son quickly freed the three that were inside. Firemen with their Indian tanks worked frantically atop the house to keep flaming cinders the wind dropped upon the shingles from inflaming the home's roof also. Just when they feared the dwelling might go up in flames too, providence caused a drastic change in the wind and sent a light rain. This help joined with new shingles and the fire fighters' furious bid to save the dwelling.

Out in the yard, Harriet, Mildred, the perishing pastor's wife Orla, and neighbors breathed sighs of relief that the home was safe. But Mrs. Freer was caught up in an agony of heartbreak, realizing that in terrible moments her husband had died. Her solace was that his spirit was safe with his Lord, and she would see him safe in glory.

A new blaze flared up at the barn four hours later at 9 p.m., and firemen put it out.

So on two farms, Clinton Corners and Unadilla, the family lost their barn, the first one in a hurricane in 1937, the second by a fiery blast in 1949. When the earlier one was ruined Mildred was five, and at the time of the last crisis she was 17.

God gave His all-sufficient grace to devastated hearts of the pastor's surviving wife Orla, the Freer's three children, and the Curreys. All of these were sick with shock and numbed in an ordeal of immense pain. I remember Mildred kindly keeping up loving letters for many decades to Mrs. Freer as this Moody Bible Institute graduate lived until 1996, when nearly 100. Shortly before her death, one of her children, Mark, helped her privately publish a book about her husband's two pastorates, *Moments at the Manse* [pastor's home]. The work resulted from many years of writing

The Curreys had a new barn erected soon after the tragedy that for Pastor Freer was an open door out of the silo through gates of splendor into the presence of Christ.

Mildred and Bob went to Unadilla Central High School, which had a student body of about 150. Mildred was there her final two years after two at Lauren High. She played on the girls' softball team and her strength and skill helped her become one of the top batters. As a strong farm girl, she often blasted hits to drive teammates scurrying home. This prowess won for her the teammates' nickname, "Slugger Millie." She was art editor of the school's yearbook of 1948, *The Unadillan*, and treasurer of her senior class. She and her classmates enjoyed a seniors' celebration trip to visit sites such as the Rockefeller Center in New York City in March, 1948.

As a teenager Mildred helped her mother in the home, learning further lessons in how to cook, can vegetables, fruits, and jams for the pantry, and keep the home tidy. They also loved cats and always had several that needed their tender care. In farm work, she sometimes drove the John Deere and trampled silage with her brothers in the silos. She also helped load the wagon in the field with hay to haul to the barn loft. Sometimes she would make the trek on the cow trail up the slope to drive the animals to the barn for milking. Due to her breathing shortage, the walk would involve many stops to catch her breath and wait for new strength to plod on.

She worked with her mother in Harriet's large garden across the driveway in the field. Harriet grew squash, turnips, parsnips, and other vegetables there. And beyond that garden was a small orchard of trees that bore red apples. The mother and daughter also worked over by the car garage where Will, Richard, and Bob had put up trellises for raspberry vines that grew to about five feet high.

Visiting preachers, musicians, and missionaries who ministered in the church often came to be the Curreys' guests at dinner. So Mildred and her brothers grew up hearing about all-out Christian work on far flung frontiers, being living sacrifices as in Romans 12:1, and living lives to adorn Christ and His gospel (Titus 2:10).

Not long after Mildred's Unadilla Central graduation in May, 1948, she became severely ill and had to be hospitalized in Binghamton, an hour's drive southwest. A specialist removed a part of her left lung. At first medical personnel thought she had tuberculosis, but later they diagnosed the problem as a mucoid impaction in the lungs. In subsequent years doctors would call her malady "bronciacticis." That is, her bronchial tubes tended to clog up with heavy mucoid blockage, and this required an all-out fight to get her breath by great, heaving efforts that "wore her to a frazzle." The 1948 operation delayed her entering college for a year.

So, the second Fall following the finish of high school, she entered The State Teachers College in Oneonta, NY, about 30 miles away. She was there one year (1949-1950), living in an apartment at the foot of a hill on which the college nested. Severe breathing pressures that recurred led to her doctor's counsel to try living in Arizona for a possible relief in health.

While at the Oneonta college, Mildred participated in the Inter-Varsity Christian Fellowship group. The yearbook, *The Oneontan,* at the end of that year, 1950, includes a four by six inch picture of 23 women students at a Christian meeting, one of these Mildred. She is in a white blouse and Scottish plaid skirt, hands crossed in her lap, a bracelet on her right wrist, a winsome smile lighting up her face.

Mildred's relish for humor drew the friendly "dig" that a classmate, Sally, scribbled in above that picture, "Dear Millie, You saved me money this year by providing so much 'corn' [humor] at noon. I did not need to buy any. Seriously, I've loved knowing you . . . ."

She finished one year at the college. Then she took her doctor's advice and on October 2, 1950, she and her mother flew to Tucson, Arizona to seek a climate that might give relief in her breathing. They felt Tucson dryer than Phoenix, and more suitable to help in her struggle.

God, however, was orchestrating events to put Mildred in the place of His own plan (Ps 37:23), and He would also order my steps. This was just as sure as He led Moses from Midian and Aaron from Egypt to meet to do His will (Exod. 4:14). His incredible moves would bring us together in His gracious designs.

He promised, "I will guide you with My eye" (Ps. 32:8).

3

The Heart Steeped in God's Word

FOR A BRIEF TIME of seeking God's way, Harriet and Mildred weighed prospects in southern Arizona, at Tucson. A Sidney Darling in the First Baptist Church of Tucson was from the Arizona Bible Institute in Phoenix. Darling spoke very highly of the school. There, he emphasized, teachers were true to the Bible and classes equipped students for godly service. This peaked Mildred's interest. She and her mother sensed God's guiding them to go north. So they came to ABI on West McDowell Road in northwest Phoenix.

The school, founded in 1935 as The Arizona Bible Institute, would come under the administrative oversight of Biola College from 1961–1971. Then its name would change to The Arizona College of Bible until 1997 when it would have a third name, The Arizona Bible College, until financial pressures brought its close after the May, 1998 graduation. It existed as "A Voice in the Desert with a Vision for the World."

A love for God's Word and a fervency to learn it well and serve the Lord with all her life prompted Mildred to a crucial decision.

She enrolled at ABI, a choice she would always cherish as being in the very center of God's will. The time was the Fall of 1950. The registrar assigned her to a room in a campus dorm. Her mother, confident that her daughter had found the school and the climate God had chosen for her, flew back to Unadilla to rejoin the rest of the family. The Curreys were prayerfully trusting the Lord that He would assist their daughter and sister to overcome in her breathing dilemmas.

The president at ABI, Dr. Victor Oltrogge, was quickly aware of the graciousness, poise, brightness, and trustworthiness of this new student. He invited Mildred to step into a position as secretary and receptionist in his outer office. She would greet incoming students and help them get situated, direct visitors, give tours, type letters, tend the records files, and answer the phone.

Again the New York girl distinguished herself both in her key position and as an "A" student. Her heart that hungered for a deeper life with God relished the Bible analysis and synthesis, spiritual life lessons, aggressive vision in reaching people for

Christ, theology, church history, and other classes. So she honed an already godly mind. She did special papers on such subjects as the Old Testament tabernacle, analyzed many Bible passages as her heart thrilled at God's treasure, and read rich Christian books that enhanced her close walk with the Lord and growth in having a heart like His. Out of this would blossom one of the purest, truest testimonies that any daughter of God ever exhibited. For she would always adorn the teaching with beautiful and consistent faithfulness (1 Cor. 4:2; Titus 2:10).

Not long after God led Mildred to the Bible school, the snack room near the president's office needed a clerk. Dr. Oltrogge and the proprietor, a student named Gene Adams, chose Mildred for this position in addition to her role as a secretary. So in the ABI stenciled "newspaper" of six pages called *Report of The Redeemer* (1952), a full page ad invites the hungry on campus to come in for treats. It features a student's drawing of a smiling girl holding up a tally sheet, and below this are the words: "Introducing Miss Mildred Currey. This talented young lady whose picture appears above as she really is (figuring out your bill) is the clerk in the KANDY KAHN . . . . She is famous for her quick and ready smile, and you can be completely at ease when you visit the Kandy Kahn . . . of a quick and completely satisfying snack."

"Kandy" was spelled with a "K" to fit with "Kahn," a word in some Oriental countries for "prince, or chief," or an inn surrounding a courtyard. So the idea was a "Candy Inn," or, based on the Persian "knana" for "house," a "Candy House."

Not only was Mildred a confectioner; she was the assistant editor of the newspaper, which shared brief bios of students, news, spiritual lessons, humor, and information about student ministries. She also was Adams' assistant editor for a further publication, an eight page stencil job called the "*Missionary Report*." This commented on a campus conference of guest speakers about missions labors in various countries.

This daughter of God became very deeply inspired about seeking Him in prayer. She also was a member of an ABI girls' sextet (1953–54) that sang in many Arizona churches and even on the radio. She did weekend and evening house to house evangelism in Phoenix, served in street corner evangelism as a singer, went out on some weekends to cotton pickers' camps to put up flannel graph lessons for children to lead them to Christ or help them grow. And in addition to her office tasks, she earned her way via baby-sitting on evenings when she could work this in.

In the sextet other ladies with whom she would correspond at times through later years were Valeene Hayes, director, and Janice Eagon and Margine Clark. The latter, who was with Mildred in Unadilla Central High School and came to ABI a couple of years after her (1952), would in a short while later become the wife of a man who was soon to develop into an eloquent, amazingly fruitful evangelist of the Mexican Gospel Mission in Phoenix, Dick Mercado. Janice would marry a farmer and live the rest of her days in Colorado. Valeene labored many years as a very dedicated musical missionary in Haiti, then has resided in Anderson, IN.

I had no inkling when the visiting ABI sextet sang before my eyes in the First Baptist Church of Buckeye in the summer of 1953 what God designed to happen in 1954 and onward. Incredibly, though so unworthy, I would soon be dating one of these pretty daughters of God for 27 months, and marry her Dec. 16, 1956. We would serve the Lord during our courtship, then for 51 years and four months in marriage, a total of nearly 53 years and a half. God would bless our ministry to register its shaping effects on hundreds of servants to labor for Christ in many countries. These would serve as missionaries, seminary presidents, seminary and college professors, pastors, Bible institute and school principals and instructors, youth directors, camping leaders, publishers, authors, lay ministers, and other services for Christ.

At ABI in 1950–1954 Mildred showed a diligent skill on exams and in research. Her mind, reflecting Christ (Phil. 2:5), was unusually bright and quick, and she devoted her utmost to honor her Savior. Classmates admired her for her pleasant, unperturbed, even-tempered and upbeat spirit of shining cheer (Phil. 4:4), her poised rest in Christ, her strength in always doing what was right, and her "level headed" wisdom to counsel adeptly on practical issues. They were blessed by her sunshine smile, truthfulness, faithful witness for her Lord, prayer life, reliability, and punctuality to keep her word. They observed her tidiness in the dorm, freedom from any words of spite, and her being an engaging, "fun" person who provoked laughs.

One summer (1951) Mildred traveled to do missionary work among children in rural areas near Dillon, Montana in the car with another ABI student, missionary Joan Gill. Joan later would serve Christ in Pakistan for many years. A picture that remains from this time of Mildred's service also shows her driving, high atop the seat of an old car, with the caption, "Hot Rodder Millie." In this she was continuing a skill her dad had taught her in driving the farm tractor and the family car.

In the Fall of 1952, her dear brother "Bub" also came west to enter ABI. That Christmas, both Bob and Mildred were elated by an invitation from other ABI students from Colorado, Alice and Ruth Shore, to be their family's guests back home. So the young people rode with the others to Parshall, Colorado, north of Denver. They enjoyed fellowship with these Christians, played in the snow, and went sight seeing in Colorado's colorful mountain grandeur.

In the Spring of 1953, these two Curreys received a message from "Cousin May" Roosa, who had retired from her clerk role for the government in Washington, D. C., and moved to San Diego, CA. May was slowly dying with cancer and wanted

Mildred to have her 1951 black Willys car. Her caretaking nurse "had her eye on the car," but May wanted Mildred to own it. So she wrote to Mildred that if she would come to San Diego, she would let her have the vehicle for $100. Then May could honestly tell her nurse that she had sold the car.

Mildred and Bob drove to San Diego, taking with them a class mate, Pat Simpson, who later would marry a Don Denind, live near us in California, and often visit Mildred as I would teach at Talbot Theological Seminary. While visiting Cousin May, Mildred followed up her compassion to share Christ, but to her heartbreak the Unitarian relative coldly pushed aside the witness. So, once the Willys deal was finalized, Bob drove his car back to Phoenix, and Mildred drove herself and Pat in the car that was now hers. Cousin May died in 1954, and at her own insistence perished eternally, not knowing Christ as Savior.

Earlier, in the summer of 1952, both Bob and Mildred spent part of the vacation back at their Unadilla home. In their return across country to resume school at ABI, they went to Ohio to join some others and ride in two cars, the men in one and the ladies in the other. In Bob's case, occupants took turns driving, and Bob was asleep on the far right as three were in the front seat and one in back sleeping after his stint at the wheel. As the car passed through Oklahoma, Bob suddenly stirred, only vaguely awake. Still in a grog, he glanced to his left as the dash board lights did little to clarify the semi-darkness and shadowed faces. Imagining he was with people kidnapping him, he felt desperate. Before the other two realized what he was doing, he heaved the door open and stepped out daringly to "make his escape."

Once Bob's foot touched the pavement, the momentum of 60 miles an hour viciously whipped his dropping body end over end in a wild, rapid, and savage fling and roll, scraping pavement and gravel. The driver, shocked, slammed on the brakes, stopped, and backed up. Bob must be dead. But amazingly conscious, the bale out rider was slowly picking his hanged body up. He now realized his mistake. His heel had been torn drastically, holes were ripped in his clothes, and blood spurted profusely in several places. His friends did their best to arrest the bleeding, and rushed him to the nearest hospital. Elaborate wrapping of gauze left Bob looking like a mummy.

The teenager could not eat and keep down food for a couple of days. People stared at the walking mummy at restaurants. The car load finally pulled in to the ABI campus and Bob, "the talk of the place," was helped to a bed in his dorm.

The ladies' car in which Mildred rode arrived at the campus some hours later. Students met these arrivals and excitedly filled Mildred in on her brother's mishap. She hastened to the dorm to see how "Bub" was. Then she beheld the "mummy," but breathed her thanks to God for sparing his life. He was in fairly good spirits, and would be "on the mend." God had plans for him in His service for years to come. He kept up ABI studies, then interrupted these for a hitch in the Air Force (1956–1960), and after that returned to finish the Bible school and earn his degree in 1962.

In his graduating year, 1962, Bob would marry a fellow student, Jeri Parnell. They moved to California and soon began a ministry of compassion, taking foster children into their home. In the nearly 45 years since, at least 600 children have felt their love, some coming to know the Savior. Jeri has held state and area offices as one of the foremost leaders in foster child care, and she and Bob have devoted selfless service helping abandoned children through difficult years. When Jeri died in June, 2008, at least eight foster child leaders stood up at her memorial to voice high tribute to her for leadership that they had admired. Bob is continuing the ministry at their home in Citrus Heights, east of Sacramento. These Curreys' lives are examples of "much fruit" (John 15:4, 8).

Mildred's brother Richard also married. He and his wife Bea had five children, Jim, Ruth, David, Lois, and Mark. Richard's work in his grown up years has been stone cutting of flagstones for decoration, walks, and the like, and with New York Electric and Gas as a meter technician. In a few years Bea died. Richard now lives with his second wife, Phyllis, on spacious acreage near Norwich, New York.

At times Mildred and other ABI students formed teams to witness and hand out evangelistic tracts at cotton camps near Phoenix. They would gather children and share Bible stories in "flannel graph" on a tripod backboard. During an ABI vacation time, one of the institute men students, Jerry Russell, drove Mildred and two other students, Irene and Leona Bendure, from Phoenix to the Los Angeles area to enjoy sight-seeing (1950). The four students visited a lookout point on the Pacific Coast, and also went to see The Bible Institute of Los Angeles, which at that time was on Hope Street in downtown Los Angeles. This, in a shorter name "Biola," would shift in the 1950's to a 78-acre campus cleared from an olive vineyard in La Mirada, south of the big city.

Mildred had no idea on her visit that years later, she and I would come to Biola for me to teach 22 years at the graduate school on the northwest corner of the campus, Talbot Theological Seminary (1965–1987).

ABI would later be, for a time (1961–1971), associated with Biola. The institution was destined for a glorious ministry. One of Mildred's classmates, Jerry Russell, would volunteer after the eventual 1998 closing to put out *"The ABI Newsletter."* This gave copious updates on alumni fulfilling the will of Christ. This organ has been via email (ca. 1998–2009, etc.). Jerry has sent this yeoman publication from his home in Covina, CA, an outskirt city of Los Angeles.

Graduation from the institute came for Mildred May 27, 1954. It featured the song "Faith of Our Fathers," choir numbers that fellow student Valeene Hayes led on "Jesus Saves" and "Only One Life," the class's song "Great is Thy Faithfulness," Scripture reading, prayer, and a class speaker. Visiting speaker Dr. Harold Lindsell gave the address. He would later write the famous book contending for inerrancy of Scripture, *The Battle for the Bible*. The president's wife, Electa Oltrogge, had written in 1952 the school hymn, "Our Preeminent Lord" based on Colossians 1:18. The entire congregation sang it before the school's most beloved professor, Dr. John Hubbard, gave the benediction.

The song's words exalt Christ.

> We praise our God and Father, Who sent His only Son,
> To purchase our salvation, and make His people one.
>
> We praise our Lord and Savior, Our risen, living Head,
> Our Alpha and Omega, the first-born from the dead.
>
> O Father, Son and Spirit, Almighty three in One,
> We pray, with glad thanksgiving, in us Thy will be done."

The chorus zeroed in on the key verse:

> That in all things He might have the preeminence,
> That in all things He might have the preeminence,
> That in all things He might have the preeminence,
> Jesus Christ our Lord.

In years to follow, this song would often distill its melody and message in our home as Mildred sat at our baby grand piano and softly sang the words. My heart, lifted as I sat in my study, would feel a new fire of devotion. God would move me, too, to resolve, "Yes, Lord—in all things!"

Mildred, when finishing her biblical studies, longed to devote her life to Christ in teaching. But where to get further preparation? She asked, seeking direction for her next step from the God. Had not He promised, "I will guide you with My eye" (Ps. 32:8)?

Mildred at Arizona Bible Institute

Top left: Dr. John Hubbard, a man mighty in the scriptures; Top right: Mildred drives an old car in Dillon, Montana during evangelistic outreach with children (1950).

Bottom left: Mildren as secretary at ABI; Bottom right: Mildred waves before leaving ABI for summer at home in New York.

More Photos from Arizona Bible Institute

Top: Mildred is ready with ABI men for church.

Bottom: Sextet that sang in churches and on the radio, left to right, Marqine Clark, Mildred Currey, Janice Eagon, Leona Bendure, Alice Shore, and Irene Bendure.

4

God's Guidance to Arizona State

THE LORD'S NEW LEADING fixed its conviction on Mildred's heart. She enrolled as a sophomore at Arizona State College in Tempe. This was just a short drive southeast of Phoenix, and the time was September, 1954. She yearned to keep near her beloved Bible school, her brother Bob there, and friends in the area. And ASC had a name for preparing teachers. Her major, building on studies earlier in Oneonta, was secondary education.

God put in her heart to attend the Sunday evening youth group at the First Baptist Church of Tempe about two blocks from the campus. She lived at first with Georgia Wilson, her roommate, on Maple Street less than a half mile west of the college. Soon she was teaching a Sunday morning children's group at the Buena Park Mission Church where the pastor was another ABI graduate, Eddie Matchett. The church was less than a mile east of Arizona State. This witness was on the south side of the main highway, Apache Boulevard, which skirted the southern side of the campus and ran on eastward a few miles to Mesa.

It would be in the first days of Mildred's sophomore year that God's providence brought her into an English Literature class. This course, among other things, focused on Shakespeare writings such as "The Tempest." And, quite incredibly, against my natural uncultured instinct, the Lord inclined my mind to choose that same class! That is not all. He directed us <u>both</u> to the First Baptist youth group in Tempe. And we would see one another at Campus Crusade for Christ meetings, just as Mildred had been in Inter-Varsity at Oneonta. Besides these venues, God would incline us to a regional, Arizona Conservative Baptist youth "Valley Rally," held monthly, each time at a different church. The rally was named after the vast "Valley of the Sun," embracing Phoenix and several cities within a great circle about it.

In the summer after her sophomore year (1955), Mildred returned to New York to stay with her folks. One of her activities was with a fellow-Unadillan and ABI classmate Margine Clark, and a younger church friend, Margaret Wright, doing Vacation Bible School teaching children. Margaret emailed me after Mildred's death, in 2009, with one of her memories. "Your picture," she remembered, "went with us wherever we would go." Mildred carried and showed off the photo of me, whom she had begun dating near the outset of our Arizona State sophomore year.

Margaret would marry Leon Blosser, and they would serve many years as missionaries in Egypt, later in pastoral work in the States.

During her stint in college, Mildred kept close ties with ABI, teaching two night classes at her alma mater. She drove her black and white '51 Willys from Tempe to lead her adult lay-people students in "Child Psychology" and "Pedagogy," the latter on how to teach. One night she invited me to go with her and sit in on the class.

I was amazed at how collected she was as she sat behind her teaching desk. Her lectures were very clear and sensible, and she was adept in answering questions of lay people far beyond her own age. That was my impression as I watched and listened, my awe sky rocketing. I, too, wanted to teach like that.

More is due later about ABI. But before this it is necessary to catch up on my own early life that led to God making our lives "one" in serving Him (Gen. 2:24).

5

Jim—The Youngest Years

I WAS BORN IN a small, crude shack on a wind-swept hill not far from Eufaula, Oklahoma. The land was a pioneer area where Cherokee Indians roamed the countryside and sometimes ransacked homes when people were away. It was 1934.

My parents were Ruben and Tiny Allen. Mother was one of 12 children, eight brothers and four daughters, from the James and Bertha Fraley family. My sister, Anna Mae, preceded me by three years (1931–1995). Tiny had been born April 23, 1911 in Crowder City, Oklahoma. She told me that she had a severe struggle giving birth to me, her son. A midwife helped her.

James Edward, as my parents named me, became a tow-headed, blond lad, almost constantly in motion, and often gravitating to deviltry. I demonstrated early and often that I was "in Adam."

On one farm wash day two miles from Liberty, AZ, when I was around five, Mary Chesshir was helping my mother by washing the clothes in a Maytag machine sitting in the back yard. My mother was inside resting near the time when a brother, Frank, would be born in what would eventually be a family of 10 children. Mary had the wash tub filled with water heating over a Mesquite wood fire. Nicknamed "Pat," I slipped near the tub behind Mary's back and, for a "Dennis the Menace" prank, dumped several fistfuls of dirt into the water.

Mary turned, was instantly aware of the mischievous deed, and her anger flared. She stormed after me brandishing a Tamarisk switch. I beat a retreat in panic, ducked through a barbed wire fence, sped across the corral as if shot from a gun, and dug hard up a hill. For a time Mary was right on my heels, but the desperation of facing her wrath put enough "jet" fuel in me that my legs set some kind of kid's sprint record pulling away. Then I skulked at my fugitive distance until Mary, hours later, left for her own home.

My mother happened to gaze out a window and see the fugitive laying down flying feet in the terror of the getaway. The awfulness of the damaging misdeed struck her mind, yet the desperation in the young boy's flight caused her to erupt with laughing. All this she hid from the outdistanced lady who was after "a piece of my hide."

Dark times had shrouded our lives about four years earlier, in Oklahoma.

The family like many had become dirt poor, scarcely eking out a farming existence in days that tried many people's souls. Desperation had turned into the famous "Dust Bowl" era. Then many formerly successful farmers and their children would watch, helpless and aghast with tears, as government agents came in to shoot their cattle down and get rid of entire herds. These visitors with their guns were driven to stop a disease among cattle from spreading. Besides this loss, a disastrous famine tortured the land.

My father "Rube" often jogged away astride a mule to toil on nearby farms. Mom looked after my sister and myself, did the housework, and kept a few hens so that she could sell the eggs.

Mom told me years later that Rube from the beginning had never shown any love to her. She was just a convenience in his selfish life. He looked at us children as just in his way. Her own previous family had had feelings that, with so many children to feed, eventually 12, Tiny ought to marry and be "out of the nest." They pushed her into a wedding in 1930 at 19. Rube was a hardened man, riveted to nursing his own thoughts, lost within his own desires, surly, raging to get at hard drink, and at times fitfully cruel.

One day a country salesman stopped by and Mom traded a hen in exchange for extract, a liquid flavoring for a cake. Her excited hope was to surprise her husband with a special pleasure when he returned home that evening from farm labor. He came riding his mule into the yard, and as a young bride elated with her secret Mom ran out to meet him. Surely he would like the dessert she had baked, and maybe he would be more tender toward her. But, knowing how the shelves were nearly barren of food, he cut curtly right to the question of where she got the flavoring to make a cake.

"Why," she said in the jubilation of her surprise, "I traded one of the hens." That was meant to be a victory and a treat of celebration to ease their penny-pinching misery.

"You—what?" Rube's face flared to crimson, fury exploding in his cheeks. He snapped up his mule quirt, and began to lay stripes of meanness upon Mom's back and legs. For he had coveted to swap the hen to rake in drinking money. The shocked wife began to shriek from the cutting lashes and from a broken heart. Anna Mae, my sister, who was a small girl of three, fled in terror to scream for her aunt. The visiting sister came out, eyes wide with terror, scarcely able to endure the brutality. A wonderful surprise that love planned had erupted into a nightmare of pain, despair, and heartbreak.

On other occasions, Rube would go in the rumbling wagon with the family to a Church of Christ some miles across country. On the long ride home, Mom remembered how he would rip the preacher to shreds and scorn things of the Bible, putting his worldly slants on things. Years later, after much neglect of church going, Mom would realize that in all her early visits to church she herself had never personally known the Savior. She would look to Him and be saved (John 3:14-15). The family has no knowledge that Rube ever came to Christ, although we hope he did.

The larger Fraley family of which Tiny was a part did back-breaking work in farming. They devoted exhausting days to picking cotton, milking cows, and some of the older boys hunted possums and coons to put meat on the table with beans, cornbread, okra, and black eyed peas. In his final years, the family's father, James Thomas, was frightfully wasting away in a losing battle with stomach cancer. He would die at 45 in 1933 shortly after the 12th Fraley child had been born. Tiny would be visiting, sitting in vigil by his bedside, suffer the stinging grief that he was gone, and sob in breaking the news to her mother.

When my sister Anna Mae was four and I hardly past one, most of Mom's desperate family, the Fraleys, had "pulled up stakes" and migrated westward to Arizona to scrape for work in bleak times. The long lines of cars that Oklahomans drove westward on the narrow roads leaving the state to search for new hope found description in John Steinbeck's famous novel. Out of it came the movie by the same title, *The Grapes of Wrath*. For many of the migrants went on to eke out their existences in California's grape vineyards.

Several of Tiny's brothers would valiantly work their way out of despair, skimp and save, eventually buy farms, and in a few years become very successful. Bill, Tom, and Vernon all worked until they could secure land for themselves. Ed and Russell became foremen in the circular pit copper mine at Ajo, AZ, one of the largest open pit copper mines in the United States. The name "Ajo" (pronounced Ah-ho) was derived from a wild, desert onion. Another brother, Pete, did a stint in the Navy and later worked at various jobs. James Thomas or "J. T." was a Shafter, CA fire marshal, later an operator of a Fresno, CA filling station, then a forest ranger, and a lay preacher. Gennis taught school, then ran a grocery delivery service, stocking stores.

The four Fraley daughters also did well. Dorothy or "Deanie" married Clyde Dodd, who became foreman of a large McLaughlin cattle ranch in California. Margaret wedded Ralph Scott, a mechanic and later a worker in the California oil fields. Ellen Ruth, the baby, married a preacher, who died rather young, and she later married Larry Brannon. Her two sons would become pastors of large Church of Christ congregations. Among all these 12 Fraleys, several received and loved the

Lord—Bill, Tom, J. T., Gennis, Deanie, Margaret, and Ellen Ruth. And Tiny would come to know the Savior as well.

Rube and Tiny still lingered in the Eufaula area until early Fall, 1935. Here they were reduced almost to a penniless poverty. Finally, getting mail telling them that for a time other Fraleys had landed jobs west of Phoenix, they sold their pitifully scant belongings, scraped together barely enough money to buy train seats, and chugged away to Phoenix themselves. Fresh off the train, Rube had just two dollars. He bought milk and crackers for the family, and the parents set out walking, taking the children along the dusty highway westward to find Liberty, about 27 miles away. They knew that the "Hollywood Turkey Ranch" where some of the Fraleys were picking turkeys was somewhere near Liberty, "a wide spot in the road" with two grocery stores, a filling station and garage, a couple of houses, a well, and a court of laborers' cabins.

A Hollywood movie producer had bought land and started a turkey haven, hence the place came to be called "The Hollywood Turkey Ranch." It was a mile east and three miles north of Liberty. Liberty sprawled about six miles east of Buckeye and 27 west from Phoenix.

The trudge was a punishing one with Rube and Tiny trading off carrying me, the year-old baby, and four-year old Anna Mae pattering along behind or at times also being carried. Several hours brought the family, in colloquial language so "plumb tuckered" that they were ready to collapse, to a roadside field arbor. There a merchant sold fruits, vegetables, and soft drinks. They sank, pitifully worn out and disconsolate, upon wooden boxes outside the arbor near Highway 80. The parents felt almost at their wits' end, at the back side of a biting hopelessness.

A man in a Ford Model T came chugging toward Phoenix from the direction of Liberty, and wheeled in for a stop at the arbor. Rube went to the driver and asked if he knew where the turkey ranch was. The man owned that he knew fairly closely where it must be, and could ask and find it. When Rube pulled his last dollar from his pocket to offer the driver for a ride, he agreed to haul the downcast "Okies" to the ranch.

Once there, Mom immediately pleaded for a job picking turkeys. For it was urgent to earn money, or the family would have no food. And, like Joseph and Mary at Bethlehem, we as yet they had no place even to lay our heads. Mother's older brother, Bill, was a foreman of the ranch, and a broad-shouldered, six-one stranger, Francis Rosscup from Rolla, North Dakota, was the head turkey killer. Workers were rapidly stripping feathers from turkeys hanging along racks. The meat was to be trucked to Thanksgiving markets of 1935. Lola was absolutely "green" at this new task, and was fumbling, clumsily desperate but game to get the feathers off one of the birds. She must not fail, for it was critical to provide for her family.

Francis came over from killing turkeys and his eagle eye fixed on the newcomer's pathetic ineptness and her ordeal. Her panic was obvious. He was moved by her need, kept "coaching" her on how to "pick" a turkey quickly, and would not cease until her hands became a flurry of skilled action. He stood back and bragged about the job she learned so quickly. He did not realize she was doing it for her very life, her husband, and her children's sakes.

Rube, a proud, obstinate man, perched high up on a tractor seat in the farm yard, idle, fingering an empty tobacco pipe wistfully. He felt too good for the demeaning turkey job Francis offered him. It was beneath his dignity. He did not seem willing to dirty his hands at such a task. So Bill Fraley at least persuaded him to dig a trench nearby. The Fraleys, already having a small house packed like sardines with kinfolk, mercifully secured one of the tents set up in the area as a temporary home for Rube, Lola, and us two children.

Soon the 1935 winter's slashing rains began relentlessly to drench the area. Turkey killing and picking had to be suspended, and all four in our family huddled, shivering in the miserable, biting freeze of a canvas tent, living on a dirt floor. The tent was even invaded by waters rising to defy heaped up ridges to seep in. Francis came driving up from his own home two miles southwest of Liberty. He stood outside the tent, appalled at the heart-wrenching ordeal of the family. He pulled out candy for Anna Mae and me, and surveyed the pathos of the four suffering in such pitiful discomfort, subject to punishing and repeated downpours. Deeply touched, he invited us to come with him to live in his two-room board farmhouse. He turned the home over to us, sacrificially volunteering to live elsewhere himself. He just asked, in return, that the family feed his chickens and pigs, and milk the only cow he had so far, "Jersey." Even for this he paid a small salary.

When I think back on those days now, I am brought to tears of gratitude to God. He saw the wretchedness and mercifully had a heart to help us long even before we knew Him! It was like the line in the song, "He loved me ere I knew Him."

Mom took care of the chores outside as well as in the tar-covered board house. She was glad to have a roof to shield us from the winter's wet onslaught, and the warmth of a wood stove blazing in the kitchen. The only other room was the bedroom. Rube began to leave the family, sometimes leaving us alone for several days on visits to Buckeye six miles away. There he used Mom's turkey picking and farm savings he pilfered from a cup he sought out in her hiding place behind cupboard dishes. It held her meager hopes, which he squandered to bolster himself in his despondent condition with beer at one of the saloons. When he would show up again at the house, he was absorbed in his own thoughts, shiftless, surly, and caring only for himself.

Francis had hauled a wagon load of mesquite wood from across the nearby Gila River and gotten Rube's word that he would chop winter firewood. Rube briefly did some of the job, then abandoned the axe, quit, and trudged off to town. When he was gone Mom discovered upon coming in from chores that he again had taken the money by "turning the place upside down" to locate her cup's new hiding place.

She stood outside the door hiding her emotions from us children, utterly "wiped out." Leaning with her head against the wall, she heaved with heartbroken sobs. What would she and the children she loved so dearly do?

The man from Dakota broke upon the scene unexpectedly. When he stepped around the corner of the house he caught sight of Tiny in tears. He froze in his tracks, taken aback. His question about what was wrong caused Mom to erupt in new sobs and words filled with pain. Rube's ransacking had turned up the cup with its few coins, he had confiscated the money they needed, and left us again, apparently to waste what he pocketed. Francis bit his lip, not knowing what to say, walked to the wood pile, chopped a load of chunks for the fire, carried these into the house, and poked some of the fuel into the stove. It was a wet, cold, miserable day, and he sat beside the stove warming his hands. He kept shaking his head in disbelief, then reading *The Buckeye Valley News*. Mom answered his troubled questions about the merciless pattern that now had been going on for some weeks.

"Don't you worry, little lady," he consoled, peering over the top of his paper. "You and the kids won't go hungry. I'll never let that happen. I'm going right now to get groceries and make sure you all have enough. You just see you take care of things here. For the life of me, I don't know what's got into that man--your husband."

When Rube showed up again after several days, he dropped a bombshell on Mom. He had made up his mind. He was going to return to Oklahoma. She would find out later he left her to borrow money from her folks, the Fraleys, who lived two miles away near Liberty, to buy a train ticket. "I want all of us to go back," he said. Mom would tell me her face went white as a sheet. "We can't," she moaned. "We came out here because there was nothing there for us. Nothing!. We wouldn't have a chance. We've already seen that. Our only hope is here. The rains will end, and I can work again. I'm staying. Anna Mae and Pat have to stay with me."

Rube was flustered, angry, calloused, and cutting. Finally he slammed his few belongings into a beaten up suitcase, and walked stiffly past Mom and us children without a goodbye or a sign of caring. In time, it would become sadly apparent that he had heartlessly deserted the family. Mom's shattered heart sank to a new low as she kept watching him walk out on us, plodding along the road, eastward, on his trek toward Liberty.

Week followed week far into 1936. No mail arrived from Rube.

Francis came again several times to check on his farm, and was aware of the plight. He asked what this lady wanted to do, and she said she must stick it out, if he could extend use of the house a bit longer, for the children's sakes. In warmer weather the three of us could then move back into a tent. More weeks slipped by, and word came from Oklahoma to the Fraleys from some who knew Rube that he really had abandoned the family, left us "in the lurch." He had turned, in a hard, willful way to his own life.

Francis heard that, mulled it over. Later he came back and told Mom he loved her and us children. Whether she would have him or not, he wanted to take care of us all. They talked it over and decided to drive to Phoenix to have divorce papers filed. Later, when they got hold of Rube, his word came that he agreed to that. They took the deadness of his interest as a case of calloused desertion. Lola remarried, this time to a man she adored, and whom she knew truly loved her and us children, the Dakotan. The wedding was May 4, 1936, in Albuquerque, New Mexico. The couple went there with Mom's brother Bill and his wife Emma from the Hollywood Turkey Ranch.

When I think of the events, as mom so truthfully told me, my mind sees a similarity in Louis L'Amour's novel of the west, *Hondo.* John Wayne starred in the movie version and dubbed the tale the greatest western he had ever read. A man, Hondo Lane, cane to the rescue of Angie Lowe and her son at a desolate cabin deep in Apache territory. Angie's husband had left her in danger to pursue gambling and drink that led to his death. Hondo fell in love with Angie, and protected her and the son in loving care.

This new husband of mother and father to Anna Mae and me had come from Rolla, North Dakota, in 1929. His father Frank had made a profession of faith in St. John's Church of North Vernon, Indiana on April 9, 1876, but there was no evidence of genuine conversion. He had been born September 6, 1858, the son of Jacob and Elizabeth Rahskopf who had come from Germany to Indiana sometime around Frank's birth date. Due to English spelling problems, as on a census, they had the name smoothed out to Rosscup, a name that may have meant such ideas as "horse's head" or "head [crown] of a hill." Frank married Rosa Cooper in 1883, and the couple migrated to Langdon, North Dakota where he ran a meat market in 1885–1887, then they moved to Rolla to farm in the Turtle Mountain area in 1993. Francis was born there Aug. 3, 1900.

This man from the north was one of four brothers, and his family had two sisters. One sister's granddaughter Shannon Hartnett from the San Francisco Bay area, would distinguish herself as holder of about eleven women's world records in Scottish highland festival athletic contests in the 1985–1995 period. She was a cover girl on sports magazines and appeared on TV.

Francis was a very caring husband and precious "daddy." Anna Mae and I loved his constant playful affection, and soon snuggled into his arms as our very dear father. I from an early age helped feed the chickens, milk the cows (for Francis was adding other cows than just "Jersey"), slop the hogs, and ride "Old Dick," a pet work horse. As Anna Mae and I grew, our gracious father gave us animals as our very own. The first was a gift to Anna Mae of the calf "Heifer," which won a district 4-H prize at Tempe, and to me, "Pat," his gift was two pigs which I fattened and sold in Phoenix to finance buying several little pigs. Dad saw that whatever money we earned was our own. For he was teaching us to be wise to save, invest, and build with vision for the future.

I can say now, I believe that all of our difficulty was in the compassionate providence of God. He meant it for our later good. This Dakotan, our new father, rescued us out of an oblivion that we could not help, and was there with a father's love. Beyond him was the heavenly Father we would one day know. Without God giving us this help, even before we knew Him, and all the good things that would come later, our lives might have been shattered and pitiful, wrecked on the dump heap of disaster.

It is an opportune time to draw a life portrait of Mom. Precious, precious mother! She worked extremely hard, caring for her children in tender love, helping milk the cows by hand, carrying armloads of wood in for the stove, and cooking for what would eventually become a large family of 10 children. She did the washing, at first laboring over a ruffled scrub board and later with a Maytag washer, ironed, and made most of the children's clothing for several years. She held quilting bees in which women made quilts to warm against the winter's cold. She fed the chickens, and drove a mile to haul cans of drinking water. She fixed school lunches for the smaller children, made decorative flowers of crepe to beautify the simple home, and crocheted "doilies" that looked nice on kerosene lamp tables.

This woman made constant sacrifices for those she loved. She was ever the tender comforter and the encourager. She would do without nice clothing herself to make sure we had what we needed. And she was a wonder in the kitchen, patting out flour biscuits, stirring white gravy, fixing a lunch of chicken and dumplings, and sometimes shortcake with mashed strawberries. She cranked a freezer to make ice cream, and went out in the ranch yard to chase down a chicken, wring its neck, pluck its feathers, and have a meal on the table in minutes.

Mom stuck by her man, loving him with all her heart. And to his dying day he was always loving and faithful to her. Just about in the middle of her life of 86 years (1911–1997) she would receive Christ in 1957. And after this the Bible became her precious "gold mine" as she trusted the Lord and prayed. Dad died in 1965. In her elderly years Mom lived in Scottsdale, near Phoenix, and I in Whittier, CA. I wrote her every week, and phoned to see that she was all right.

Once when she as a widow phoned me, she was desperate. In a senior citizens' mobile park, she had tried and tried to get the cover of the air conditioner on but could not. I could tell by her voice that she was at her wits' end. I was about 360 miles away, so I could not be there to help. So I said, "Mom, let's ask God to make it go on." I led us, beseeching the Lord to cause the cover to fit. After this Mom said she would try again. A few minutes later she called me back, and she was excited. "You wouldn't believe it! I put it up there, and it went right on, pretty as you please."

I could believe it. What a happy moment. God answers prayer! "And whatsoever ye shall ask in prayer, believing you shall receive" (Matt. 21:22).

This durable little woman of five feet five inches loved her children, I am convinced more than she loved her own life. And even before she knew the Lord, she was a person the world credited with integrity, just as our Dad Francis was.

Mom had not gotten past the eighth grade. She spoke in simple farm land lingo, often slaying the grammar as hillbilly "Festus" did on the long-running TV "Gunsmoke" western series. But she was a marvel of a mother, as honest as the day is long. I remember waking to see her sitting very far into the night in the pale light of a kerosene lamp at a Singer sewing machine mending clothes or making new ones. All her children would hold her in very high regard.

One day when I was just a small boy, a neighbor boy swiped one of my toys and made off with it. So I walked the quarter mile to that boy's yard under a spreading canopy of tall cottonwood branches. Nobody was in sight, and I spotted the kid's toy tractor in the dirt. For spite to "get even," I hid the tractor in the brush on the way home. Mom "pried" out of me where I had been and the sorry deed I had done, scolded me for the deceit, and laid down Rosscup law. "You go get that tractor and put it back in his yard right where you found it—I mean, now! And don't you come back 'til it's done." She believed in doing unto others as one would desire that they do in return, though she did not yet know the Lord's "golden rule" on that (Matt. 7:12).

I learned from Mom's stand to do what was right. A few years later at about 10, I found myself in a grocery store with a young cowboy from a huge cattle ranch. The two of us had ridden our horses, hitched them, and gone inside. My friend caught the proprietor not looking and pocketed a candy bar. I saw the theft, but would not follow his example. We swung back on our horses, the friend with candy and I without any. But my heart felt right that I had done what Mom or Dad would do.

How mysterious are the kind dealings of the gracious God. Even before those of the family were to know Him as Savior, He was doing compassionate things for us in preparation for the years to come. We were in a long line of those who received grace from God. He was the Lord who brought Abram from Ur of the Chaldees, out of a family of idol-worshippers, before He made the Abrahamic covenant with him (Gen. 12:1-3). He was the Lord who preserved a poor couple's baby, Moses, in a desperate case by a basket in the marsh of the Nile River, and in a pharaoh's palace, to prepare him for leadership in later years. He was the God who watched over Joseph and Mary in their poverty and even cared for the Christ child when there was no room in the inn.

He was the God of hope. He was, He is, the God who "raises the poor from the dust, and lifts the needy from the ash heap" (Ps. 113:7). And He is the God before whom all humanity, in their unsaved state, are dead in sins, undone, in a poverty of utter desperation, without Him and without hope (Eph. 2:11ff.).

This God, so faithful, looked compassionately on a mother at her wits' end and her children in a destitute misery of rain. He showed pity. In providence and in great kindness, He had put it in the heart of a North Dakota farmer who did not know the future to migrate to Arizona in 1929, eventually buy a 20-acre farm, and come splashing along a boggy, muddy road to show a heart for a family in stark need. He was the God who permitted our unfaithful, blood dad to commit a heartless, neglectful, low life, selfish desertion. He was the God who allowed the heart of a lonely Arizona farmer to fall "head over heels" in love with a woman and her children, abandoned and seemingly in for a miserable future. But he swept us into his arms of care. He was the God who defeated human failure and gave the family a hard-working, loving husband and precious "daddy." How mysterious are the ways of God even when human resources plunge to a hair's breadth from dead zero.

Humanly speaking, what would have happened if God had not been a God of rescuing pity? This was the God who found Jerusalem as a forsaken child (Ezek. 16:3-14), and compassionately gave her a future and a hope! He is not only the God of immaculate theology when things are pretty and ideal, but the God of all comfort who can work in conditions gone awry to the outrageous, last outpost of dire need.

Once we children began to catch the Liberty School bus that came along the dirt road near the farm, we both excelled in studies. I became a voracious, avid reader, in those nights by a pale kerosene lamp light in a house that had no electricity until I was in the fifth grade. For the library at Liberty School had a fine collection. I checked out books constantly—Fran Striker's Lone Ranger series, Edgar Rice Burroughs' 24 Tarzan books, the multi-volume Bobbsey Twins series, *The Wind in the Willows*, many western novels like Zane Grey's 63 or so, and the Powder Valley series by Peter B. Field, the novel about a horse named *Steeldust*, Mary O'Hara's trilogy *My Friend Flicka*, *Thunderhead*, and *Green Grass of Wyoming*, and such stories. Later I would pore through dozens of Franklin Dixon's *The Hardy Boys* mystery novels, Clarence E. Mulford's famous "Hopalong Cassidy" books of the Bar-20 ranch, and several of Walter Farley's nearly 20 stories about *The Black Stallion* and the boy Alec Ramsey who rode that fast horse. Then there were comic books about The Lone Ranger, Red Ryder, Roy Rogers, Gene Autry, Hopalong Cassidy, Superman, Captain Marvel, Batman and Robin, Woody Woodpecker, Donald Duck and Mickey Mouse.

In school we read *Treasure Island*, Jack London's *The Call of the Wild* and also *White Fang*, *A Tale of Two Cities*, *A Tree Grows in Brooklyn*, *Forever Amber*, *Jane Eyre*, *Robinson Crusoe*, Samuel Clemens' *The Celebrated Jumping Frog of Caliveras County* and *Tom Sawyer*, Harriet Beecher Stowe's novel of slave days called *Uncle Tom's Cabin*, and other works then famous.

Anna Mae and I, now answering to Francis's nicknames, for her "Sis" or "Sit," and for me "Pat," took to school paper bag lunches with sandwiches of a great variety. The taste at noon time might be ham within slices of Roman Meal bread or flour biscuits. Or the filling could be scrambled eggs, or cheese, or peanut butter and honey or jam, or mashed potatoes, or avocado, or sausage or bacon from hogs I helped Dad butcher, or if nothing else was available, pinto beans or just plain churned butter on wheat bread or biscuits.

This fare was almost always better than Mom had taken to school as a girl. On walks to class through Oklahoma's winter cold, she took a hot baked potato. This "portable heater," tucked into a pocket and switched from side to side, kept her hands warm, then when it had become cold was her meal at lunch time.

6

Growing Up and Meeting Christ

ONE CHRISTMAS THE LIBERTY School must have been desperate. When I was about seven, I was tabbed to play Santa Claus in a children's play before the parents. In the sixth grade, I became one of the fastest sprinters of my smaller, Class C size in the school, and won district ribbons in track, second in broad jump and fourth in high jump. Anna Mae learned to play the clarinet and marched in the Buckeye Union High School band. Later my sister Joyce would be in that band and after that in the prize-winning Arizona State University band.

Francis' 20-acre farm had once been part of a vast, unusable white alkali area of desert brush and arroyos. Around 1889 a man came from Ohio, the Buckeye state, named this due to a tree's brownish nut about the size of a buck's eye. He and others started Buckeye. Some farmers a few miles east of the town dug out a canal, put in pumps to fill it with water, and "cleansed" the wide table land area by a series of irrigations, flooding water across the soil from north to south to spill over cliffs into the Gila River basin. So they ridded much of the white substance, alkali.

After watering the area enough time s, the farmers waited for the land to dry, then found the dirt rich to till. Tractors stirred up clouds of dust. Men began to start farms all across the "Buckeye Valley," in all directions from the small roadside town of Liberty.

Some of the childhood games on the farm were riding downhill inside a rolling barrel, doing leap frogs over board calf pen fences to elude a pursuer, hide and seek, cowboys and Indians, building huts out of branches, kicking the can, marbles, yoyo, skip rope, hop scotch, "mumble de peg" with a knife, sawing out toy wooden guns, making leather holsters, and "skinning up" into trees. "London Bridge is Falling Down," softball, riding a horse, "Lone Ranger" and other activities were fun. At grade school, I was one of the most elusive runners in a game in which children lined up and ran across the field where players in the middle had to pat them three times on the back to conquer them and join them to their own ranks.

Anna Mae and I threw up tepees made of tamarisk tree branches. We liked to huddle inside these, imagining we were in some stirring western drama such as we heard on Lone Ranger radio episodes. At times we hunted for turtles in an irrigation drainage ditch, swam in that stream, or sought to find quails' eggs in their brush nests near the farm.

One day I lay in heavy Bermuda grass just staring at the sky. Eagles maneuvered high in the blue, drifting this way and that. Dazzled by their incredible flight, I formed a poem, "On this green blanket where I lie, I love to watch the birds fly by, and wish that I could soar so high." I had no inkling that later God would save me, that one day I would soar on eagle's wings (Isa. 40:31), and even fly away to heaven at death (Ps. 90:10), or in the rapture (1 Thess. 4:13-18)! In my pagan state, I knew nothing yet of these.

At small Liberty School, one of the girls about seven years older than I distinguished herself by uncanny classroom oratory and acting. She was Jacque Mercer, daughter of the principal, Arthur Mercer. Later when at Arizona State College Jacque would be voted "Miss Tempe," then more amazingly "Miss Arizona," and even very incredibly "Miss America." Another student, Jim Parks, a friend who lived about a mile and a half from our farm and rode horses with me, would in a few years be one of the top national AAU sprinters. Jim even beat the heralded Duke speedster, Dave Sime, in a 60-yard dash. Sime and Bobby Morrow of Abilene Christian College became the most famous collegiate sprinters for a time in the 100 yards (later this would be renamed "the 100 meters" and be about nine yards longer).

Another student, Otha Dee Arnold, rode with her rancher father to cowboy competition in the "rodeo circuit," places such as the famous Cheyenne, Wyoming Frontier Days Celebration. That rodeo was dubbed among cowpokes "The Granddaddy of them All." In the arena competition at such cities as Salinas, CA, Calgary, CAN, and Fort Worth, TX, Otha Dee's dad Carl Arnold piled up points to win the world steer roping championship in the mid 1940's. He was a lean horseman who many years later would be one of the pallbearers at my Dad's funeral in February, 1965.

In Buckeye High School, encouragements came. God gave me the privilege to be chosen president of the National Honor Society, president of the Pan-Am Club, editor of the school newspaper, *The Buckeye Hawk,* and secretary of my senior class. At church, the young people chose me as president of our Sunday School class, then of the Sunday evening young people's union, and after that of the Buckeye Valley Singspiration, composed of youths in area churches. After that, He blessed me to be president of the mid-Arizona, larger Valley Rally of many churches. Then, unexpectedly, the youth voted me in as state president of the Baptist young people for two years (1954–1956). In retrospect I would come to realize that God was training me for leadership in ways that got me ready to teach students who would take Christ's message to various countries. The earliest offices in the home church, strangely, were even before I came to know Christ as Savior. All glory goes to Him, the great "I AM," who has His plans of grace, and is always ahead of us (John 15:16).

In the earliest of those days, none of the Rosscups were Christians. But Francis and Lola were highly moral people who showed "true grit." They helped their neighbors in all sorts of ways. Some of these were quilting bees, sewing clothing, Francis slaving in the harvests or helping farmers who were ill, and his sitting in vigils by people's bedsides to tend them, or helping extract Mesquite honey on a huge nearby bee farm.

Dad was a kind of John Wayne, an iron man, a man's man, as the most famous western writer Louis L'Amour would say, "a man to ride the river with." At six feet one inch in height, he weighed in at around 215 pounds, about the same size as Joe Louis, who hammered his way to be the heavyweight boxing champion of the world as "the Brown Bomber" in the 1940's. God had gifted Dad with mind-boggling strength. Once in a farmhouse fire, two or three men tried to carry a stove out to safety, but gave it up. Francis rushed in, got hold of the stove alone, and lugged it out. On another occasion while driving, he came across a man trapped under a car that had fallen on him when he was trying to change a tire. Francis lifted the car off the man and got him free. Farmers said in my hearing that my dad could do the work of three men.

And he would toil for long days in the torrid Arizona hay fields, forking mown alfalfa into "shocks," i.e. rounded piles that later could conveniently be loaded on a "float," a flat hauler that horses or a tractor dragged over the ground for unloading at a hay stack. Before and after a day in the field, Dad would be at home to milk the cows of his growing dairy. As the years went by he soon built a milking herd of around 30, fattened out many "vealers," i.e. young cattle, and raised hogs, calves, chickens, and sometimes turkeys and ducks. We heard at his funeral that a family had nothing for Christmas, and Dad showed up at their door with bags of groceries as well as toys for the children.

This Dakotan seemed to know a bit of everything. He had been a butcher in his home state, and was a voracious reader. His perusals were mostly of news such as in his paper from back home in Rolla, North Dakota, *The Turtle Mountain Star*, and *The Farm Journal*. I remember listening nearby when he and other ranch men would talk, and was amazed at how much he knew about a lot of things. The men would lend their ears as he described how to do this or that, or commented on events of World War II in the early 1940's.

I rode to the roadside town, Liberty, with Dad many a time and watched him beat opponent after opponent in pool, snooker, or billiards at Cleve Hardin's recreation hall beside his grocery store. Dad said he had honed his skill in cold North

Dakota where one of the few pastimes in freezing weather was playing at a pool hall. A bread man used to run his route out of Phoenix and stop by to have contests with Dad. Both could make incredible shots that banked a ball in just the right ways to sink in a pocket, or hit other balls in. One would win, then the other as onlookers stood by, at times whistling or gasping at impossible shots that worked.

Dad would labor many nights, walking the fields to check on the progress of water as he irrigated. I often would see him during the day when he had come in from the field in a gray farm shirt just drenched with sweat from laboring in the scorching sun.

During some of the war years, Francis added to his various farm jobs a role of guarding planes at Goodyear Air Force Base in Goodyear and Luke Air Force Base north of there. Goodyear was about 15 miles northeast of the farm as one drove toward Phoenix.

I recall that as a small boy noises often awakened me from the next room long before sun up, about four o'clock. I could hear Dad's and Mom's preparations for Dad to be off to work at those air bases. I knew the clank and thud when they poked wood into the stove, and the clink when they set the iron stove lids back in place, or the buzz of voices in the kitchen, the sizzle and aroma of bacon or sausage, the ting of Mom sticking a tin of biscuits on an oven rack, the aroma of coffee, the clatter of plates and tinkle of silverware. And the tantalizing lure of frying eggs and bacon, and steaming honey-brown biscuits drifted into the bedroom. These laid an awesome sensation on a young boy's nostrils.

I sometimes would go, in my pajamas, to join Dad and Mom at the table. After the meal I would follow Dad into the bedroom, and gape in amazement as he strapped on his big belt, holster, and revolver. To a kid's eyes he was a hero of a man, something like the Lone Ranger with his ivory handled six guns and silver bullets.

Speaking of the Lone Ranger, one incident comes back clearly from the years. The Holsum Bread Company put an ad on loaves about sending in a certain number of labels to win a Lone Ranger star. For this ranger of Fran Striker's masked man novels had been the only ranger who survived when outlaws caught a band of rangers in a canyon ambush. Off went my order. I waited, scarcely able to stand the delay, for the days to drag by. Then the mail man delivered a small package. Tearing it open, I pulled out the star, pinned it on, and felt like "the Lone Ranger rides again"! It was like the kid in the movie, *"A Christmas Story,"* fondling hopes of getting a Red Ryder air rifle with an image of Red Ryder himself carved into the stock so he could ride the range and stop outlaws.

One very early morning a tramp rapped at the door. Such "bums" were numerous in those difficult days. This wanderer's huge pack was slung over his back. His pitiful words, like those of Jean Valjean in the 1998 movie version of Victor

Hugo's famous novel *Les Miserables*, were that he was very hungry. Could he have just anything to eat? Dad piled a plate full for him. The man started to turn to take the food and a tin of coffee out under the Tamarisk trees. Dad stopped him for a moment. Mom told me later of his words, which were not like the loving bishop's life-changing act of kindness to Valjean, but thick with ringing authority like John Wayne's.

"Now I have to go to get to work on time," he said, tapping the revolver riding his hip. "We've been good to you, but if you do any harm to my wife or children, I'll be back. Believe me, I'll be on your trail, and I won't let up 'til I catch you."

The man cast wary eyes at the gun butt, and swore he just wanted his stomach filled. By no means would he harm a soul. So Dad left, with the stiff, powerful warning behind him. He would come back to find that the tramp had soon returned the plate and cup, thanked Mom, and tromped off on his way.

On several occasions as I was the oldest boy, Francis would take me, his son, with him high on the wagon seat behind a team of work horses, Old Dick and Charley. The wagon would rattle for miles along a dirt trail to a spot where Mesquite wood was abundant. First the team had to ford the Gila River, then make the trek out into the wastelands and breaks to find great stands of Mesquite. It would be a day's work, Dad chopping limbs, and me dragging them to the wagon and loading what I could.

On one occasion the branches of trees suddenly were whacked aside. At the thunder of a new voice, I looked up to see a menacing, bearded man stalking toward my father. A wild intruder, he was brandishing a shotgun and his angry words boomed out like cannon shots. I cowered near a wagon wheel in grave fright for my father, as the gunman angrily claimed that the land was his and Dad was taking his limbs. Yet they were there by the thousands and would go almost altogether to waste. Dad reasoned with the man that this was government land, as it was, and tried to cool his fury. The shotgun continued to swing and jab, and the man sent chills up my spine. Finally, Dad quieted him, he was satisfied, and stalked back into the brush.

I stood trembling, yet very grateful. The two of us later finished the loading of winter wood and rumbled homeward over the rough, rutted trail. I wanted to drive the team, so Dad laid the wide leather reins into my chubby fingers. He kept his own large hands near, and when he saw need closed his fingers over mine to guide the great horses.

Our cattle's grazing area was limited on the 20 acres, so Dad often sought out pasture lands far from home. I remember at least 15 trail drives to push the livestock to these ranges. In each case we would go morning and evening to round up the cattle in a corral and milk them by hand, Dad milking perhaps 20 and myself 10.

Mom also worked "her fingers to the bone." As the family increased finally to 10 children in the years of 1937–1951, she made shirts, dresses, bedspreads, sheets, and bonnets. Her hands were busy hustling up three meals a day to put on a long table for what would in a few years be 12 in the family. When neighboring crews came to help us harvest our grain, Mom would fill the long kitchen table with food—fried chicken, mashed potatoes, white or brown gravy, sliced tomatoes, stringed beans, churned butter, honey from our hives, plenty of milk and iced tea or "Kool Aid."

She and Francis were often home doctoring the children, for the winters were punishing. Often somebody had the "croup," or "measles" or "mumps," or "pink eye," or pneumonia, fits of coughing, or a splitting headache. In the summer the problem might be a bare foot cut from running over broken glass or a ground weed called "goat heads" or "bull heads" that was a menace with knife-like points called "stickers."

Frank was born as the third child, then Ethel, later Jerry, Elmer (Tommy), and others joined the family quite rapidly—Mary Ellen, Joyce, Betty Lou, and Catherine. The children almost reached the number in a famous book at that time, *Cheaper By the Dozen*.

Frank would grow up to become a railroad repairman for arms at crossings; Ethel would go to Arizona State University and in marriage be a teacher, housewife and mother. Jerry became a grade school teacher; Mary Ellen would go various places with her U.S. Air Force husband Jim, who would become a Lt. Col. and fly Phantom Jet missions over Cambodia and later be a commercial pilot for American Airlines. Mary Ellen would become a member of a beauty group for a time, teach grade school, and write a book on Saudi Arabian customs, such as the treatment of women. Joyce went to Ecuador for Peace Corps service and later has lived as a housewife. Betty Lou would marry a whiz at painting and wall papering, and an expert church organist. Betty was a secretary in a missions organization for many years, then at a Christian senior citizens' estate. Catherine would wed a man in shipping and herself become manager of the Neo-Natal Care Department at the University of Washington Medical Center in Seattle.

I was to be converted to Christ in 1952 during my junior year of high school. All the others in the family later followed in becoming Christians or professing Christ. One child for a time professed to be a Christian, but for years has claimed, and it is a heart break, to see as nonsense the belief that God exists.

One little brother, Elmer, or "Tommy," died at a year and six days after the family's desperate drive to a doctor's office in Phoenix. Mom carried the lifeless body back to the car where some of us other children waited, and Dad drove on the way home, everybody sobbing. At the funeral held at the Liberty Cemetery, a Pastor

Sell from the Church of Christ in Buckeye officiated, and everybody sang, "What a Friend We Have in Jesus." But at that time none of the Rosscups knew the Lord.

I was very hard hit by the loss of my baby brother. In those days at about age seven I had no understanding of my need for God, or the way of salvation. God was not even in our conversation, except in Dad's and my curse words. For weeks I would seek out a lonely place to sit behind the house, lean against the wall under the spreading limbs of Tamarisk trees, and cry my heart out. But the words sang at the funeral would keep coming back, even though I did not yet know the Savior, "What a friend we have in Jesus . . . ." That was in 1942, and God was planting thoughts in the soul.

Years slipped by. We were "separate from Christ, excluded from the commonwealth of Israel, and strangers to the covenants of promise, having no hope and without God in the world" (Eph. 2:12).

But God . . . (Eph. 2:13)!

One Sunday morning at the age of 18, I was striding in corral filth from working with cattle to the ranch house around 100 yards away. A young couple drove into the yard to pick up my three years younger brother Frank to take him to Sunday School at the First Baptist Church in Buckeye four miles from our place. The unexpected, soft purr of an auto engine behind me fell upon my ears. I was trapped and embarrassed. The two visitors' faces were radiant, their words gracious, and they invited me to go also the next Sunday. Their cordiality was a magnet, and I did. It has been said, "You need to be winsome to win some." Not long after their contact, I received the Savior, as I will recount a bit later.

This couple I only knew then as Charles and Jo Helene Green. Charles was from a ranch a few miles west, and Jo Helene a daughter of the Buckeye high school principal Herschel Hooper. How could I know that in that same time frame (1950–1952), Charles took classes at the very school, the Arizona Bible Institute, where God was preparing my wife? Jo Helene devoted herself also to a life of all-out service. The couple studied at Redlands University and Westmont College, and Charles at Western Seminary in Port-land. Then he was pastor of the Northwest Baptist Church in Portland. Language study followed in Costa Rica, and church planting missions in Argentina (1963–1974). After that, the two did church planting in Farmington, New Mexico for four years, and Charles pastored Bible Baptist Church in Phoenix in 1978–1985.

The pair were missionaries in Caracas. Venezuela in 1985–1990, followed by a two-year pastorate to senior adults at First Baptist, Prescott, Arizona. Symptoms of Parkinson's disease caused a move to Phoenix for three years, then they lived in a home on their son Steve's property near Franklin, Tennessee. Charles went home to be with the Lord March 6, 2004, and Jo Helene Dec. 9, 2005. Among the five children God gave this couple, Steve would become one of America's top Christian singers. Barby, one of two daughters, married Mark Bailey, a man destined to be the fifth and current president at Dallas Theological Seminary after the legacies of Lewis Sperry Chafer, John Walvoord, Donald Campbell, and Chuck Swindoll. A son, Randy, is President of Mission Mobilization, International, David has served in Steve Green Ministries, and Grace is a pastor's wife in New Jersey. (For the summary of these fruitful lives, I am indebted to Barby Bailey, a letter, Aug. 6, 2009).

The Greens' going out of their way to arouse my interest in the Lord points up a principle. Personal contact is vital in pointing people to salvation. Years later I would write a "thank you" letter to the Greens for helping me on the way to God. They sent back a precious reply, then we exchanged Christmas cards for some years.

Leaders at the Buckeye church in my early days put on a campaign to invite and bring children to Sunday School. They announced that they would give awards to those who brought the most new pupils. I was unsaved, a wretch of selfish, worldly motives, but I was passionate and a go-getter—not to help people get to church but in a lust to win an award. So I went around the farmlands in my pea green '41 Chevy, inviting children. Finally I convinced 27 new ones to come one way or another. When the ceremony of prizes came, the superintendent called me forward and put the award into my hands. It was a black New Testament and Psalms, the first copy of God's Word I had ever had or held.

Breathless and overcome with awe, I went back to my seat clutching the treasure. It was as if I had come across a gold mine, a bonanza. I had heard the pastor preach from a black book, and the way he spoke of it told me that it had wonderful words. My heart was caught up in the sense that there was something very special about this book, and I felt a stir of curiosity to find out what it was! I believe now that the stir was part of God drawing me (John 6:44). I could hardly wait to be alone to read this, my own copy. At home, I took the "prize" out under a vast spread of Tamarisk limbs, climbed atop the bales of hay, staked out a perch that overlooked the corrals, and felt my entire being riveted into the pages.

Eventually as I kept up frequent vigils, God attracted my focus to verses Pastors Steven Dearborn or Basil Holmes had urged when they came to their invitations to receive salvation. There now, before my very own eyes, were the words of John 1:12, John 3:36, Romans 5:8, and Ephesians 2:8-9. These were about receiving Christ, believing, taking salvation as a gift, and not relying on works of any kind as if to earn it.

All the time, in deadly error, I was striving in a merit game to work my way into God's favor. In church, I would hear the invitation to "come forward and receive Christ." I believe the message was clear, but I still was blind. My fingers would grip the pew in front of me, and in a kind of despair I would cry silently to myself, "Not now; I can't. First, I have to live a perfect week. That way I'll show I can live the Christian life. Otherwise, it's no use making a start. God doesn't want phonies, and I'm one of the worst. Next Sunday, after I've lived up to it, I'll receive Christ, then I can make it."

But I was an undone sinner in darkness. Week followed week, and each time sooner or later my bubble of fancied perfection would burst, usually on Monday or Tuesday. An ornery cow would refuse to be herded into the corral. Or a bovine critter would bang me with the "shot put" ball of hard mud on her tail as I sat milking. I would cut loose with a furious string of cursing, then feel crushed, helpless, in stinging remorse, mourning that I had doomed my chances. That week was utter loss. Next week I must start all over, and try again. It was like being in a slippery pit (Ps. 40:2a), desperate to climb out, but always sliding back to the bottom.

Many Bible verses began to reason the light of God's offer into my heart. Though I did not suspect such things, the Holy Spirit was at work. One day, while lying on a ditch bank during a break from helping my father irrigate alfalfa, the truth sank home to my thoughts. A mysterious power moved me. Why, it is a gift! The concept placed a mighty, elating grip upon my mind. "A gift! That's what God says it is—a gift! He says 'believe . . . receive . . . not of works . . . for by grace ye are saved . . . .' Can that mean what it seems to mean? Isn't God true? He doesn't lie. It must mean what it says. I do believe; I do receive. 'Lord Jesus, please come into my heart and save me—the way You say!'"

God kept His word: ". . . the one who comes to Me I will certainly not cast out" (John 6:37).

Sins rolled away. A strange rejoicing swept through me, as if the purest water was washing me through and through. According to verses I saw in God's Word, I was brand new, made right, washed white, altogether clean (Isa. 1:18; 1 John 1:7). I knew then that God had done what the church's preachers said, "saved" me (Acts 16:31).

I had been president of my Sunday School class, also president of the Sunday night Baptist Young People's Union meeting. But secretly I had felt like a crummy phony up there in front of the others. What a hypocrite! The latest pastor even had thought I was a Christian—fatal mistake—due to my leadership. Why, he had even asked me to preach two messages to the congregation. I had labored very hard to get these ready, "patch working" things I had heard from other speakers, and I'm sure I copied them very poorly. But after the rebirth I came to the youth meeting with the exhilaration that God accepted me. I was confident that at last I was pleasing before God to be leading. I broke down and poured out to those in the group the change God had wrought, and how I was no longer living a lie. Instead of condemning me, people seemed glad. Soon after that I was one of several the pastor baptized. Oh, happy days to be remembered!

After being born again, I burst off the starting blocks. Diligence in study drove me in the faith. I ordered a packet of Christian books by evangelist John R. Rice that my pastor's Christian paper, *The Sword of the Lord*, advertised. How excited I was when the mail man brought the package, and I devoured the studies. I was ravenous, and simply could not feed my soul enough. One title was Rice's *Prayer, Asking and Receiving*. My prayer life began to sprout wings. I was amazed reading Rice's examples of God's great answers to prayers. And God began to change my life with answers to my own pleas as one of his sons (Matt. 7:7-11).

Who but God knew the plans for a dear daughter of His, already at a Bible school yearning to serve Him? And who but God knew that a new son of His was the one He was getting ready to meet His daughter in a short time and walk with her through many years of life? Oh, incredible God! Oh, great God who is greatly to be praised (Ps. 96:4)!

Some of us young people used to go with burning hearts to people in cotton camps on Sunday afternoons. We passed out tracts and talked with those who would listen as we told them the love of the Savior.

I could not know that not even an hour away, in Phoenix, was a girl who also knew Christ and went out to the unsaved, a lady God was preparing for our eventual marriage! Years earlier, while living near Liberty, I and my childhood sweetheart, Norma Jean, when not even age 10 yet, had put our hands together and dropped a penny in a tree's deep crotch to sink and be sealed as the tree grew. Our heart pledge was that the coin was a token to seal our love forever. We promised we would always be true, and one day marry.

Jeanie, from Salinas, California, was visiting her grandparents on a nearby farm as her family did frequently. Our times playing together were indescribably sweet. Then at the end of my sixth grade, Dad bought an 80 acre farm 10 miles away, northwest of Buckeye, and moved his family there. I was not to see Jeanie again until nearly six years later, late Dec., 1952, in the middle of my senior year of high school. One of the former Liberty neighbors, also in high school, told me that Jeanie was visiting. So in great excitement I phoned, and she said yes to a date. There was little to do in a small town, so we drove to a movie, then went to another town nearer Phoenix, Tolleson, for fish and chips. We sat in a drive-in area by the restaurant and talked for a very long time. Then, reluctantly, I drove her back to the farm to rejoin her family.

We made a date for me to take her to the Salad Bowl football game in Phoenix 27 miles away on New Year's Day. But before our time could come her family returned to California. I was <u>never</u> again to see Jeanie. How great is my hope that God has worked in her as He did in me, so that I will see her in heaven!

The plans <u>we</u> make are not always <u>God's</u> plans. His are so very much better.

Letters between Jeanie and myself crossed in a flurry for a time, then I became preoccupied with a high school girl I began to date. Other interests were track and field, writing sports for the town newspaper *The Buckeye Valley News*, church activities, riding my quarter horse, and plans for college. No doubt life's activities caught Jeanie away to new things too.

How wonderful, how kind, is God's over-arching providence. I would go off to college, meet many girls, and I assume that this California girl would meet other fellows as well. In just a year and half I would see Mildred for the first time. All my world would change! Not a penny sealed in a tree but the Spirit as the seal in my heart and the One leading me would determine my future (Eph. 1:13-14; 4:30).

One of my best friends from the sixth grade through high school was a very fast bay quarter horse, "Molly." While the family had still lived near Liberty, Dad went to an auction sale in Phoenix and sent home a surprise to me. A rancher with a horse trailer swung into the farm yard. I went out to see what he was bringing, as my father from time to time had cattle hauled to build our herd.

"What's this?" I asked the cowman, Herb Harvey, as I peered past trailer bars at what he had brought. It was a brown filly, as I would learn, a two-year old!

"Your dad said she was your'n," Harvey replied in cowboy lingo.

"Mine?" I was swept up in awe, thrilled beyond words.

"Yeah," said Harvey, "She's out of a racin' string, so she'll be a fast one. They had a lot of horses, and reckoned they had to get rid of some."

Indeed, I would find this quarter horse to be a blur of speed. At the time "Molly" was quite young, but I was light, and could swing upon her back and ride. The two of us became close friends, and I spent hours with her. When she would hear my call, she would nicker her response, then lope to the fence to greet me and shove her velvety nose into my hands. She grew, and was a jet stream streaking along the dirt roads or around the pasture. I could not then know that in New York, another farming father had given a girl I would one day marry her own bay horse by the name of "Star."

On one occasion our family's cattle were pastured a few miles from home. My Dad and I drove there to milk twice a day. One evening I rode Molly to do these chores, tied her, and left her enough rope to graze beside a driveway. She waited for my return and make the trek back home. She got a back foot tangled in the rope that I left too long, panicked, and sawed the foot about half off.

I found my friend bleeding. After some doctoring, I walked and led her in an extremely slow trip home. Molly had to carry the damaged foot and hop. For weeks, she lay or stood in the field near the home corral, and I carried hay, oats, and water to her. Then I would hug her and croon to her for hours. Dad told me that she might never walk again. But the foot healed, and Molly recovered ability to walk, even run as before. The times of caring for the filly reminded me of the famous book I had read by Mary O'Hara, *My Friend Flicka*. In it, a Wyoming ranch boy Rod McLaughlin took care of a wounded Flicka. The Flicka classic was made into a movie and often is still in larger book stores today.

Molly did not just regain her former ability. The boy and his horse often "burned up" the dusty roads at breakneck sprints. Once, after the family's move to the larger farm near Buckeye, a cock-sure neighbor boy challenged me to a horse race. The friend had a mount from a line of horses that had won races on a Phoenix track. We lined our mounts up for a quarter mile dash, and the neighbor was brazen, bragging absolutely that his race horse would easily wipe out the untested, unprofessional Molly. And, he laughed, what could this filly do when up against his bigger, seasoned professional?

At the signal, the practiced race horse bolted forward. Somehow Molly was not ready, rearing up, and quickly fell a few jumps behind. She saw the other horse blast forward, was instantly on to the idea of things, and simply exploded as if she was a ball shot from a cannon. My heart sank, though, as I thought we had lost, and I was booting my mount to urge her utmost speed as I leaned low, far over her bobbing neck. Then jubilation surged into my breast. Molly was simply destroying the veteran racer's head start. About halfway through the race, the prodigiously muscled filly surged alongside the practiced speedster. We, the riders, whooped and called on our mounts for everything they could summon. Molly powered into the lead, "burning the wind," and kept pulling away. The other boy went home red-faced and wiped out, and I reined toward Molly's pasture, very proud of her.

But one of my saddest memories was to follow. I made a colossal blunder of crass selfishness. I have lived to regret it more deeply than any words can describe. I drove off to college and became so preoccupied with classes, going places, and dating, that I put off trips home to see my folks and my friend. I failed them and Molly so miserably.

Months passed. On one trip when I went home I asked, "Where's Molly?" She was not in the small fenced off pasture ready to hear my call, throw up her head, nicker her greeting, and come loping to the nearest fence to greet me.

Somebody ventured, "She kept getting out. You know how she learned to nudge the wire up, off the post, to let the gate drop. Dad would have to scour the neighborhood, find her, and bring her home." Joyce, a sister, sat in the car holding the lead rope, and Molly would yank and pull it through her tight fingers until her hands bled. "Dad got fed up with the nuisance, and sold her."

Stunned, and my world reeling, I asked "who has her?" The family thought a certain farmer still kept the bay, so I searched. The farmer told me that he in turn had sold her, and knew that a tallow truck had come to take Molly off to a glue factory. My heart was simply crushed and sick. I had lost my dear, dear friend. I drove back to the college smitten with dark misery over having been so selfish and having let down my "pal" of the riding trails.

The lesson was as bitter as quinine. I had learned it too late. I realized that I should have cared for my "Molly," and come to wrap my arms around her neck, croon to her, stroke her velvety nose and face, and swing upon her back. She no doubt had waited many a day in vain to hear the old familiar voice calling. But in all her ordeal, I had not come. Perhaps that was the reason, in her loneliness, for her thinking of nudging the wire on the gate pole loose so she could go along the roads we had traveled together. Was she in search of me?

That is one of the most painful memories with which I have had to live. But it is necessary to go back and pick up other details of my life.

In the years of high school (1949–1953) I had worked on the 80 acre farm to which my father had moved the family in 1947. It was four miles northwest of Buckeye and near the looming hulks of the White Tank Mountains. I also found time in the summers to write a full-length Mesan High School football novel which I never finished, and a thick western novel about rustlers pushing cattle to a hidden valley stronghold. Such writing had grown out of a sixth-grade effort in a school assignment when I penned the short story, "Jimmy Jones and the Cattle Rustlers." My young teacher, Jean Hamilton, carried that scribbled story home, typed it, and made my day with words that would boost me for a lifetime, "Jimmy, here's your story; it's good; you keep writing."

I did. The novels followed. And while in my junior year of high school God helped me get a job as a reporter for *The Buckeye Valley News* for about two years. I wrote countless articles on sports and all-around news. As a junior it was my delight when my Lord helped me win the area Veterans of Foreign Wars school essay contest with a title, "America is Everybody's Business." That essay made it to second in the state. The next year judges selected me again as the area winner, this time on the theme "freedom." God was giving me abilities before I ever would learn to pour out my praise to Him, and in the earliest days of my saved life.

At the end of my high school career I sent off for several college catalogues. One was from Bob Jones University where some from my church had gone. And I looked at schools that had good departments of journalism. But God's kind help to me to win two scholarships lured me to Arizona State College in Tempe. I was one of many from across the state which a special committee interviewed, and one of five they chose for an annual Blue Key National Men's Honor Fraternity scholarship. As I believe my Savior was in this, I feel that He also helped me be selected for the 1953 Arizona statewide Dixie Dee Gammage Scholarship for work in journalism. The latter award was largely based on grades, teachers' "plugs," essay writing promise, and articles published in the local paper. God does the things we do not deserve and cannot do; He opens doors that we cannot open.

The writing that the Lord was providentially and so graciously giving me privileges to learn would adapt me for open doors He yet meant to swing wide. My Father was kindly honing me to be ready to write papers and exams in college and seminary, and eventually gain in His grace my supervisor J. Dwight Pentecost's words for my seminary Master's thesis, "This is the finest thesis that has ever come across my desk" (it was "*Crucial Objections to Dispensationalism*," objections which I sought to answer, 1961). I now believe Dr. Pentecost was very generous, and in nearly 50 years since then thesis writers have so much more work published that helps them do better research. Standards have risen to be more exacting at Dallas. The Lord led in my being given the William Anderson Award in 1966 for what the Dallas faculty felt was the best work in the doctoral program that year. The dissertation dealt with James' use of a quotation he drew from Amos 9. It was called "*The Interpretation of Acts 15:13-18*," and it pertained to when God will rebuild "the tabernacle of David" and restore Israel to its ancient land.

In following years, I would write, at Mildred's encouragement and her unselfish helps that set me free, *Abiding in Christ* (Zondervan, 1973), *Commentaries for Biblical Expositors* (1993, Grace Book Shack; and 2003, Kress Christian Publications), notes for six Old Testament books in *The MacArthur Study Bible* (Josh., Judg., Lam., Jer., Ezek., and Dan.), several entries in the 5-vol. *Zondervan Pictorial Encyclopedia of the Bible* (1973–1975), and *An Exposition on Prayer in the Bible* (2007, Logos Bible Software), the latter a 2,900 page encyclopedic writing on prayer passages from Genesis to Revelation. God also would help me author three western novels via Tyndale Publishing House, i.e. *Treachery at Cimarron*, *Ambush at Vermejo*, and *Longhorns North* (1983–1987). The latter are patterned after works by the most best-selling western novelist of all, Louis L'Amour.

But back to September, 1953, I drove my 1941 Chevy off to Arizona State to major in journalism. A year later at the outset of my sophomore year I sat beside a girl who drew me like a magnet. She told me her name was Mildred. Our English Literature class focused for a time on Shakespeare's "*The Tempest*." I also snapped to attention at the First Baptist Church when I heard this same lady's winsome testimony as a new member in the youth group. This Shakespeare girl was a Christian, as I was! Thoughts danced in my head. An old one-liner says it all. "In the Spring time a young man's fancy lightly turns to thoughts of love."

But I was "an eager beaver." I made my move earlier, in the autumn!

7

College Days and Falling in Love

THINGS HAPPENED QUICKLY TO knit Mildred's life and mine together.

Thank Shakespeare for "*The Tempest*" and God for His leading! This girl's life manifested a rare quality, sharply distinct. Right away this seemed to set her in a class apart from the other women, as I think God impressed on me. Hers was the inviting beauty of grace, her poise in carrying herself, the peace that was aglow in her face, and the soft, pure melody of her voice when I introduced myself. I knew she was of a quality cut from a far different mold. Attracted as if by a powerful fragrance, I maneuvered to get a desk beside this student, fight past the boyish shyness, and strike up conversations. On my own part these sometimes were clumsy and with a giddy spirit.

Courtships with other girls, each for a brief time or several weeks or months, had passed in grade school with Ulene, Wanda, and Patsy, then in high school with Elaine, and later Ophalyn, and early in college Pat, Ellie, Patty, Carole, and Shirley. And the childhood crush, Jeanie from California, who helped put the love-sealing penny in the tree, was far away, pursuing her own life. I would never see her again. "The way of man is not in himself; it is not in man that walks to direct his steps" (Jer. 10:23).

Friendships with other girls had been as nothing compared with the magic now. I would not even be bothered by Jeanie's promise, or mine. This was despite even a special visit. Jeanie had even walked over to our farm when I, a sixth grader, was milking. She wanted to say goodbye that late afternoon. I asked Dad if I could take a break, and he kindly let me go. I walked Jeanie on a path along a hill part of the way back to her grandparents' place. We lingered beneath a tree's canopy, stalling the inevitable. It was a sickening pain to part as if it meant the end of the world. At last she simply had to go, and I stood riveted, wiped out, as she started across a field to return to her family, and to California. She turned again and again to wave. I stood as if in a spell, misty with tears, my heart an awful, burning thing until this sweetheart was a small, fading speck, far, far away. It was an indescribable agony to wrench myself from that spot and make my forlorn, dazed way back to corral labors. Jeanie's hand was no longer in mine.

Since my family had moved soon after that from the Liberty farm, I was not to see Jeanie in her visits again until nearly six years had gone by, as above.

No regrets. God heals wounds, and takes them away. His will is sweeter. And no regrets about Elaine of the junior and senior years in high school. She was a very nice girl, a beautiful person, but a Roman Catholic. As a young Christian and not well-established in the faith, I rationalized. I insisted, as so many do, that we could work out the differences in our beliefs. But one day Elaine came to a realization that I should have reached. As I drove her home we stopped for a while and she, though gentle, shattered my heart, telling me there was just no way it could work. For she must go to her church, and I would not budge from mine. The break-up just about ripped my heart into shreds. I drove, sobbing my heart out, to a remote desert spot, the sky caving in on me. I was broken and misty eyed for weeks. That parting was a pill more bitter than quinine.

They say "time heals all wounds," or backward, "time wounds all heels." I would come to my senses at last. I had been a "heel" in dating Elaine to go against wise biblical thinking. God was actually very kindly saying, "just wait." As He said to Israel, He was saying in principle to me, as well, "For I know the plans that I have for you . . . plans for welfare and not for calamity to give you a future and a hope" (Jer. 29:11).

God was there as a God of providence. He knows best, and mercifully can save us even from our own devices and plans. As Andre Crouch wrote, "How can I say thanks for the things You have done for me?" God never fails.

An outstanding, class-act Christian girl, Shirley, was my "steady" for weeks going beginning the second year of college.

When Mildred, the girl from New York, captured my heart, I told this to Shirley gently. Mildred was now always in my thoughts. Shirley took the break-up valiantly, and we kept on being good friends. She later married Gaylord (Rich) Jonassen, a player on Arizona State's baseball team, and they, as staunch servants of God, have exchanged Christmas cards with Mildred and me through the years. Now the Jonassens live in Pennsylvania.

An interesting note is that when my mother Lola went, in old age, to live in the Glencroft senior citizens' estates in Glendale, AZ in the 1990's, Shirley's mother also lived there. Our mothers became friends. Once when I visited "mom" in that place, Shirley also was there on a trip to see her own "mom." We all met in the dining hall for cordial and beautiful fellowship and catching up.

Three jobs gave me earnings as a sophomore at Arizona State College. Later while we were there the school would gain the title "Arizona State University." One chore was mowing lawns at First Baptist Church about two blocks to the northwest from the campus. A second job was writing two or three long, weekly sports articles about the Sun Devil team, whatever the season, for *The Tempe Daily News*, a half mile walk from my dorm to the up town office. A third task was as Circulation Manager of the campus paper, *The State Press*, in the same huge building where our English class met.

In my junior year I would be the sports editor of that campus paper, and then in the final year Assistant Sports Publicist in the school's athletic department. In this job I worked happily as I learned much under Lee Coleman, an outstanding Sports Publicist whom one of baseball's major league clubs later whisked away.

Mildred would later chuckle as she teased me with her memory. It was about this student who often shuffled in late to English Literature during its focus for several sessions on Shakespeare. The New York girl was soon on to the fact that the one tardy was ever the same fellow. He announced his identity by unconsciously scuffing his shoes' soles when he walked. He would slip in beside her seconds after a tolerant Dr. Schilling had begun her lecture. Later Mildred would learn that I had hurried uptown, about a half mile, on my jaunt off campus to *The Tempe Daily News*. I was responsible to meet my deadlines by hastening between classes to turn in sports stories. Then I rushed back, memorizing along the way my three verses a week from the Navigators' "Topical Memory System" (108 verses). I kept the Scriptures on cards in a small, brown calf-skin pouch.

I asked Mildred, "May I carry your books?" Her smile betrayed her pleasure, and she put her load into my hands. My heart almost did a flip with sheer ecstasy. I walked her to the library, was there later to greet her when she came out, and once again took over her books. In days that followed, I often walked her to her car, the black 1951 Willys with a white stripe below the windows. She told me that she lived off campus with her room mate, Georgia Wilson.

One October day as we strolled by the campus fountain, I mustered courage to ask what stirred my heart. "I was wondering," I said, feeling terribly awkward, "if . . . uh . . . you would like to . . . uh . . . go to the game Saturday night with me. It's right here, in our stadium. We're . . . uh . . . playing West Texas State." She looked up in a way that showed me—or I had a loony notion—she was surprised. I guess I gulped five times before I heard words that were like a melody. "That would be very nice." She was smiling in the same sweet way my fancy had pictured a thousand times since meeting her. I was beset by a feeling that a soft, fluffy substance was holding me up in space, and I was propelled onward through the sky while a dream unfolded.

I told her my car was not working, so we would have to walk to the stadium. I spent some time apologizing for my lack. But joy dealt its rhapsody within my heart when she replied, "Oh, how wonderful. I love to walk!" I asked for her address, and she said 928 ½ Maple Avenue. That, she explained, was six blocks west of campus, beyond the far, or west side of the main street, Mill Avenue, that then ran north and south through Tempe's main business section.

I jotted the address on a slip of paper and when I got to my dorm, East Hall, laid the precious document delicately on my desk. With my consequent studies, the address got covered over by several layers of "archeological strata." But no problem. I had no need to check. I figured I had that important number riveted in my memory. This was too big a thing for me to botch. I kept repeating the address, maybe a hundred times.

That Saturday night the kickoff of the Border Conference clash was set for 8 o'clock. I planned my walk to arrive at Mildred's home by 7:30, and we would have a leisurely stroll the half mile to reach Goodwin Stadium long before the game. I got ready well ahead of time, and around 6:45 eagerly set out to spot the address, saunter around that neighborhood until 7:30, then show up exactly right on time. In punctuality as in every other detail I must be off to a fine start. This was big-time, and I must do it right, impress my date.

Alas! I found Maple addresses such as 820, 824, and 830, but no 828½, no ½'s at all. Alarmed, I retraced my steps, even checking driveways to see if there was a ½ hidden behind some house. Minutes sped by. I was baffled, and my watch grieved me at 7:15, then 7:30. Panic began to mount within me. I should be at her door, but I could not locate it! A very great opportunity was fading fast. It was, to me, as if the earth was disintegrating as in 2 Peter 3.

"Son," one old gentleman said, "you sure you don't have your wires crossed? I've lived here for 20 years, an' I know the block like I know the back of my own hand. That address just isn't." I stumbled away in a daze. I had ransacked every alley and seen all the back doors.

Try again, I moaned in misery. Somewhere near 826 Maple, I came to a little green home, and did not see a number. Could this be it? When I knocked, a middle-aged, blond lady appeared in an apron. I knew Mildred had a room mate, an older woman named Georgia, whom Mildred had said was blond, but I had never met her. The lady opened the door readily, and looked at me as if she had been expecting me. "You must be . . ." she said, and I replied "Jim. And you must be Georgia." She seemed not to hear, but I apparently satisfied her. The uneasy feeling at the pit of my stomach had vanished in an instant. Success—at last! Suddenly I was whistling inwardly.

"Do come in. We've been expecting you. It'll just be a minute." Ah, blondish hair just like Mildred told me Georgia had, I celebrated. I was just about a basket case, too rattled to think very sensibly, and grasping for straws at this late hour. The woman motioned to a couch chair and a newspaper. "Won't you sit just for a moment?" I glanced at a sports page of a Phoenix newspaper, *The Arizona Republic*.

"Is Mildred about ready?" I asked.

This lady "Georgia" paused before she disappeared into the kitchen. Again, apparently she did not hear what I said. "It'll just be a moment," she assured me. How wonderful that everything was working out. I kept listening for a soft clue of footsteps to tip me off that Mildred was coming out. A glance at my watch told me we would not be late for the game if we walked briskly.

The lady was suddenly back. This time she held a huge bowl of steaming red stuff, maybe tomato soup. She had a towel around it. I had leaped to my feet. Alarm bells were clanging, and even more so as she shoved the hot food into my hands. "Here, take this to your mother."

My mother? Oh, my . . . .! Shock must have done a blitz job in my face. It was as if I was toppling off the end of the earth. My mother was 45 miles away, in another town! Astonishing dodo, that was me. Winner of the dummy award, one of the three stooges! How had I done this? I was in the wrong house! I pushed the pot back into the woman's hands, saw her eyes bulge, big and aghast, and backed in embarrassed shame to snatch the door knob. The woman was a study in astonishment. I could only fumble out words.

"Does M-i-l-d-r-e-d live here?" I never pronounced a word more distinctly!

"No . . . no . . . no," she cried out, punctuating her words with gasps.

"I'm . . . I'm sorry. This is a big mistake. I'm in the wrong house!" Then I ducked out red of face, beat it, and must have established some kind of all-time retreat record. I had to get my embarrassed self to the far end of the planet.

A man washing his car in his front yard called out to me, "Hey, no luck yet?

"No," I admitted sheepishly. "I can't find any 828½ Maple. I guess the only thing I can do is go back to the dorm and check. I left a slip of paper with the house number on it."

"Here, the car's done. Hop in. Let's take a run over there to see. Never hurts to make sure." On the way, he consoled me. "The same thing happened to me two years ago."

I set a new hundred yard dash timing of my own into East Hall, snatched up the address, and stared at it. Shock did a number on my face. "Oh, how could I? It's 9 . . . 928½!" I was flabbergasted at my blunder. Sprinting back to the man's car, I felt like the world's greatest "loser" in groaning out my confession. I had been a block off. He was hysterical as he said he would drive us to the stadium, tromped the gas pedal, and sped to the address. I leaped out to turn on the jets to Mildred's door. The man winked, "You're doing okay. I hope things turn out better for you than they did for me. You know, when this happened to me, I never did find that girl's house."

Mildred's residence was a small cottage set back to the left from the house of her landlord. That explained the ½. I raced up the walk, clattered on the porch, and knocked. Mildred came, smiling. I began to fumble a very embarrassed apology, my face as red as a ripe tomato. She looked radiantly lovely and not in the least bit disturbed.

"I was listening on the radio to the start of the game," she said as if the world wasn't ending after all. "The other team ran the kickoff back all the way and made a touchdown. They're ahead of us, on the first play."

The man rushed us to the stadium. We hastened to our seats, arriving about five minutes late. Our team was down, 7-0.

"I realized something had gone wrong," Mildred comforted me. "I knew you, that you would be on time if you could." Her kind confidence made my day. I, with more success than the kind driver, would marry the girl! I just did not know it then. And how could our date fail, the way Mildred pounded on my shoulder in ecstasy every time Arizona State did something great. The Sun Devils did great things often that night. I owed a thank-you note to them. I was thrilled that there was a lot of pounding. And her excitement sometimes joined the burst of rockets. For in those days when our team scored handlers fired off rockets that exploded their colors far above the field, across the night sky. Three rockets went off that evening. Our team came out on top, 21-14, and the date was a win that meant even far more to me.

The name "Sun Devils" is somewhat like the Duke University "Blue Devils." A "sun devil" in Arizona's sun is a ferocious wind gust that rages with powerful momentum to whip up objects and sweep them along in its fury. At times, as some other teams, Arizona State lives up to its name, and at times it does not. As a name, "Sun Devils" is similar to the Iowa State Cyclones, Miami Hurricanes, and Tulsa Golden Hurricanes.

A few weeks after the date, on January 11, 1955, my professor in "Advanced Composition," Dr. Ratliff, stunned the class. "Take out your papers and pens," he said. "Write a short story on the most embarrassing event of your life." I sat dumbfounded and horrified. Not a clue. And soon time would be no more. What ever happened to me that . . .? All of a sudden, that Maple Street date leaped into my mind. I had gotten behind the other students, I suppose, but I began to write furiously. Later, the professor handed the graded essays back. I sat in amazement starring at the "A" he had penciled on mine, and under it the words, "Real sharp for impromptu." I forgot some details of that paper, and these many years later I came across it in a folder of treasures I did not know Mildred had kept.

As seasons passed, come Fall football, Mildred and I would watch NCAA college games on Saturday afternoons, especially when Arizona State's winning teams of the legendary Coach Frank Kush were televised in a great 1970–1976 run of season records such as 11-0, 11-1, 10-2, 11-1, 12-0, and 9-3, and six bowl game victories. The unbeaten Devils topped North Carolina in the 1970 Peach Bowl, 48-26, Florida State in the 1971 Fiesta Bowl, 45-38, Missouri in the '72 Fiesta Bowl, 49-35, Pittsburgh with its fabulous running back Tony Dorsett in the '73 Fiesta Bowl, 28-7, and the No. 2 team in the nation, Nebraska, in the '75 Fiesta Bowl, 17-14 to plunge into the No. 2 final ranking with a 12-0 mark. In that 1975 campaign's rankings ASU was edged out of the national championship by an also undefeated Oklahoma Sooner "Big Red" juggernaut.

That October, 1954 date started things for Mildred and me big-time. I think our next outing was on a Sunday night, after church. We said yes to an invitation of Neal Nichols (from Douglas, AZ) and Beverly Watkins (from Morenci) to go for a ride with them. It was fun sitting in the back seat with Mildred, the exhilaration interrupted only by her getting car sick as Neal whizzed around some curves west of town out by the Tempe Cemetery. We had to stop so Mildred could walk around a bit and deal with nausea. Maybe the problem was that we had gone to the Tempe Dairy Queen and had sundaes, then buzzed around the highway's curves.

Neal and Bev married, now live in Overland Park, Kansas, and have sent us a Christmas card each year.

After Mildred's and my first times out, we had many dates. My Chevy was sometimes able to take us, and on other occasions we rode in her Willys. Any destination was our joy—to Chandler a few miles south through what then was open ranch country, to an ice cream parlor; to a popular Tolleson drive-in west of Phoenix for fish and chips, to the Phoenix Theater for Shakespeare performances such as "*Macbeth*" and "*King Lear.*" We saw more football and also basketball games, and went to the First Baptist Church for services and young peoples' meetings Sunday night and mid-week Wednesday fun times. Several outings were to picnics.

Some meetings were just to sit on a campus bench and talk about studies or the Word of our God. Mildred amazed me by her astounding knowledge about that Book. Whatever the situation, music was a rhapsody in her words, and Christ the light shining in her life.

Mildred was crazy about the cherry cokes at the fountain in Laird's Pharmacy in uptown Tempe. We would often stroll to this "oasis" on the main street, Mill Avenue, several blocks from campus. At the cherry coke haven, we would lounge on stools at the counter, or linger at a table, sip the treats, and in our fellowship enjoy a bit of heaven before heaven.

Another thing we enjoyed was taking drives to a butte north of Tempe. We made treks up a gentle slope. Mildred's breathing would require numerous halts for her to catch her breath. She was game, so was I. Once at the bottom of the butte, we sat on a great, shaded slab of rock to gaze out across a panorama of Tempe and part of southeast Phoenix. The blessing of the friendship was "out of this world."

It also was pleasant when I walked Mildred home from the campus, or from church. Arizona State at that time had the original building of "Old Tempe Normal" that had been a bastion on the campus in the state's territorial days before statehood in 1912. It was on a lot immediately across a small street west of our church. But by this time the famous building was vacated, and soon to be demolished because a shopping center was coming. We would sit on the front steps, which pointed away from campus, west toward Mill Avenue, with massive columns of stone looming behind us on either side. The great hulk of the edifice towered above us. There we would have jubilant fellowship before I walked Mildred the rest of the way westward to her Maple Street cottage.

Our church youth group then was quite large on Wednesday night, 50 to 60 attending. Milt Winterberg, the youth director, would lead us in a Bible study and singing, then the kitchen off the fellowship hall would open a window to serve cookies, cake, and hot chocolate (winter) or goodies and cold drinks (spring, summer).

That sophomore year at Christmas break I went home, which was 45 miles from Tempe, near Buckeye. The vacation days dragged for me since Mildred was back in the college town. I went to Nichols' Florist Shop in Buckeye, where my high school friend Earl Nichols' mother Frieda helped me select a very nice poinsettia arrangement to have delivered to Mildred. My date told me later that it was a thrill when the man from a Tempe florist shop handed the poinsettias to her at the door. The flowers were beautiful in her living room, and with their arrival my stock went soaring.

While I was dating Mildred, Joe Findley was going with Georgia, her room mate.

One staff "heckler" of *The Tempe Daily News* published a serious condition that beset these ladies' cottage, owned by Carl Spain, who ran an auto shop in Tempe. "A plague of a certain variety of bug has been infesting the rancho of one Carl Spain. It is an epidemic of a certain rare type of creature that seems virtually impossible to exterminate. Mr. Spain [living next door] is helpless to rid his premises of this pesky little varmint which has seemed to attack the residents of the apartment. These tenants are Georgia Wilson and Mildred Currey. The bug, not yet dealt with, is the one released by cupid, known as 'the love bug.' This reporter's blessings are upon Miss Wilson and Miss Currey, and my sympathy goes out to the Spains."

The bug survived, and Mildred and I took Dr. Herbert Staunky's famous biology class at ASC, sitting together. He had his students go out and gather scorpions and snakes so that he could study the venom. We drove past Buckeye to Palo Verde where, behind the Bruner farm home, a huge pile of old lumber and Cottonwood tree limbs was an "apartment house" for scorpions. There we scraped many into our bottles. In the class, Mildred "pulled" an A and I got a dose of humility from a C. She always was a sharp student, and she was on to Dr. Staunky's multiple choice tests, while his tricky wording threw me. Hard study did not appear to help me figure out the mind of the professor when several possible answers seemed correct.

"Through many dangers, toils, and snares . . ." is quite an apt description.

Arizona State Years

Top left: Mildred; Top right: Jim.

Lower left: Mildred with her Bible at Forest Home College Briefing Conference near San Bernardino, CA, after junior year of college; Lower right: CCC Banquet at ASU (Jim and Mildred are at far left), beside Mildred is Bill Bright, CCC President and one of God's most fruitful men in leading collegians to Christ.

8

A Bible Lady Who Lighted a Flame

MILDRED HAD COME FROM student days relishing God's Word at ABI. What she said about knowing Christ as in the Bible began to light my heart with a candle flame. The fire kept growing.

She told me how she had loved godly mentors who "made the Bible live." Classes she most cherished were by Dr. John A. Hubbard, who led in rich times of Bible synthesis, analysis, and spiritual life. Hubbard, who had come to the school in its 12th year, 1947, focused on a walk of fruit in the Spirit, winsome sharing of Christ to lead people to salvation, and prayer. He was a bright and powerful example. Mildred had diligently prepared papers on the Bible, and her stories of such riches ignited a burning hunger in me. I, too, felt a longing to study God's Word under men mighty in the Scriptures, men who were after His own heart.

Others among the ABI "men of God" at that time were: Victor C. Oltrogge, president; Eugene C. Eymann, synthesis, theology, and biblical introduction; John Van Kommer, hermeneutics, church history, church administration, and registrar; and Rev. LeRoy Thomas, Pastor of Palmcroft Baptist Church in Phoenix and teacher of Bible geography and prophecy. Mrs. Victor C. (Electa) Oltrogge taught English, and was the school librarian. Valeene Hayes, a student, was director of the choir and the ladies' sextet that sang the songs of Christ's power in many churches.

Members of the sextet with Mildred were Margine Clark, who later married Dick Mercado, leader after his father of the Mexican Gospel Mission in Phoenix, sisters Irene Bendure and Leona Bendure, Alice Shore, and Janice Eagon.

I wanted to be like these people of the Word. God had made a special, lasting impact of godliness on Dr. Hubbard's students. This man to follow after was one of the Lord's finest servants, and lived to be 86 (1876–1962). At 19 as a promising player on the cornet but unsaved, he accepted an offer to play in a brass quartet for a Christian band on the Chicago streets. Hearing the gospel several times in the meetings, he realized his need of the Savior. He wrestled for five weeks not sure of how this would affect his music career, but finally yielded to God. At his job as a music store bill clerk he refused to falsify figures. He paid the price for integrity; the boss fired him.

A book by the Moody Bible Institute's famous Reuben Archer Torrey came into John's hands. It was *How to Bring Men to Christ*. This led to study at the institute, and his taking as his life verses Hebrews 12:1-2, about "looking unto Jesus." At conferences he heard some of the most famous speakers in spiritual things such as F. B. Meyer, G. C. Morgan, A. T. Pierson, C. I. Scofield, Dwight L. Moody and Moody's song leader Ira Sankey. Moody died in 1899. Then Hubbard was the song director traveling with evangelist Lewis Sperry Chafer. Chafer would later become the first president of Dallas Theological Seminary in 1924, and write the famous *Systematic Theology*, 8 vols., which I would read in the late 1950's and early 1960's when I was a student at the Texas school. Chafer also authored the books *Grace, He That is Spiritual, Major Bible Themes, Winning Souls by Prayer*, and *Satan*.

Hubbard led in three pastorates and pursued a year of study at Princeton Theological Seminary while he kept teaching the Word. In 1901 he married Frances Betts, and the couple had three sons and a daughter. In 1920 Torrey, who had worked with Moody, transferred to be head of the Bible Institute of Los Angeles, also called "Biola." He secured Hubbard to be dean of men. Nine years later Hubbard took on a full-time teaching ministry there. In 1931 Dr. Chafer and Dallas Seminary honored the outstanding servant of the Lord by conferring on him an honorary doctoral degree.

Hubbard was God's key instrument in igniting many students to go to the mission field, and Mildred looking for God's path to devote her whole life to Christian ministry. He taught at ABI 15 years in the full bloom of his career until his death in 1962. To sit in this teacher's classes made some conscious of Acts 12:24 being fulfilled anew. "But the word of the Lord continued to grow and to be multiplied." On April 4, 1962, the Lord called the mighty man of valor home. I will never in this life find adequate words to thank him for his outfitting of the godly woman who would help me serve God.

Mildred often told me in deeply loving terms of what a godly influence this instructor had on her and others. She felt the impact of a man who looked at Jeremiah 1:7 (". . . on whatsoever errand I shall send you, you shall go") and saw himself as God's "errand boy"—prompt, obedient, and on hand to deliver the message when the Lord speaks. Students in his Bible classes often felt their hearts burning within them as he opened the Word, spoke the truths of God, and pleaded principles the Spirit of God printed with flame on his own heart.

One of this professor's sayings stuck in Mildred's mind. He would tell students that when their minds wandered to snatch back their thoughts with "Come back here, you vagabond!"

Men such as this awesome teacher of the Book shared in fashioning the woman who was to be my wife. And she would live out the best ideals of the school God used so powerfully. John Hubbard's name would certainly be in a Hebrews Chapter 11 Roll Call of Faith, if there was a Vol. 2, or 3, or 4, along with so many other godly people. For, to borrow a biblical phrase from Genesis 6 and use the thought in relation to the spiritual realm, "there were giants in the earth in those days," in this later case good giants. Dr. Hubbard was one such giant.

This faithful leader kept to his ABI post after his wife Frances and two of their sons went to heaven. And in 1962 the school named a new library in his honor the "John A. Hubbard Memorial Library" (For the history I am indebted to Electa Z. Oltrogge, the wife of the school's president, Dr. Oltrogge, for she wrote "God's Errand Boy, A Brief History of the Life of Dr. John A. Hubbard." The school passed out this 3 pp. leaflet the day it dedicated the library).

God empowered chapel speakers in the training school to register a life-shaping impression on Mildred. She heard some of the nation's finest Bible teachers whom ABI invited in, and always greatly stirring messages by the Spirit led Dr. Hubbard.

ABI was to continue by this name until 1971, then as earlier stated change in name to The Arizona College of the Bible as a school affiliated with Biola University. In 1981 Biola would step aside, and in 1997 until the witness for Christ closed in 1998, the name would be The Arizona Bible College.

Some of the students I later helped train at Talbot Theological Seminary (1965–1987) would join the faculty at ABI or a name that succeeded it. These were Robert Bowles, in a wheel chair, John Bechtle, a brilliant student, and David Macy. And Dr. Vernon Doerksen, who taught in the Talbot Bible Department for several years, transferred to this faculty in the 1980's and published a commentary on the Book of James.

It would be my privilege around 1968 to deliver a week's spiritual life messages at the ABI chapel services on the life of faith in Abraham. A woman who had come from off campus to hear this series invited me to join several at a dinner. It turned out that the hostess was Mrs. Harrison Green, formerly of my home town, Buckeye. Her son Charles and his wife Jo Helene had first invited me to ride with them to church, a kindness that led to my knowing the Savior. As mentioned earlier, one of Charles' and Jo Helene's sons, Steve, would later become nationally famous as a Christian singer.

Some years even after my series on Abraham, when the name of ABI had changed to The Arizona College of Bible, the faculty asked me to give a chapel series at another location to which the school had moved. So I gave four messages expounding the Spirit-filled life in Ephesians 5:18-21. In this I used many of the truths

I had discovered in my own digging and in assigning my hermeneutics students to turn in at least 35 observations on 5:18. Some of us found far more than the 35!

Mildred and I were elated with the privilege of attending an ABI alumni banquet in Phoenix in the Summer of 1998. At that time about 50 came together from far-flung ministries. We saw joy and commitment to carry on various works for Christ even shortly after the sad news had come of the school closing due to severe financial problems after holding forth God's light for 63 years.

At that banquet, for example, we had a joyous talk with Dick and Margine Mercado. Margine had sung in the ABI sextet Mildred was in, and Dick was and is one of the men God has used in many countries to bring hundreds of people to Himself. He heads up the Mexican Gospel Mission and for many decades God has made him a highly effective, rousing speaker.

Mildred treasured in her heart certain good Christian books, but chiefly fed her spirit on good things of the Bible. In this resource, she lived out the life as Paul did, "to me to live is Christ" (Phil. 1:21), and "Christ lives in me" (Gal. 2:20). Early in our courtship and into our marriage, she would mention the keynote song that ABI people held as their theme, based on Colossians 1:18, with the repeated emphasis, "that in all things He might have the preeminence." Another song frequent there, which she also celebrated in her life, was "Great is Thy Faithfulness."

I have always had a very deep appreciation for and breathless awe at the God-exalting ministries which leaders, students, and alumni of ABI have fulfilled. I am deeply convinced that Mildred adorned the highest standards that the school prized. The essence of the school, and Mildred's testimony, was the words of the song from Colossians 1:18. And when I would study Bible under the great expositor, J. Dwight Pentecost, the beloved "Dr. P" at Dallas Seminary, I would learn that this was his life verse.

9

Deepening Love Amid Studies

It was by God's appointment, since I had flunked the fourth grade, that I would be at Arizona State for my second year at the same time when Mildred came as a sophomore. So we could graduate together in 1957, and go on to my own Bible training for our lives of service!

At Tempe, Mildred was helping another ABI alumnus, Eddie Matchett, pastor of the Buena Park Mission Church in town. So Mildred was there for a time on Sunday mornings teaching a children's class, and I often went with her on some Sunday evenings to help minister with the young people. Pastor Matchett occasionally invited me to speak to the youth.

In the 1954 summer between my freshman and sophomore year at ASC, I had been elected president of the State Baptist Young People's Union for the Conservative Baptist Church movement. I would be re-elected for a second year in 1955–56.

In this capacity, I would travel to sectional rallies in various parts of the state and give brief greetings as the state leader. Memories return of trips to Clifton, Douglas, Morenci, Phoenix, and Tucson. Mildred would not go with me on these jaunts, when I rode with the state director of young people, Clarence Stauffer, whose Arizona Baptist Convention office was in Phoenix.

One of my sweet memories is what happened at the annual summer "Youth Assembly" at "Prescott Pines," the Conservative Baptist camp a few miles into the forest from Prescott. This was in 1956 after Mildred's and my junior years at Arizona State. I was still state president, and leading in youth business meetings at the camp as well as teaching a seminar on personal devotions. On the afternoon of the special banquet that was highlighted the week, I looked up and saw Mildred driving in from Tempe in her little Willys. She had come to join me for the banquet, and I remember her smile that lighted up my life.

A scary time had confronted Mildred and me in the spring of our junior year in college (1956). Her breathing grew perilous, and she had to be confined in the Mesa Community Hospital a few miles east of Arizona State. She was bed-ridden there about three weeks. I hitch hiked to visit her several times. When she was released, she had missed so much school that she had to drop several classes, and did not have enough units to gain a <u>secondary</u> education degree. Still, she did have sufficient units to graduate at the same time with me by a major in <u>elementary</u> education (1957).

During our senior year (1956–1957), Mildred's brother Bob, still a student at ABI, worked at a filling station and lived in north Phoenix. We often would go over to visit Bob at a boarding house, and also to call on Mr. and Mrs. Ercel Clark, friends Mildred and her folks had known in Unadilla, New York. One of Mildred's best friends while at ABI, Margine, was the daughter of the Clarks and married the Hispanic evangelist Dick Mercado, mentioned earlier. We sometimes would drive to Phoenix for a Saturday night "Truth for Youth" meeting, at which Mercado, an electrifying speaker, would stir us with a passionate message. I still have his 1950's booklet, *Don't Dare Today's Demons*.

Mildred had been one of several sharp students at ABI, plus God had fashioned her to show a mature composure of "having it all together." The faculty recognized her teaching skill, and invited her to instruct two courses on campus as related earlier. A thought came to me as I watched her expertise, and I would often realize it throughout life. I was way above my head in having the privilege of going with a girl of her quality and godliness. She was not only attractive and sweeter than a peach, but resourcefully versatile to become adept at whatever the challenge in her servant life.

Throughout Mildred's days, I would have more surprises at her all-around prowess. She could put a nice meal on the table, keep the home spic and span, maintain good business files, paint, hang up wallpaper, sew, crochet, and knit. She was a wonder of a wise mother and a counselor, and a Sunday School teacher who invested her whole heart and love into her lessons. She was a tasteful, charming, and pleasant hostess, and an engaging conversationalist who had the finesse of class and confident poise. I really believe that had God led her life in such a way, she would have acted with a graceful carriage in a king's palace. At any rate, she was of royalty as believers are kings and priests in Christ (Rev. 1:4-5). She was always confidently and serenely composed no matter what the group. Ladies would look to her for her wisdom that came out of a deep well of careful thought, "homey" wit, and a profound trust that God was always her adequacy.

She would become quite proficient in doing computer products of creative interest, and write countless cheering notes that ladies would brag to me about.

Besides, she was a very careful driver, and on snowy or icy roads, or in dense fog, she could keep the car hugging its lane. Not only that, but she seemed always to know her direction, having the instincts of a homing pigeon. In later years, she wanted to drive us, assuring me that it was not because I was unsafe, but "because I just like to feel the wheel, and have something to do." So I would have a chauffeur going here and there.

I have mentioned Mildred's ABI participation in a girls' sextet that sang for Jesus in many churches and on the radio. I heard that sextet when they came to the First Baptist Church, Buckeye in days before I even knew Mildred. Later I would put two and two together and realize she was one of the six who had thrilled me in the soul-stirring music about the gospel and living for the Lord. And I would remember the talented Valeene Hayes, who directed the group.

Georgia Wilson, Mildred's room mate on Maple Street, married Joe Findley after our third year at Arizona State, and Mildred was the maid of honor. After this time Mildred moved into an upstairs apartment in a two-story building also in west Tempe. Then her room mate was Jo Ella Henry, who was in the youth group at First Baptist Church.

After Mildred and I had dated for several months, I worked up the bravery to ask her if I could drive her to meet my folks. She said "yes."

Then came the crisis. Showdown time!

We rode the 45 miles to the 80-acre cattle outfit four miles northwest of Buckeye at the southwest corner of Broadway and Oglesby Rd. Mom was preparing a supper for the family and us. I was quite apprehensive, I am sure in foolish immaturity and a lack of trusting God. For Mildred was from a farm too. It was just that her family was a Christian one, and my parents did not yet know Christ. More than that, she had only two brothers, Richard and Bob. I had eight siblings. Would such a large family overwhelm her, and chill her interest due to a wrong idea of what I might have in mind?

An even more troubling thing was that our Rosscup house, though always "Home Sweet Home," was a sort of bizarre, shoddy eye sore. When Dad had bought the place from a man named Caruthers, the long, gray cement ranch house came with it. The former owner due to some strange quirk about design had gouged many deep slashes in the wall cement while it was still soft. That was his idea of a decorative effect, but a hideous one. We called these ugly marks "chicken scratches," but those chickens must have been as big as ostriches!

Of two things I was certain. Mildred would win my family's instant approval, for she was the fairest of the fair. And Dad and Mom would be cordially gracious in their simple, "down home," country hospitality.

We got out of the Willys. Dad swept Mildred up in a big, gentle hug of welcome. Mom came to her with open, loving arms. My five sisters who were still there (Anna Mae had married Gene Arter and was gone) and my brother Jerry gathered around the very long kitchen table. All my fears began to fade like snow melting in the sun's glow, for we had a happy time. Mom had fixed one of her marvelous meals, my folks were so joyous, and Mildred took to my family. Right there, God wrote an exclamation of jubilation on the evening.

I had gone with several girls in high school and into my second year at college. But I saw that by comparison Mildred was in a class all by herself—the finest lady I had ever dated, quality par excellence. I was so proud of her, knew I was courting "way above my head," could only shake my head in a wondering awe, and my heart was exultant.

Mom boasted later, "She's one of the most beautiful girls I've ever seen!"

Well into our dating life, Mildred showed her fun loving way of a good tease. I asked her to go out with me, and she said she could not. She was having a date, instead, with "Richard Hudnut." That rocked my world. Heaven and earth fled away. Agony was at the pit of my stomach. A few days later, after Mildred's fun had registered its full effect, she let me in on her secret with a twinkle in her eye. "Richard Hudnut" was the brand name of a hair-do formula. What an uninformed "ignoramus" I realized I had been.

We often would go to visit Dora Hilton a few blocks from the campus. She was an elderly lady, a lonely widow, who ran the switchboard at Arizona State. Mildred always was kind to seek out and encourage people who appeared to be left out or a fifth wheel in a couple's world. And I so admired her for this. Mrs. Hilton invited us for a number of meals, and we did thoughtful things to brighten her world.

It was the summer between our sophomore and junior years at what was then Arizona State College (ASC). Some time toward the close of our collegiate experience, the school would win the title Arizona State University. I yearned to visit Mildred who had gone back to her Unadilla, New York farm for the vacation. She invited me, in turn, to come and meet her folks. So I had to earn money to pay for a Greyhound bus trip back there, and for school that Fall.

One job came to me from Mr. Rhodes, father of Laura, a girl in our church youth group. Laura would marry Dora Hilton's son, Larry. Her dad pursued a professional truck driving career in several states, and was recruiting drivers to move a large number of new 1955 orange Dodge dump trucks from Detroit to Fort Sumner, New Mexico. There, a car dealer had won a contract with the state highway department to supply the vehicles. Despite my youth at 21, Mr. Rhodes picked me as one of his drivers. He also took on several New Mexico cowboys that the dealer in Fort Sumner had lined up.

I was in on three trips. Each man drove a truck and hauled another piggy back in a cavalcade. Mr. Rhodes went first, then me, and behind me the several others. On each venture to Detroit, we rode on a bus. Some of the cowboy driving recruits could make only the first trip. On one drive to New Mexico, a span of more than 1550 miles, we pulled in to gas up, and I spotted a nearby pharmacy. Once my truck's tank was full, I parked my rig, raced into the drug store, found a Billy Graham paperback just out, *Peace with God*, and took it away for 50 cents. It was a blessing to feed my soul after fast eating at many a trucker's rendezvous along the way. I still have the old, worn, scotch-taped copy. It is a memento of God's faithfulness to satisfy my spiritual hunger.

On the first trip out of Detroit at a highway's "clover leaf," the cowboy driver in third place behind me dragged a bit behind. So he did not see which way Mr. Rhodes and I had turned. Frantic since we were nowhere in sight, he stepped on the gas, and the cowboy drivers behind him stuck with him. They were unaware that they were headed on a road that would lead north to Canada! Mr. Rhodes and I drove several hours, then pulled in at a roadside restaurant. We expected the cowboys soon to show up.

An hour or so went by, and no ranch hands. The New Mexico car dealer was driving his big car on the route, but had tarried in Detroit. Knowing the highway Mr. Rhodes was taking, he walked into the restaurant and the two compared notes on the missing drivers. The dealer hurried back eastward to locate his vehicles and errant drivers. He shrewdly guessed that they had made the wrong turn at the clover leaf, and spotted the trucks at a restaurant stop far to the north. They had been "stepping on it," thinking they were on the right road and needed to catch up. We waited a long time at a later truck drivers' eating paradise, and finally the lost drivers walked in red of face.

I worked later that 1954 summer for a Claude Arnold in home construction in southeast Buckeye a block south of the main highway through town and the Dairy Queen. That ice cream "oasis" then was on the corner at Jackson Street beside the main drag, Highway 80. We built homes, one of which my folks would later buy (1958) when Dad sold the farm and they moved to town. In August, I left the construction in heat as blazing as 119 degrees. The local newspaper said it was the hottest spot in the nation that day. I rode the Greyhound Lines to New York to see Mildred and meet her folks, a grueling, four day jaunt. It made me wonder, "if this is comfort, what must the stage coaches of the old west have been like?"

Meanwhile Mildred had spent much of her summer helping her mother in the farm house and working with Pastor Weatherbee at the Unadilla Baptist Church. She taught Sunday School and assisted in the "Daily Vacation Bible School." She would be ready for my arrival after my ride that seemed it never would end.

My sweetheart met me when I stepped off the bus in Unadilla. And oh, how refreshing she looked. Worth the trip. It was one of the happiest hours of my life. I think we both were "in seventh heaven" as we walked to her Willys. The stay was for two weeks before we must drive back to Arizona with Mildred's brother Bob. She took me to her Unadilla church, and to a Sunday night youth rally in another church. There, one of her favorite preachers, Archie Benedict, spoke powerfully on Gideon's soldiers breaking open their pots with lamps for a momentous victory (Judges 7:15-23).

Mildred's sense of teasing humor again came out as she introduced me in the youth group. Her description was picturesque. I was "one of the savage Indians of Arizona." That was because some in New York, never having ventured west, had bizarre ideas about Arizona still being a dangerous badland of rampaging Apache warriors. They had images of the old days from cowboy movies that were graphic about the early, wild, raw, dark and bloody west. The young people hooted it up, having a good laugh at this terrorizing "brave's" expense.

I loved my girl friend's Dad and Mom. He was a tall gentleman, she a stocky, gray-haired lady's lady with a dancing warmth in her eyes. That is where Mildred got it. I helped Dad milk his Guernsey cows in the big barn. It stirred my life to hear this muscular, wiry layman talking rich theology so winsomely made practical as he went from cow to cow. He had never been to seminary, but he was a seminary professor to me there. If only my Dad had a love for the Savior like this! We had wonderful times at Mom's table eating boiled potatoes, beef, gravy, squash, stringed beans, and turnips from her garden, with a dessert such as German chocolate cake or apple pie, and cold milk.

Mildred took me on a hike along a cow path in the lane behind the barn, trudging slowly up the slope into "Currey's Mountain" (like the "Walton's Mountain" on the old TV series, "The Waltons"). The hill top beauty was a forest of trees. She often paused for a couple of minutes to get her breath. We went to round up the dairy cattle that grazed in a hidden, grassy meadow and follow them back to the milking. I also helped Dad and his crew mow, fork hay into "shocks," and haul wagon loads from a field up on a hillside terrace to hoist it into the barn's loft.

I reached into my shirt pocket and my heart felt a sting of dismay. My brown-haired, calf-skin pack for Bible memory verses had apparently flopped out, lost. Crying out for God's help to find this immense treasure (Ps. 130:1), I retraced places I'd been in the meadow and after a long search my eyes caught sight of what was worth more than silver or gold. The pack lay partly concealed where the long grass grows, near a wagon wheel rut.

On one occasion, braving summer heat, Mildred led me up the slope and veered off to the left, through timber. There we rested on a slab of flat boulder below an enormous heaping of stone. She reached around an outcropping, tinkled a hidden, tin cup left there, rinsed it in icy water that trickled down, and handed me a refreshing drink. It satisfied like the Pepsi in an early jingle, "Pepsi Cola hits the spot, whether it's cold or whether it's hot." In this case the drink was "Adam's ale," delightfully cold. It slaked my thirst.

In another venture, I rumbled in a wagon with Dad up the slope and watched as he and some helpers sawed down a cherry tree. We worked the trunk on to the wagon bed to go down to the wood pile. I recall the fragrant scent of the fresh cherry wood, so distinctly tantalizing in the air, so appealing with its pleasant sensation of cherry aroma.

The Curreys were people close to God. To me this was a compelling thing. How unlike my own folks at that time, who, although I loved them with all my heart, had not received the Lord. I was enthralled at the ways, so new to me, that a truly Christian family acted. Dad came in from the morning's milking, finished the cereal in his bowl, then opened his big Bible and Sunday School quarterly to study. He sat engrossed for about an hour each morning, obviously thrilled with his bonanza. For years he taught every Sunday, and his mind was a treasure lode stocked with God's riches (Matt. 13:52). I marked how steadfastly he clung to this diligence, and learned from it.

Conversations at meals and in the living room centered so often on Christian things to drink in. I never heard a foul word or any tidbit of gossip. It was a joy to have "rivers of living water" surging into my own hungry spirit (cf. John 7:37-39).

But oh, the ache—and the prayer! If my own Mom and Dad could have this! Yes, and all my brothers and sisters! My heart burned that this could be realized, and I poured out my heart longings to God. Mildred had taken up these prayers too.

Things were happening. My brother Jerry and sisters Ethel and Mary Ellen had trusted in the Lord, and they were helping other children in the family want to go to Sunday School.

The God who hears was at work.

10

God Answers Prayers—Eternally!

GOD WAS ATTENTIVE TO my intercessory vigils and those of others.

Shortly after that, about 1957, my own mother drove some of her family to town and dropped them off for Sunday School and church. Then she turned the old Buick homeward. Church going had not been her own custom for a very long time. She would come back in a few hours and pick up my siblings.

But as she pulled away, our church's tower bell was tolling. She recognized an old, familiar tune from her childhood Church of Christ in Oklahoma. Mom's ears picked up the chimes, and memory began to fill in words. God rocked her life with a powerful yearning that flamed in her heart. She just broke down and began to sob at the wheel. She suddenly was pouring out to the Lord how she needed and simply must have Him. Along the miles she told God she longed for Him to forgive her and come into her life (John 1:12).

He did!

She somehow kept the car clinging to the road despite the cascading tears. The car going north hung a left, turning westward into the ranch yard, and coasted the rest of the way to the house. Mom flung open the door, jumped out, and touched ground running. She hurried through a shower, dressed, and drove back in time for the church service. In God's providence that morning all the Rosscup young people were sitting in one row together. But the seat nearest the middle aisle was vacant. There was still room for one, there and at the cross!

Our indescribably precious mother slipped into this seat.

"Mom!" gasped my surprised sister nearest her. Our mother had never been to this or any church in years except at Mildred's and my wedding a year earlier. But all of a sudden something was new. "What's happened?"

"The Lord's in my heart now!" Mom whispered. The word buzzed down the family line as if it was a powerful electric current. It shook hearts, and tears began to trickle. At the end of the service, Pastor Leroy Crossley asked if anybody would like to come forward to make a decision, or to testify of one. Mom turned into a human catapult. Her feet went a flying to the pastor, and he grasped her outstretched hand as she daubed her eyes with a handkerchief. The scene was stirring. Many had prayed for my parents' salvation. Now God had done part of His blessed work! Great rejoicing gripped hearts because of the God who answers!

Mom, a new creature (2 Cor. 5:17), then joined others of us in prayers for Dad's salvation. A few years later, around 1964–65, Francis, or Dad as we called him, still was a hold out, unsaved, the self-sufficient, impossible hard man. How strange that he could be so thoughtful toward people, yet so insensitive to God. Mom would lie in bed at night, grip his hand, and silently plead her fervent cry for the Lord to save him. I was praying at Dallas Seminary, and had friends interceding. Buckeye church people kept up their prayers, as my sisters and brother Jerry did, and the latest pastor Roy McGuffy and his wife cried out to the One who hears prayer.

The Rosscups had sold the farm in 1958 and retired to a house in Buckeye.

Pastor McGuffy used to walk down the stairs to the basement youth hall that Dad ran now that he had left his cattle. The hall was located a few doors south of the main street through town, on 4th Street. Dad and some other older men would shoot pool or retire to a side room to play dominoes. McGuffy often would sit nearby, chat and tell jokes. Dad picked up on how he was quite human and a really winsome man after all. Before that Dad had put down ministers. He was counting on his good deeds to his neighbors to assure him a pass at heaven's gate. One day my parents invited the McGuffys to dinner. In that itself the God of the impossible was showing what was possible to Him.

"I've checked, and Billy Graham's on TV right after supper," Dad confided to Mom. "That'll keep the pastor quiet, just hearing that other preacher. By the time the TV program ends, it'll be late, and I can steer the talk some other way. He won't have time to talk that God stuff to us." I now know that Mom continued to pray to the Lord that the evening would go His way.

How strange and how wise the ways of God that out-smart us. What a God of surprises. His wisdom is higher than man's to "head us off at the pass."

So the iron-willed ex-rancher, one of the toughest of the men of flint, had it all figured. Supper ended, and the group went into the living room. Dad clicked on the TV. Right on schedule—Billy Graham. Soon the evangelist was preaching. Dad leaned back in his couch chair, smug. Mom went into the kitchen to get the dessert ready, and was gone for a while. Graham preached a powerful message, gave the invitation, stood with bowed head, and waited as people filed down out of the stands and came to stand before his platform.

Does God answer prayer? Really?

The seemingly unbelievable happened. Nothing is too hard for God.

Dad got up from his seat, deeply stirred, and plopped himself down on his knees before the TV set. Something very mighty was moving him (John 6:44, 65). This was his time, his way of "coming down out of the stands," and God's drawing urge was irresistible, bidding him to "come" (John 6:44; Rev. 22:17).

Mom stepped into the doorway from the kitchen and glimpsed Dad down. She thought at first he had fallen, and cried out in shock, "Dad! What's wrong?"

Nothing was wrong. Something was right.

"Mom, I'm a different man." Dad was completely humbled. Tears were coursing down his leathery cheeks—the jaws of an old, proud, long-resistant rancher. He was a man who had always said if anybody could make it to heaven for doing good, he was that person. His merits would get him there. Now Dad was down, leveled, broken, undone, crushed by utter need, stripped bare of any merit, with no words to explain things away, simply taking a gift. Mom just came apart with joy.

Pastor McGuffy pushed himself to his feet and brushed his teary eyes. Recognition touched his soul. He laid a firm hand on Dad's shoulder, and could hardly choke out the words, "Brother Rosscup, I believe you've been saved."

Dad dropped to the floor in a different way a few months later. He fell, instantly dead of a heart attack, in his youth hall—knowing Jesus. This time he did not leave the ranch, or depart for the youth hall, but went to be with his Savior. Safe at home!

I would not find out he had been saved until somewhat later.

In Casa View, an outskirt of Dallas, Mildred, Dianne, Carolyn, and I had just sat down to supper in February of 1965 in the final months of my doctoral studies. The phone jingled, and I went into the living room to answer it. My brother in law Larry Wood's voice came into my ear.

"Jim, I'm sorry I've got sad news for you. Your Dad passed away today."

I was dazed, scarcely able to believe it. How could it be? How could it be? The family's rock, one of my heroes, my beloved Dad? My world reeled.

Mildred and the little girls could not go. I drove 22 hours to be at the funeral. Mom was in such an awesome shock then, and had so many people around her, that she did not tell me the story of Dad's conversion until some weeks later once she had recovered a bit from her numbness. I heard the pastor say nice things, but did not get to talk with him to see things as they really were.

Later, Mom related the story above to me.

I delayed for some time, but later wrote to Rev. McGuffy who in a short time had left Buckeye to take another pastorate. Did he too remember things as Mom retold them? How did he see the entire matter? He wrote a two-page letter back, telling me that he remembered it the same way. Dad, he confirmed, was one of the most remarkable conversion cases he had seen in his years at Buckeye.

Mom told me of Dad's joy after that. What a change! As an unsaved man he had once sat at a table of fried chicken and announced in a cocky way that he would say grace. Those of the family bowed, and he said, "Grace divine, the biggest piece of chicken on the platter is mine!" Then he speared the piece and burst out with a haughty laugh, thinking he was being smart. After salvation he came to the table, bowed his head contritely, and spoke tender, reverent words of gratitude to God.

On a night shortly before Dad's home-going, Grandma Bertha, Mom's mother, was visiting from Lemoore, CA. Dad went alone to the Nazarene church that evening, for a special speaker much talked about was there in a revival series, and Dad was eager to hear him. He returned home, face beaming, spilling over with good things the preacher had said. How differently a "new creature" sees things (2 Cor. 5:17)!

At Dallas Seminary, little groups used to pray. I had often asked the men to plead with me for my dear Dad and precious Mom. And Mildred and I had prayed. People in the little Buckeye church were praying too, and some of my siblings by that time had been saved, and were beseeching the Lord for the parents we loved more than words can say.

I have often thanked the Lord that He is sensitive to prayer. Mom and Dad have flown away to heaven, Dad in 1965 and Mom in 1997. Our elder sister Anna Mae, who received Christ some years into her marriage and became a very godly Christian and woman of prayer, went in 1995. Another very godly Christian sister, Betty Lou, joined the Lord Nov. 2, 2007. Now our beloved and godly Mildred is also at home with the Lord as of April 15, 2008.

The person faithful to pray will find that God is even more faithful to answer.

11

More Growing, and Diplomas

GO BACK WITH ME again to college days at Arizona State.

Mildred and I continued studies, went to more home football games, a Harlem Globe Trotters uncanny game of shooting baskets at our gym, church services, youth meetings, rallies, plays, and Truth for Youth gatherings. Mildred and I would begin dates with prayer and often Bible study. At different Christmas times her gifts to me were Christian books that nourished my spirit. How they blessed my spirit! Some were Andrew Murray's *With Christ in the School of Prayer*, F. B. Meyer's *Abraham, The Obedience of Faith,* another a book on Christian evidences to support the faith, also Edwin Hartill's *Hermeneutics* [principles in how to interpret the Bible], E. H. Bancroft's *Elemental Theology*, A. P. Gibbs' *Worship, the Christian's Highest Occupation*, Andrew Zenos' *A Compendium of Church History*, and others.

These I devoured. And they were to me as vital as cool, refreshing water to a man thirsty in a hot desert trek. They also helped me grow in Christ.

Further books she brought from ABI, and I still have, were J. F. Strombeck's works, *First the Rapture* (pre-tribulation rapture view), *Grace and Truth, Disciplined by Grace* (I have re-read that one several times), and *Shall Never Perish*, a simple book on Christ keeping His own saved. Strombeck was a Christian business man and chairman of the trustees board at Dallas Theological Seminary. His writing on being disciplined by grace is one that I have treasured through the years as it developed concepts such as Titus 2:11-14.

I became the richer due to these works which stimulated spiritual fruit in my own young Christian life. The sharing of them also led to fruit abounding to Mildred's account (Phil. 4:17).

She also introduced me to the Keith L. Brooks prepared booklets on Bible study. Brooks headed up what then was known as the American Prophetic League, headquartered in Los Angeles. Brooks did paperbacks on *Basic Bible Work for Young Believers*, also the *Christian Character Course* and other topics such as Ephesians and prophecy. He would present several pages of questions and places for answers one dug like gold nuggets out of passages he specified. Often Brooks interspersed his own rich comments to clarify things. In such a guided study, I felt the impact of great wealth and sweetness on a subject (Ps. 19:7-10), and became stronger in my Lord (2 Pet. 3:18).

When the two of us had Bible studies together, Mildred would let me take the lead though her home and institute training had grown her to be unusually adept in the Bible. By contrast I was about as green as they come, and relatively ignorant. How humble and non-pushy she was. Her pleasant voice would gently suggest things that were wise and good. Her grasp often caused a fresh, apt, and wonderful light to glow on passages. This good sense about God's truth helped me even beyond what I got out of personal Bible study using the Navigators' "Search the Scripture" sheets to fill in, and Brooks' study booklets with their guiding questions.

Another fine Brooks booklet of those days that I have often gone back to check is his *The Cream Book*, an 89-page collection of arresting one-liners on many subjects, sub-titled *Sentence Sermons* (1938 and following). These have often helped when I was preparing messages, or just to be spiritual stimulants to live the Christian life.

A further thing that helped me spiritually during college was talks with my pastor, Bob Warren. I would go to him for counsel, sometimes when quite discouraged. He had a way of turning my eyes to the Lord and sending me out of his office elated by a focus on my Savior. One day when I was concerned about where God might be leading me, Bob said, "Jim, God hasn't promised to show us the whole road all at once, just one step at a time."

Mildred and I drove several times to a picnic area in the South Mountain Park, south of Phoenix. There we would unpack our food and drink on a table beneath an arbor, talk, look at the cacti, ironwood trees, and brush, listen to scurrying desert animals and tweeting birds, and revel in the land of the whistling wind. Those times of heart-knitting seemed like "heaven on earth."

We kept up our studies and our dating into our senior year. Early that school year a fear clutched at my heart. Uncle Sam's military draft letter summoned me. Our plans had been to finish college and I would go to seminary, but it looked like I was being swept away for some years before I could finish at Arizona State. The ache of possibly being apart from Mildred put a "shot put" weight on my heart.

We prayed, and I went to ask help from Dr. H. D. Richardson, vice-president of the college. There I sat on the other side of his huge, polished desk, explaining my need. He took up my case, sent off a special letter on my behalf, and the draft service re-classified me IV-D, the "D" for divinity. So I stayed in school, freed up to marry and go on to seminary. After that, the draft never again summoned me. God had other plans.

How distinct is the memory of the preparatory events for induction that the Army summoned me to in Phoenix, and my thought that I was soon to be on my way out. My prayers went up to the Lord because of Mildred, graduation, and the flame of desire for Christian training. Our Lord who even raises up kings and takes other kings down (Ps. 75) shut that induction door for me, and was about ready to start opening other doors.

Our graduation together in May, 1957 was at Goodwin Stadium at the south end of the campus, in the stands overlooking the field where our team then played football. There were more than 700 graduates that May. Mildred received a B. A. in elementary education, and my diploma was in journalism.

But something else had happened five months before this (Dec., 1956). God's providentially sparing me from the draft permitted it.

Glad day! Glad day!

12

Wedding Bells

IT WAS A SPECIAL day in the summer of 1956. I visited Mildred at the upstairs Tempe apartment where she lived with Jo Ella Henry. Her roommate was away at work, and I had come to take my sweetheart on a date.

But first, I needed to deal with an issue of awesome magnitude.. I had been working up the courage to say something to Mildred. This, apart from Christ's salvation, was the most important thing in my life.

I fumbled out the words asking this captivating lady to marry me, and watched her open the box that held an engagement ring. Her eyes twinkled, and she said "yes." Oh, day to be remembered! "He who finds a wife finds a good thing, And obtains favor from the Lord" (Prov. 18:22). In years to follow I would experience a continual succession of favors from God that Mildred would share with me. After she would pass into glory, I would look at her large picture every night before pillowing my head, and say, "Good night, Mildred (or Dumplin'). Thank you for everything—and that's a lot!"

We kept our engagement secret for a few days so that we could spring our surprise at a large church youth banquet. The group met in Phoenix at the Marine Room of the then popular Golden Drumstick Restaurant. At first we were just milling around, socializing. When we were summoned to gather at both sides of a long series of tables set up in an "L," Mildred and I had become at a distance in the crowd and the youths filled the seats quickly. Rather than disrupt things, we wound up sitting on opposite sides of the table, across from one another, rather than side by side.

Reviewing our wedding album these years later, I found Mildred's program for that dinner. Happy tears came back as I found her note about her green formal and white daisy corsage as well as my brown suit and white carnation boutonniere.

I had the engagement ring stowed in a pocket and, at a signal on the sly, sneaked it to Mildred under the table. She then slipped it on. When our youth sponsor, the elderly Carlton Nason, beloved "Pop" to us all, stood and began to announce our secret, Mildred flashed the ring high. Pop could finish his speech only after the "oohs" and "ahhhs."

The theme of that night was "Love One Another" (John 13:34). Our speaker was Carl Hodges, Director of Truth for Youth in Phoenix. Hodges spoke on knowing God's love—its breadth, length, height, and depth (Eph. 3:18-19).

Shortly before that dinner, as I also discovered in treasures Mildred had kept, I had written her a little note with a bronze key taped at the bottom. My words were, "Mildred, I am a funny fellow, so I am being funny tonight. I am giving you this key to my heart. You may keep it as long as we live, and it and the heart it is symbolic of opening are completely, unreservedly yours. Your own, Jim."

In days that followed Mildred made her own wedding dress, crafted and sent out invitations, planned for flowers, photography, cake and punch, and other arrangements. Our wedding was at the First Baptist Church, Tempe, December 16, amidst Christmas decorations, in 1956. Our dear, dear Pastor Bob Warren officiated, Milt Winterberg, the marvelous youth leader, played "Saviour Like a Shepherd Lead Us" on his saw. His skill was tremendous! And Clarence Stauffer, state youth director, led in prayer. Midge Bjorkland, a standout singer in our youth group, offered a solo.

We said "I do" and kissed.

My Dad and Mom and the family had come from Buckeye. Most of my siblings were there. The bakery that was to deliver the cake had not shown up with it when we came out of the ceremony, and Mildred phoned. They said they somehow had taken the cake by mistake to Buckeye but were rushing it the 45 miles to Tempe. In a little while they had it set up in the fellowship hall, and the reception was a success.

Mildred was a refreshingly beautiful bride. She had been sick those days right before the ceremony, but now God held her up. I looked around and saw Dad so well-dressed, beaming, and realized it was one of the very few times I ever saw this ranch man decked out in a suit. Beloved Mom lighted up my life with her smile of happiness for us.

One of our college friends, Rod Purdue, and his date Chalma made secret plans with us. He brought his big Packard car and speeded us away to evade the car loads of young people who were lurking in fun to pursue us. Our plot had been to block the alley behind the church after the Packard made its getaway, but some avoided the road impasse by speeding around the block. So they were not far behind, on our trail anyway. Rod got out on a dirt road southeast of Tempe, raised a heavy dust cloud behind him, then simply ran off and lost the slowed down followers. Safely away, he drove us to our secret apartment at elder Max McKinley's cottages on McAllister Street a few blocks east of campus.

Bill Stambaugh, best man (from Prescott, AZ), and Gloria Bushell, maid of honor (from Gila Bend), were at the apartment to help us pack to leave that very evening on a honey moon trip. We were off in the little Willys to New York, a four-day drive. Mildred's folks had not been free to leave the cows that needed to be milked, so Mildred carried their telegram of joy for us during the wedding. By agreement we were on our way to celebrate especially with the Curreys back at her former home.

Bill and Gloria later married one another and farmed south of Tempe.

Mildred and I took turns driving day and night, except that we stopped in Virginia at a motel one night as I recall. In New Mexico's bitter winter cold and in the highlands, anxiety clutched at us very early the morning after the wedding as we looked for a filling station open. Our tank gauge was plunging to a menacing low. A couple of towns had nothing open. We spotted a sign that said the next town was a few miles. We thought we had gas to make it. But the Willys ran out, and we drifted to the shoulder of the road not far from the edge of a cliff.

Mildred wrapped herself in blankets and curled up on the car seat. I locked the vehicle and started "hoofing it" to go get gas at the town. I labored about a quarter of a mile up hill, and the December highland freeze was so overpowering that I began to feel the cold shutting down my body. Death seemed but a few steps away out there in the open. The icy chill of desperation gripped me. Turning around, I stumbled back in a perilous bid to reach the car, and a sudden terror told me that I could never make it. I cried out to God for help in my agony of need. Then I had struggled only a few steps when I saw lights approaching. I lifted my hand in an awesome bid for life. A cowboy came in a pickup, stopped, and asked if that was my car back there run out of gas. I chattered yes as I felt as if I was in a cold storage locker, and he invited, "Hop in, I'm goin' to town."

He got me to a gas "filling station" that was open in the early morning. Another car that sat at the pumps was pointed the way we had come. The driver agreed to take me back with my can of gas. We poured the fuel into the tank, Mildred and I were off again, and we returned the can at the station, where we filled the Willys tank.

How merciful is our God of rescue (Ps. 34:4)! "Great is the Lord, and greatly to be praised" (48:1).

In Virginia after a night at a motel we heard the clippity-clop of horse's hooves in rhythm on pavement. Gazing out, we saw an Amish man seated in a buggy. We ourselves went on toward New York.

Our Christmas in the farm house was filled with happy hours. I got to exult again in how an all-Christian family worshiped the Lord. We shared our gifts from beneath a beautiful tree in the corner of the living room. Mildred and I usually sat up late at night loving one another, and twice each day I helped milk the cows, put down oats, fork hay, clean out the barn, and wash the utensils after morning and evening milkings.

On our long journey back to Tempe, we got to Charleston, West Virginia in the dark of night. I was driving around hairpin turns on a two-lane road in extremely dense January fog, and could scarcely see the painted line dividing lanes. A long day's drive had wrung almost every ounce of strength out of me. I said to Mildred, "The strain's so great, I'll pull off, rest a few minutes, and get my bearings." When I angled off the pavement, I did not figure on rain's mud on the shoulder of the road. Our Willys went into a skid and finally came to a stop. We started to climb out to stretch our legs and revive in the cool air. Mildred, the passenger side door open, looked down and shrieked. Nothing but depth of space was below. Our right front tire was hanging some feet out over a cliff! Heavy mud, apparently, was bogging the car from plunging over!

Did I say "mud"? The main reason was God! He had other plans for us.

He kept us safe as Psalm 121 assures He does for His own. The psalmist makes this point in v. 2, "My help comes from the Lord, who made heaven and earth." And He repeats His faithfulness to keep (vv. 3, 4, 5, 7, 8). God "shall preserve your going out and your coming in even forever."

We cautiously eased out the other side and stood trembling. The Lord had kept us from a catastrophe, plummeting into oblivion—and probably early deaths!

Through the fog we could faintly make out the blur of lights on a hill above. But we were alone, without help. No, never alone. God almost instantly brought a man in a big Packard car. He stopped, whistled at the scene his lights up close revealed, and said he had a chain. In moments he had backed us onto the pavement, to safety, and we were on our way—alive!

The rest of that trip, things went well until we got to New Mexico. What was there about New Mexico? Many miles short of Lordsburg in the southwest area of the state, one of our rear tires blew out. I struggled to keep the car under control and drift off to a stop. Soon I had put on our spare. But alas! A few miles later that spare blew out as well. We were stranded.

Mildred went across some railroad tracks to hide beyond a pile of boulders where we felt she would be safe. Then I hitch-hiked into Lordsburg to buy two "repossessed" tires. Somebody took me back, and Mildred emerged out of concealment.

We got to our first home together, a Tempe cottage. Then came semester finals. Our last semester began in the Spring of 1957 in a haven of wedded bliss.

Jim and Mildred are Married

Top left: Mildred at her wedding (Tempe, AZ); Top right: first Christmas card from the newlyweds.

Bottom left: Mildred feeds cake to Jim at their wedding; Bottom right: Jim and Mildred exit First Baptist Church, Tempe, AZ as newlyweds.

13

At Dallas in Seminary

HUNGER WAS RAVENOUS IN my heart for more Bible training. Mildred regaled me with ABI stories of how wonderful such learning was. I could taste it. Besides, I had talked with several people who gave me counsel that seminary was the path for me. Our Pastor Bob Warren, a Bob Jones University graduate, said, "Jim, if I had it to do over again, I'd pack my bags and head for Dallas [Theological Seminary]." Elmer Lappen, leader of Campus Crusade and a dear friend, advised "go to Dallas." Wes Darby, a Clifton, AZ pastor who had given me a copy of Maxwell Coder's fine paperback book, *God's Will for Your Life*, said "Dallas is the place." Others agreed.

Mildred had heard that Dallas had built a name as a school of Bible-believing excellence. Her ABI professor, John Hubbard, had worked in earlier days with the man who would be the first Dallas president, Dr. Lewis Sperry Chafer, who led the school in 1924–1952. Chafer had awarded this man of God an honorary doctorate in 1931. And Hubbard said that Dallas was the seminary to attend.

Mildred's opinion, after her beloved mentor's, "sealed the deal."

Come summer (1957) we loaded our few worldly goods into a small trailer, had a church mechanic Carl Spain put a hitch on the Willys, and set out for Dallas in June, sight unseen. We were just two young people who loved the Lord and hungered to know more about Him. We went by faith as Abraham (Heb. 11:8), for we did not know the place to which we were going, or a person there.

Except God. And any person, with God, is a majority.

Len Sharp, who owned one of the largest dairy farms in Arizona, near Tempe, and was an elder at First Baptist Church, had written one of the letters to recommend me at Dallas Seminary. His daughter Linda, who was in the Tempe church's youth class that Mildred and I led, would come years later, several times, to my Talbot Seminary faculty office, for counsel. For she was a student at Biola on the same campus. Linda married Bill Young, a seminary student and friend of mine, and I saw her graduate on campus and chatted with her visiting parents on the school green. That was the last time I saw Bill and Linda, or the Sharp family, all these who meant so much to me.

On our way to Dallas, we got to one stretch where we were clinging to a narrow ribbon of highway. Treacherous winds rocked the Willys and its trailer in a bravado that caused terror. We were swept beyond good control. It was all I could do to keep the car and trailer on the road, for the wind whisked them in zig-zag fury. A coming car was bearing down on us, and I was desperate to hold to our side of the road as I slowed down and hauled at the wheel. Our hearts leaped into our throats. Just in the nick of time God helped me get both car and trailer to swing to our side, and the onrushing car buzzed past. Mildred and I got out, shaken, and walked around thanking God for the narrow rescue from possible death. It was a great deliverance.. How good is God! Two frightened, but finally relieved young people climbed back in the Willys and forged on.

"Through many dangers, toils, and snares, I have already come;
'Tis grace has brought me safe this far, and grace shall lead me home."

We got to Dallas one early evening. Our first quest was to find a Western Union office where we could send telegrams to Mildred's folks and to my own that we had arrived safely. Then we came to a small motel for the night a few blocks from the seminary. The next day, with soaring hopes, we drove to Swiss Avenue and pulled up across from the seminary's front gate and sign. Our dream was for real. Excitement gripped us. We strolled hand in hand up the long walkway to the main, central hall where the business offices were.

The excitement that electrified our hearts was one of the great things in this life. Here we were, a dream being realized!

Dr. Donald Campbell, who years later would be president of the school after Dr. John Walvoord, had a home for us. It was at what they called the Carroll Avenue Apartments, a two-story building with eight family units. We moved in upstairs on a corner facing Sycamore Street where it intersected Carroll Avenue. We had a kitchen, small dining area that partly served as a study for my foot or so of books, a large living room, a bathroom, and one bedroom.

Dr. John Witmer, Professor of Systematic Theology at the seminary, surprised us by a visit one afternoon. He had seen that Mildred had an elementary teaching degree and needed a teacher for a grade school with which he also was affiliated. Mildred was ecstatic at the prospect of realizing her dream--teaching. However, she suffered a sharp disappointment. Shortly later in that summer her breathing became difficult, and we had to inform Dr. Witmer that she was unable to go through with the agreement. A bit further along, instead, the seminary invited Mildred to take a role at the main office switchboard and be the receptionist. She would do that while I attended classes, and we could eat together in the lunch room.

The apartments were about eight blocks from campus. But we usually drove the Willys and Mildred went to the office, I to my 7:30 a.m. Greek class. She soon became a darling to the faculty as she did many considerate things for them with a winning smile, and her sense of good humor captured their hearts. She would sort out mail and put it in faculty and student boxes, answer calls at the switchboard, help people who came to the window, and such tasks. Her ABI office job had trained her well. She knew how every student was doing because she put graded papers or exams back into their boxes.

The seminary's yearbook, *The Heritage* of 1958, has a section called "Staff." There, at the top on the first of four pages, is postcard sized picture of a lady at the seminary switchboard, phone in left hand, right hand making a plug in to connect a call. Below the photo are the words, in two lines, "Mrs. James E. Rosscup, PBX Operator."

Near the end of June, 1957, a job agency located a possible placement for me. I drove about 30 minutes out to the east of Dallas to a "bedroom city," Garland. There I inquired at *The Garland Daily News* for Bill Bradfield, Jr., the publisher. Bill walked me across the immediate State Street to a soft drinks place and we sat taking sips from bottles of soda pop, and talking. He told me that he had just lost his fine sports editor of four years, Jim Reapsome, who had gone to Dallas Theological Seminary. Reapsome later was an editor of the famous *Sunday School Times*, a Christian tabloid that nourished many lay people throughout the country.

"Really?" I replied, mulling over this astounding revelation. "Dallas Seminary is where I'm just starting."

Bill looked at me incredulously from behind his spectacles. A smile of pleasure and instant decision broke across his face.

The publisher liked my credentials that included work on my hometown weekly, *The Buckeye Valley News*, sports writing for my college town's *The Tempe Daily News*, being sports editor of the campus weekly, *The State Press,* and serving a year as the college's Assistant Sports Publicist. I had also gone to college, partly, by being selected for the annual state scholarship in journalism. I had majored in news writing, and sports was one of my great loves. God had kindly prepared me.

Reapsome's model work for those years cleared the way for me. Above and over all was the sovereign, guiding hand of the Lord (Ps. 32:8; Jer. 10:23). He does that for his sons and daughters (Ps. 48:14; Rom. 8:14; Gal. 5:18). A familiar song at that time had the lines, "Life is a symphony, since the Man of Galilee changed my discord into song, made life sweet the whole day long. . . . No more a stranger, He is the arranger of my symphony."

Bill hired me on the spot. I soon loved the job in a football-crazy city that backed the Garland High School Owls in their black pants and white jerseys. People there picked up, "copy cat" style, on the "Black Knights of the Hudson," the West Point or Army football teams that in the 1940's featured the fabulous running backs Glenn Davis and Doc Blanchard. The fleet Davis was "Mr. Outside" who scored around the ends, and Doc Blanchard was "Mr. Inside" who blasted for big gains through the line. Getting their cue, Garland fans called their Owls "The Black Knights of Duck Creek." Two years before, in 1955, Garland's storied All-State running back Bobby Boyd had rambled on incredible touchdown runs to lead the Owls to the state championship game. In that battle, Port Neches edged Garland, 20-14. The next year, 1956, the season before I arrived, again in the Texas title game, Garland had outlasted Nederland in a snowstorm to win the state's crown jewels, 3-0.

Boyd went on to distinguish himself as starting quarterback leading the mighty Oklahoma "Big Red" Sooners. After college, he was a starting cornerback for the Baltimore Colt pro team that fought to the Super Bowl.

In my year in Garland (1957–58) the Black Knights won their way to the state quarter finals. Then they suffered a stunning upset on a sprinkler-soaked field (some said deliberate) at Cleburne, 20-0. The story was that somebody had inadvertently left the water on the night before, and puddles on the gridiron looked as if rain had delivered a down pour. The boggy, slippery turf stymied the especially fast Garland running backs Chock Bailey and Bobby Norvell. These breakaway "touchdown twins" could not make their usual quick, evasive cuts, but often lost their footing and went down on their own.

An attorney friend who helped me keep statistics in the press box, Chuck Cabaniss, and I ate our cheese sandwiches before the game, then sat in shock. Our team, favored to win big, never got untracked. Later, while I was in my doctoral studies at Dallas Seminary, Garland would win back to back state titles in 1963, beating Corpus Christi Miller 17-0, and 1964, storming from behind in the final seconds to break the hearts of Galena Park rooters from Houston, 26-21.

I led a couple of Garland's high school athletes to professions to receive the Lord, one an all-conference tackle and the other a standout on the basketball team. I hope those decisions proved real for eternity.

After a year, I found the seminary's six courses so demanding that I had to give up the sports editing to focus full time on studies just to "stay in the hunt." Mildred continued to work in the seminary office. Editor Bill Bradfield has remained a friend throughout life. He sends emails to me every few weeks. He came to know the Lord and has written a book on great quotes about the Bible. Christmas cards also come from Bill and his wife Claire. Bill would hire me again as his sports editor in 1962-65 when I worked on my doctorate at Dallas Seminary, but by this time he had become owner of *The Texas Mesquiter*, a weekly in Mesquite, a few miles from Garland. Mesquite had had a name as one of the wild towns in the old west days.

In the summer after our first seminary year (1958), I had a tonsillectomy and was painfully sore, unable to eat anything but the softest food, and even that was agony. My family, having sold the farm and moved to Buckeye, had gotten a Ford Edsel Station Wagon and was making a trip through several states. They came to us in Dallas, and Mildred, after a day at the seminary office, took them out to eat while I suffered the agony of the tortured throat. What a trooper she was in her cheerful, giving spirit, as I would find her always to be.

One of life's huge scares befell us around February of the first seminary year (1958). I was working as sports editor of *The Garland Daily News*. I was driving Mildred and myself home from a Garland High basketball game in a drizzle on slick pavement, following Loop 12 that belted Dallas. I drove under an overpass, and suddenly Mildred cried out, as her eyes darted off to the right, "Look, Jim, he's in the ditch!" My eyes flashed to the scene near a bridge of a side road that sloped down a hill to meet Loop 12. A semi-trailer had jack-knifed on the incline, failed to make a turn to the bridge, and the rig had plunged into a creek ravine.

A driver just ahead of us was a "look-e-loo" so foolishly that he had slowed to a stop on a speedway to gaze. My eyes diverted ever so briefly, I did not imagine that he had paused—my fault—and when my eyes snapped back it was too late to brake in time. Our little Willys slammed into his vehicle, and the impact flung Mildred through the windshield on the passenger side. I was stunned by my nose and forehead banging into the steering wheel, my glasses shattered, but I managed to pull my wife's limp body out and carry her around to the median grass just to our left. Another driver graciously spread down a blanket, and my darling was crumpled, unconscious, her face bleeding. I bent over her, seeking desperately for a sign of life, my own heart racing in a terror that ran riot.

What had I done to my darling?

In minutes a screaming ambulance arrived, and sped us off to Baylor Hospital in Dallas. I had climbed in beside Mildred and the stretcher. A tow truck took our dear friend, the Willys that was battered beyond description. It would be consigned to a "graveyard" of cars. The front was caved and twisted into grotesque ruination. But God was <u>our</u> help (Heb. 13:6). Mildred regained consciousness at the hospital. A thousand thanks! A doctor removed her spleen and a specialist sewed stitches in her cheek, pulling flaps of her face together from deep cuts. After a frightening night ordeal, she was released the next morning to recuperate for days at the Carroll Avenue apartment. In time the healing God (Exod. 15:26) made her face free of signs that she had been in an accident. This was another comforting kindness of His boundless love.

I was stunned and unable to go to class for a couple of days.

Bill Bradfield, kindly boss at the news office, told me of a bank repossessed blue 1956 Plymouth that he personally would buy for me. He took me out to look at it, I liked the way it drove, and he let me have it for a low sum that my salary could gradually pay off. "Goodbye, Willys, our good friend of Arizona, New York, and the road to Dallas."

It was one more time of gracious acts in God protecting us for service He had in store!

We moved during our sophomore year to another seminary dwelling right on the campus. It was on the school property side of Apple Street, which skirted the seminary land. A kind couple, Ralph and Dorothy Braun, she the sister of Shirley who would become a fellow student Henry Holloman's wife, heard we needed a place near the school. Their sacrificial love prompted them voluntarily to relinquish the home for our sakes. It was a green cottage on campus, where Mildred had only to walk about a minute to her office work.

There we again were surrounded by seminary couples. Seminary houses were in a row along the street.

It was during our fourth, final year, later on, that Dave and Sande Sunde came to the seminary, Dave from Western Michigan University and Sande from Hope College and Western Michigan. Their presence would be one of the biggest blessings of our lives. Sande secured a job in the office alongside Mildred, and we all became dear friends, our hearts bonded for life. That Fall (1960), the four of us had a happy drive to Abilene, Texas, to go to the football game pitting Mildred's and my Arizona State team against Hardin Simmons University's Cowboys. The foe was a power in the Border Conference (such teams as Texas Western, West Texas State, New Mexico, Arizona, and Arizona State). But the Sun Devils shut down the Cowpokes to grab a 28-0 win.

We stayed at the Sands Motel, and went to look at the famous Church of Christ in Abilene. There we gazed dubiously at the corner plate claim, "Founded in AD 27 by John the Baptist." We also had sausage "puppies in a blanket," that is, rolled pancakes, at the restaurant that operated with the Sands.

Dave struggled in Hebrew and Greek as well as theology and Bible, and it seemed that he might have to drop out of seminary. I took him in hand and tutored him so that he jumped from failing to passing, stuck it out, and weathered his first, threatening year. Then I graduated, and he, greatly improved, went on gamely to complete the next three years, graduate, and become a youth pastor in a city called Southgate, CA., an outskirt of Los Angeles.

When Mildred and I and our two daughters came from my doctoral studies at Dallas to California in the summer of 1965 for me to begin teaching at Talbot

Theological Seminary, the Sundes were our host and hostess for a few days. Then we moved in for a two-week stay at a Talbot faculty couple's home, Bob and Nancy Saucy's place in Anaheim while they were on vacation. We found a small rental on Pecos Street in Norwalk, just off Imperial Highway, for a year until we could begin to buy a home in La Mirada (1966–69). After that, we bought our present home at 10909 Grovedale Dr. in east Whittier (1969–).

God would give us 39 years yet before Mildred would go to her home in heaven.

To this day, Dave Sunde reminds me just about every time I see him of how God let me help him stay the course at Dallas. We have gone to their three daughters' weddings, and Dave graciously flew from Louisville, CO on April 19, 2008, to read Scripture and share moving words about God's faithfulness at Mildred's memorial service, based on Lam. 3:22-23. In a very close heart link, we and the Sundes have sent many a prayer for one another to God.

Mildred in seminary days was a great help to Sande to grow in the Lord. The two ladies had splendid fellowship, and we often met as couples for meals. A friendship was kindled that would be a treasure all our lifetimes. Sande's tribute to Mildred appears in Chapter 29 here.

Dr. J. Dwight Pentecost was very pleased with my Th. M thesis, "Crucial Objections to Dispensationalism." In it, I sought to answer objections to that system. God encouraged Mildred and me when "Dr. P" said it was the kind he liked to see. Before and after this appraisal, he was a special help to us. He visited Mildred on three occasions when she was in a Dallas hospital desperate with a collapsed lung, was by her bed, and prayed for her. He welcomed me often to his office, and when I graduated with the Th. M degree urgently encouraged me to return from a stint with Campus Crusade.

"Jim," he insisted, "God has given you what it takes for teaching. I think you should plan to come back right away and work on your doctorate."

This counsel came from a man mighty in God. It was like a beacon light that kept drawing me on the sea of life.

14

Editing "The Collegiate Challenge"

WE FINISHED MY TH. M degree at Dallas Seminary in May, 1961, and for a year served in Pasadena, CA with Campus Crusade for Christ. The Crusade president, Bill Bright, asked me to be managing editor of a campus magazine, *The Collegiate Challenge*, which CCC was launching nationwide. It would grow as the years went by.

The magazine office was in what then was called the Arroyo Seco Building, a many-storied edifice on Pasadena's main artery, Colorado Boulevard along which the annual Rose Parade moves. The office had two rooms where the magazine had its birth and infant months. Today the publication is much expanded as *The World Challenge*. My boss was Bill Bright, and my mentor under Bright's appointment was Dr. Wilbur Smith, Professor of Bible at Fuller Seminary in Pasadena, who did the editing of the campus organ. Smith was one of the most widely read Christian evangelical scholars of his day, a Bible conference speaker, and author of many books, such as *Therefore Stand* and *Profitable Bible Study*.

I put together for each issue a two-page spread on testimonies of students, and wrote a monthly series of two-page articles on the Christian foundations of famous colleges and universities—Harvard, Yale, Princeton, Columbia, Dartmouth, Northwestern, Stanford, Baylor, etc. For this I did a lot of research and boiled down the findings to fit the space. Our Christian artist, Raymond "Smoky" Smokel, put in his skilled touches that dressed up the presentation. "Smoky" had been unsaved, a top artist for Hunt's Tomato Juice and also for Schindley's Distilleries, plus doing the art for some famous publications. He told me that at one time he had had about 40 people working under him. Converted to the Lord Jesus, he had devoted his time totally to Christ's cause via CCC, World Vision, etc.

Work on the magazine had just begun when Harold Ankeny, Youth Minister of Bethany Church in Sierra Madre, just east of Pasadena, contacted me. He wanted to take me to lunch. At the meal, he pleaded with me to be the regular teacher of the college and careers Bible class Sunday mornings at the church. After a few days of thought and prayer, I accepted. For a year I poured my whole heart into that ministry as well, and had a great rapport with some beloved, sharp young people. I taught in the mornings, and in the evenings the group always met for fellowship after the regular service in some church members' homes.

That was one of many classes I have taught. An earlier one was a high school class at Reinhardt Bible Church, outside Dallas, during my Th. M studies at Dallas Seminary for two years. After that I taught the college class two years, as well as a high school boys' group for a year in the garage of a home. Later when in the seminary doctoral program, the Scofield Memorial Church a few blocks from campus asked me to teach its "Co-uni-bus" class. The name meant college, university, and business. So I taught the 50-60 who attended during my doctorate years (1962–1965).

When I completed the doctoral work and we traveled to California in 1965 to begin my seminary teaching career, I would accept an invitation to teach the college and careers class at the Church of the Open Door in downtown Los Angeles (1966–1972). There, after my class, Mildred and I would get to hear the church's famous pastor with his southern brogue, J. Vernon McGee, preach some mighty messages. From there we would shift to Calvary Baptist Church in Whittier, and my teaching of the young couples' Joint Heirs group (1972-74). In following years I taught a number of different classes at this, our "home" church (1976–2008), and series in many other churches or at mountain conferences.

Mildred went with me when her health allowed. In some of the church classes she played the piano for the singing. And we attended a number of group parties in homes.

But permit me to return to Pasadena and our year with Crusade (1961–62).

Mildred did things that boggled my mind that year. Despite her illness, she was pregnant with Dianne, who would be born in April. And when Campus Crusade staff members would come from out of town to be our guests, she would be hostess at meals. One occasion stands out. Three high up leaders came unexpectedly, and I phoned Mildred to see if we could have them over in a little while for lunch. She, a real trooper, readily agreed.

Those were tight times. On the "shoestring" CCC salary, we often came down to a crisis before the next pay check. How much more I should have trusted God! Our cupboards were nearly bare, yet in a resourceful skill, Mildred's incredible, quick planning pulled us through. Like Elisha with the widow who had the pot of oil, she trusted God, came up with food that was needed, and we all had a good meal. I think of Proverbs 31:15b, she "gives food to her household." What an amazing woman the Lord fashioned from that trusting New York girl! How greatly He worked through her.

After a year as managing editor for which I had agreed, I said goodbye to the magazine work. This was after Bill Bright, national president of Campus Crusade, sat in my car and pleaded many arguments to keep me in this ministry.

"Jim," he said, "we need people on the front lines. We want you here."

"Bill," I replied, "I realize how important it is to be on the front lines, or anywhere for Christ. But God has put it in my heart to do doctoral work for teaching, and I believe that is 'front lines' too. It can have its impact to shape hundreds." So that would prove to be true, thank God!

Dianne had been born at Huntington Park Hospital south of Pasadena on April 5, 1962, and was our tiny baby. Both of us parents were beaming with joy. Mildred and I drove back to Dallas for me to pursue a doctorate degree in Bible. We were following Dr. Pentecost's prized counsel with a passion exploding toward teaching (cf. above).

Summer heat lashed out with its furnace blast along the route. The Plymouth's air conditioner could not contend against such warmth, so we kept wet towels to bathe Dianne's face and our own, and to hang in the car windows to help air coming in cool us all along the way. We visited Mom and Dad (the Rosscups) at their home in Buckeye along the way to Dallas, and showed off our prize, Dianne, amid "oohs and ahhs." Everybody in the family loved our baby girl, and they all thought I had a princess bride. Princess Mildred. I knew I had married far above my head, high class, the finest sterling, "the purest quill." I have often felt a humble awe at this wealth that God gave out of His great riches (Phil. 4:19).

Psalm 84:11 was coming true for us, even in our imperfections, "No good thing will He withhold from those who walk uprightly."

15

Going Deeper—in a Doctorate

WHEN WE GOT BACK to Dallas, the seminary had a four-room apartment suite reserved to be our new home on Apple Street at the edge of the campus. That was our abode in 1962–63.

Some time later we found a house to rent in Casa View just outside Dallas, nearer the job that paid our way through the doctorate. My former Garland boss, Bill Bradfield, had moved to become publisher and editor of another newspaper, *The Texas Mesquiter*, a weekly named after its town, Mesquite. The news office was a few miles from Garland, east of Dallas. Bill put me on as his sports editor, and that was our "bread and butter" throughout the three-year doctoral stint (1962–1965). Besides sports, I wrote feature stories and covered a beat with the city manager, city planner, and school superintendent.

The news training was excellent, for it was my privilege to talk almost daily with very sharp people, and this put me "on my toes." One of many things I learned came as I often sat in the office of the city manager's secretary, waiting to see the manager. A motto by her phone read, "Remember, you are talking to a <u>person</u>." I took that to heart for my own career in teaching. "Remember, you are talking to <u>persons</u>."

Mildred was a light shining in our home even as her breathing struggles were constant in one stage or another of difficulty. Yet she did some of the shopping, all the cooking, much of the housecleaning, and took care of Dianne. Often she was sewing, writing letters, keeping up our business records, or puttering in the flower beds. If she had any energy, she was always fruitfully doing something. We drove at first from Apple Street and later from Casa View to Dallas' Scofield Memorial Church on Swiss Avenue a few blocks from the seminary. There I taught for three years in the co-uni-bus class. Among the attendees were several seminary students, so I studied as if to be "loaded for bear." Those men knew how to ask hard questions! It was a constant test to be set for them, and also to "keep it simple."

When we could we went to the "El Phoenix," a fabulous Mexican restaurant in Casa Linda. We enjoyed not only the mouth-watering combination plates but the singing of a male quartet that stood on the balcony in their decorated "South of the Border" outfits and in lofty sombreros as they strummed guitars.

Our first of two doctorate homes was on Apple Street in one of two bottom apartments of a two-story building. Next to us on the ground floor were Terry and Jean Hulbert, returned missionaries from Africa. Terry would complete his doctorate a year after I finished mine, then have a long teaching stint at Columbia Bible College. We had many blessed times with Terry and Jean. Above us were Ed and Ann Blum. Ed would later be a Professor of New Testament for several years at Dallas Seminary, and after that president of the Christian Medical Association. He wrote the fine commentary on the Gospel of John in the seminary's two-vol. *Bible Knowledge Commentary* (1983–1985).

Our second home during doctoral studies, after about a year, was east of Dallas, at a house in Casa View. This was nearer my news writing job.

We had fun at Sunday night after-church fellowships of our Scofield young people. We always met in some family's large home. These were lively times of singing, testimonies, prayer, and assaulting the table of varied sandwiches and desserts. Dianne, a "butterball" in perpetual motion, was a hit. Not able to keep still, she buzzed all over the room, getting a rouse out of people. Our second daughter, Carolyn, would join us the first semester of our last year in the doctoral program (Oct., 1964).

Under Dr. Pentecost's supervision, I labored on a doctoral dissertation that would, in 1966, turn out to be *"The Interpretation of Acts 15:13-18."* It dealt with what James meant in citing a prophetical passage from Amos 9. I also took key courses such as Exegesis of Galatians, Revelation and Inspiration, Bible Manners and Customs, Biblical Chronology, The Apocrypha and Pseudepigrapha (Jewish materials written during the so-called 400 silent years between the Old Testament and New Testament), the Parables of Jesus, Miracles, and the Pentateuch.

Since Dave and Sande Sunde were still in his four-year Th. M at the seminary, he in his last two years, we again had many joyous times. My doctoral studies extended a third year, and a year before this ended the Sundes left to take up a church youth ministry in Southgate, CA, near Los Angeles. Once I too graduated, our family would go to California as well. I would speak at a mountain youth retreat at Dave's invitation, giving five messages on Samson, "the Hercules of the Hebrews" (Judg. 13–16).

At the end of the Th.D. program, to our amazement and encouragement, the seminary named me the outstanding doctoral student of the year (1965–66). God has His surprises. The school awarded to me the William Anderson Award. With God's grace, and Mildred's tremendous help, I passed the six three-hour final doctoral written exams, then celebrated the faculty's approval after their penetrating, oral three-hour cross-examination. How kind the God can be who shapes us, and gives success (Josh. 1:8).

The word had buzzed around doctoral students before these exams that we had to be ready to tell what was the main point in every chapter of the Bible. That did not come up on the exams after all, but I "ran scared," primed diligently to get ready, and I am sure I would have fallen very short had the committee drilled me on chapters of their choosing.

To prepare especially for those climactic doctoral exams, I would take Spring and summer lunch breaks each day from my Mesquite, TX news job. This went on for several months. Driving to the Mesquite Lake, I would sit by the water, listen to the quacking ducks, and pore over the studies. By diligent study, I would not be a "quack" myself!

All the success I credit to God's faithfulness and to the wonderful help Mildred was in many ways. She was "a real trooper," adept at handling pressures, selflessly committed to keep herself occupied when I needed to study, and always encouraging me. She was ever a plus, never a drag. God will reward her for her fruit (Eph. 6:8), probably with a capacity such as ten cities depict (Lk. 19:11-27).

While Mildred and I were in the Dallas area for that doctoral program, Carolyn was born at Baylor Hospital to be our second daughter. This was Oct. 28, 1964. We referred to our girls as our "Miss Rose Bowl" of Pasadena (Dianne) and our "Miss Cotton Bowl" of Dallas (Carolyn). For those are the cities where the famous New Year's Day parades are festive events, and teams clash in the football games.

How blessed is God (Eph. 1:2; 1 Pet. 1:2). Mildred's physician for a while in Dallas during the Th. M program had been a Doctor Hust. This physician told her, as he assessed her breathing ordeals, "You should never plan on children; in your precarious health, you could not live through it." But behold what God went on to give—two daughters, later two sons in law, then two grandsons! As Billy Graham's Los Angeles 1949 "sawdust trail" convert Stuart Hamblin's song says, "It is no secret what God can do." A Hollywood actor said to Hamblin at a party, "I hear you've been converted to God." Hamblin replied, "'It's no secret what God can do." Then he went home, sat at his piano late that night, and wrote that famous song. Exalt the Lord as the God for whom nothing is too hard (Jer. 32:17, 27)!

May God help me not to blunder, as has often been my failure, by underestimating His Majesty!

16

Teaching at Talbot Seminary

WE PRAYED FOR GOD'S guidance. Where would He have me teach? The months of the doctoral program rushed toward their climax.

Just at that time, in the providence of God, Talbot Theological Seminary was looking for a Bible professor. Dallas leaders Dr John Walvoord and Dr. J. Dwight Pentecost recommended me to Dr. Charles Lee Feinberg, dean at Talbot. This Hebrew-Christian scholar hired me, so we packed again, this time to head for La Mirada, CA.

We would join Dr. Feinberg, Dean and Professor of Semitics, with his small faculty. This included Dr. Robert Thomas (New Testament), Dr. Robert Saucy (Theology), Dr. William Bass (Apologetics), Dr. Jim Christian (Church History), Dr. Bill Bynum (Christian Education), H. Norman Wright (Christian Ed./Cou nseling), and Dr. Arnold Ehlert and Gerald Gooden (Librarians). I would be the only Bible professor for a few years. And my dean would start me off teaching an extremely trying, underline double load, six courses!

Dr. Feinberg, an expert in Old Testament Hebrew, had written or would author commentaries on all the Minor Prophets, *God Remembers* on Zechariah, Jeremiah, Ezekiel, Daniel, and Revelation, also *Amillennialism or Premillennialism?,* and other works. He knew several languages and would boggle the minds of other faculty members by talking with visiting chapel speakers fluently in these languages. He also had an uncanny memory of people's names, and the names of their children. We found that he often was quite comical, as in his quip, "the problem in the Garden of Eden was not with the apple, but with the pair!" And he said that when the infant Moses was taken from the basket to the Pharaoh's palace, "the devil had to pay the baby sitting bill!"

An interesting thing happened before we got to Talbot. Dr. Feinberg's letter of invitation had not yet come, and a letter arrived from a dean, Dr Alfred Martin, at Moody Bible Institute. He enclosed an airline ticket for me to fly to Chicago to spend a few days interviewing to teach Bible. I was about ready to leave when the Talbot letter came. Mildred and I reflected and prayed. We followed the trusted counsel of Dr. Walvoord and Dr. Pentecost. They had felt that with my love for detail I would fit into a seminary level more happily than college survey. So, to save Moody money, I phoned the Moody dean, then returned the ticket with a letter of thanks, and we put our trust in God for the California open door. Once God put the decision on our hearts, we did not look back.

Moody was a wonderful school. But Mildred and I never doubted our move, and did not regret the decision we felt God impressed on our hearts. How could one rightly question the providence of God? From this decision came happy years at Talbot and later at The Master's Seminary. From it sprang the marriage of Caleb Gutierrez and Dianne, and after this the wedded life of Randy Long and Carolyn. From it have come two grandsons, Zachary and Benjamin, God-given spiritual fruit, and so many friendships rich in blessing.

It bears saying that Mildred and I often prayed as our daughters grew up for the men they would marry, if they did marry. We asked the Lord to shape the men ahead of time. And when the girls started dating, we sat up many a night praying during their times out. One of us would be awake to welcome them back.

We got to Talbot in August, 1965, and lived on Pecos Street in Norwalk six miles away for a year, then in La Mirada three years. After this we bought the home at 10909 Grovedale Dr., Whittier, in 1969. There Mildred would spend the rest of her days (1969–2008), days that God gave (Job 14:5; Ps. 139:16). Now I continue this side of glory after her blessed home-going.

While we were Pecos residents, Carolyn elated us. One of us let our baby loose, she took a few wobbly steps, stayed upright, and surged into the arms of the other.

Dianne and Carolyn would sit in the Pecos home's patio and mother their dolls. Little friends from the area joined them.

We moved to the home in La Mirada, right beside a north/south artery from Whittier called Santa Gertrudes, in the summer of 1966.

17

Looking Back at Crusade and the Doctorate

THINK BACK TO THE time (1961–62) when we lived a year, part of it on what then was Ford Street right across from Fuller seminary and part on El Molino Street in Pasadena (cf. above). I was managing editor of Campus Crusade's *The Collegiate Challenge.*

My sister Mary Ellen lived in Pasadena for a time while attending Pasadena Nazarene College. The school sometime after this moved to the San Diego area under the new name Point Loma College. Betty Lou, another sister, came to live in Pasadena as well. These two roomed together for a while, but Betty went to Pasadena College.

Mary Ellen often would go with me, or Mildred and me, to the Sunday School class I taught for collegians at Bethany Church in Sierra Madre, nestled in the lower slope of the San Gabriel Mountains east of Pasadena. Mildred and I felt so blessed one night four years later (1966) when Betty came to visit us on Stanbrook Dr., and introduce us to her boy friend, Glen Waughan. We had supper together, and our hearts were strongly drawn to Glen. Sometime after this Glen and Betty were married in the Chapel of Roses in Pasadena as Betty's pastor, Raymond Ortlund of the Lake Avenue Congregational Church, officiated.

Several from both our families were there.

Mary Ellen married Jim Edwards and lived in various places such as Enid, Okla., San Diego, CA, and a city in Florida, as well as a stint in Saudi Arabia where Jim trained Saudi pilots. Jim had spent his years as a U.S. Air Force Phantom Jet pilot, one of our nation's most skilled. They later have lived in Peoria, AZ where they have hosted several family reunions.

Now let us return to the later time, back to Talbot.

The Talbot dean, Charles Feinberg, assigned six classes to me in my rookie, "new kid on the block" year, 1965–66. This double load kept me hard-pressed to survive each day, Monday through Friday. I taught Missions, Old Testament Survey, Isaiah and Jeremiah, Ezekiel/Daniel and the Prison Epistles, Hermeneutics [principles for interpreting God's Word], along with Genesis, Exodus and Leviticus, and an elective. Not only that, but Biola University invited me to deliver the spiritual life messages at the outset of the year to collegians. I spoke on Christ the vine and believers as branches (John 15:1-6). A few years later, in 1973, Zondervan published my book on this, *Abiding in Christ, Studies in John 15.*

I think that Dr. Feinberg was such a brilliant scholar that he set high standards, sometimes perhaps too lofty, for others. He had two doctorates, one from Johns Hopkins University under the renowned scholar/author William F. Albright. Another was from Dallas Seminary, where as a Jew steeped in rabbinic studies, he was so adept in Hebrew that seminary leaders asked him to teach that class while he was a student.

Feinberg had been an unsaved Jew spurning Jesus. A neighbor lady whose husband was a railroad worker and had eight critical maneuvers a day would, at those eight times, pray for Charles' salvation. Then another Christian, Joseph Solomon of the American Board of Missions to the Jews, gave Charles a tract on the Gospel of John and this rabbinical school student tossed the gift in the trash. Mr. Solomon gave him another, and continued to love him and explain how Jesus was the Messiah the Jewish Old Testament anticipated. Charles read, was drawn to the Savior, and became "a completed Jew." Then he devoted his life with all his God-given intellect to the Christ who gave it.

His unsaved Jewish family then held a funeral, pronouncing him "dead" to their faith and renouncing family ties with him. Later he leaned over his mother, on her death bed, and said "Mom, this is Charley." She turned her face away, in final rejection of him and his Christ, and it broke his heart to see her believe not and die in her sins (John 8:24).

Due to the heavy preparation load, I often could not get any sleep. After times with Mildred, studies persisted far into the nights. It was that or not be ready. At other times the sleep was only two hours or so. Classes began at 7:30 a.m. and I had to "keep ahead of the pack." Mildred was resilient here as well, understanding, committed, gracious, and always doing her best to take care of me. We cherished weekends with their bit of relief. How I praise God for a wife so truly surrendered to meet the disciplines of ministry. He had prepared her well in a godly home and at a great school, ABI, to grasp the discipline of this as Jesus said, "for My name's sake" (Matt. 19:29). And I praise Him for the strength and resiliency He gave me to overcome bodily weariness.

Normally Mildred and I would eat supper, have our family devotions, and talk for a while. Then I gave myself to study to be set for my teaching (Rom. 12:7). At times I would take breaks from the "grind," and we would enjoy sweet respites.

One thing that put fear in me to "bear down" was this. The Bible professor the year before I came to Talbot had arrived with high accolades. Leaders expected great things from him. But students beat a path to the dean's door complaining that he exhorted but did not teach in any profitable grasp and depth. Dr. Feinberg called the teacher in to see if he could remedy the problem, and exhorted the man to study more. He must "turn the ship about." The dear instructor seemed not to have been trained in how to do this, so after a few more weeks the dean reluctantly told him God must have different plans for him. Other members of the faculty, such as Dr. Robert Saucy and Dr. Glenn O'Neal, added his classes to their own to ease them through that school year.

This crisis opened the door to my teaching invitation. I came as "the new kid on the block," with little experience, "not dry behind the ears" in much fear and trepidation. My concern was that if an older man of much acclaim did not "cut the mustard," how could a "young buck" like me ever do it? I threw myself desperately on the Lord, the Faithful One, and Mildred prayed fervently.

How did I keep going? Caleb's words to Joshua unfurled a banner. I often would repeat them. Joshua was allotting portions of Palestine to tribes (Josh. 13–22), and Caleb came to apply for land. He told Joshua in effect, "Give me the mountain where the giants [enemies, the most feared, the greatest challenges] are. If God be with me, I can take it." Joshua assigned such an area, then Caleb went with the Lord's help and valiantly wrested the portion from the Canaanites' stronghold. For God can remove difficulties that loom like mountains (Zech. 4:7; Mk. 11:23-24).

God was with Caleb! And God was with Mildred and me. I had a dear and faithful wife utterly devoted to serving Jesus. I profited from her patience, love, soft words, pleasant spirit, and hard-working zeal of the Currey heritage. I lived in the constant testimony of how Mildred rose above her trials in breathing and maintained an awesome spirit of victory. That encouraged me. I had the Spirit of God enabling (Gal. 5:16-17), and a very merciful Lord. The Word of God lifted me as I pored over it night and day (Ps. 1:1-3). I had the light of the Lord (Ps. 119:105), and God was ordering my footsteps (Jer. 10:23; Ps. 32:8; 37:23). We had a good God who answered prayer, and when we cried out of the depths of need (Ps. 130:1), He strengthened me (Ps. 86:16; 138:3; Isa. 41:10).

The discipline of getting up very early, by 4 a.m. most of my youth to go round up cattle now was steeled into my life to stand up to a rigorous regimen. God prepares those who will be His servants long before they come to know Him. Though certainly not in the class of Abraham, Moses, and Paul, I followed in their pattern.

Mildred boosted me. Her life was one of quiet strength that shined a light into me giving new vision. I would wake up many mornings with a song on my heart and lips, "Blessed be the Name, Blessed be the Name. Blessed be the Name of the Lord!" Weary in the work, but not weary of it, I felt God's renewing strength to go on (2 Cor. 4:16-17). He kindly "quickened" me in a way often mentioned in Ps. 119 (vv. 25, 37, 40, etc.).

Never did Dr. Feinberg "call me on the carpet" because a student had complained. I sometimes dragged to classes feeling only half there, like our Air Force pilots flying struggling planes back to their bases "on a wing and a prayer." Even much study could not "prep" me to anticipate or answer all the students' questions, often unfairly far afield from subjects we were on. I was certainly not able of myself, rather my sufficiency was of God (2 Cor. 3:5). Often I would have to say, "I'll find an answer." I leaned hard on God, cried out many an 'S.O.S.' to Him, and without Him could do nothing (John 15:5). He showed pity, was wonderfully gracious in sparing me from failure, and never let me down. I took Lamentations 3:22-23, which says "great is Thy faithfulness," as not only for ancient Israel, but for me. And this was one of Mildred's favorite passages from ABI. Such need of the Lord reminded me of John the Baptist's humility, "He must increase, but I must decrease" (John 3:30).

Sometimes student questions came "out of the blue," or so it seemed. They had an uncanny skill of thinking up the most difficult, "stumper" questions, often with no apparent link to the subject at hand. Their "stumpers" about all sorts of things almost swept me away at times. With severe misgivings, I wondered if teaching was my thing. Hard pressed, I groped, stumbled, and dispatched quick "telegram" messages of utter crises heavenward. God was "on my right hand that I should not be moved" (Ps. 16:5; Acts 2:25). I often came apart to Him in prayer, and so I did not come apart. I was like the London preacher, Charles Spurgeon, who would pause when struggling for words, breathe a cry to heaven, and feel that the Spirit would come winging to help him.

My own heart often felt like caving in, but God steadied me to keep a straight face, not give away how wiped out I felt in my inability. He always pulled me through. At times I had to tell the students I would get back to them. I saw to this, and they respected both my honest willingness to admit I did not know, and my later answer, often typed just for them. How much God taught me when doing extra study to get back with those answers!

Mildred prayed for me. How many others did, such as students, God knows. Their faithfulness they will see again in that day when Christ gives degrees of reward.

I survived tidal waves. I was thankful that at home I had a wife who knew how to reach the throne, and was sensitive to my dilemmas. She cared utterly for me, and poured out her heart on my behalf. She had a habit of putting the positive "spin" on things, keeping a bright outlook, and being a "Wonder Woman," not the actress Lynda Carter of TV but Mildred Rosscup of heaven's wonders, at lifting my spirit. How she did this when she often was having indescribable difficulties with breathing only the God who is sufficient can answer (2 Cor. 3:5). Oh, the sweet, enabling grace of God! Oh, the marvel of it all, that God is always enough (2 Cor. 12:9)! Thank God for Annie Johnson Flint's song that had it right, "He giveth more grace when the burdens grow greater. . . . For out of His infinite riches in Jesus, He giveth, and giveth, and giveth again."

Often I would come home to Mildred who had her breathing pressures, much weakness, such difficult trials. I would open the door, start to step inside, and call out, "Hello, Mildred."

A voice, sometimes faint, would greet me from the bedroom down the hall. "Hello," or "Hello, Jim." That was sweeter than Julie Andrews' "The Sound of Music."

This woman had learned in the school of suffering how to trust God, receive from Him, and rise to the occasion. It has been said, "great saints are only great receivers." Meals were almost always on time. My dear one had the clothes washed, dried, folded, or hung up. She kept the house dusted and tidy, and could spot dust where I thought my cloth had totally routed every last speck.

When we had guests, Mildred always resourcefully hit upon a way to find enough food and set it on the table. This was true even in early years when often we just skimped by. She knew how to make something out of nothing, it seemed. At any rate, God did and could show her, for did not God make the world?

Like the song of Bette Mittler has it, "Have I ever told you you're my hero? And everything I'd like to be. You give me wings like an eagle, you are the wind beneath my wings." And even another part of that song was so true of my "dumplin'" as I called Mildred. "I never once heard you complain." She would tell me she was hurting, but she did not whine or question the Lord. In those many times, how my heart went out to her, I felt stings of pain, and I wished I could step into her shoes and take her struggle to breathe, bear it myself, to let her feel relief! But as God's Word says we can bear one another's burdens in some ways (Gal. 6:2), yet in another sense each must bear his or her own burden (v. 5). God's particular reward stored up for eternity will prove it was worth it all!

Once Mildred was in the La Mirada Hospital with her breathing illness. People were praying for her, and my own heart was constantly asking God to help her get better. I knew that she enjoyed sports of our alma mater, Arizona State, and just at that time the "Sun Devils" were playing in the national NCAA baseball "College World Series" in Omaha. ASU had won three national titles (1965, 1967, 1969), and this year, in 1972, had swatted their way to their finest record, an unbelievable 60-4 season mark coming out of regional playoffs. I took a radio to Mildred's bedside so that she too could hear one of the games. Listening to the game helped my darling in some degree to forget the misery she felt.

Arizona State had won their first two College World Series games, but now was up against Southern California's Trojans. Both of us were so pleased when ASU's pitching shut down the pride of the West Coast, 3-0. The Sun Devils would go on to win their fourth game as well for a 64-4 season mark that guaranteed them the finals. USC, however, fought back through double elimination to face us for the national championship. So the Trojans had to beat the Sun Devils twice.

But another matter first.

We needed help with the two little daughters. The three of us visited Mildred at the hospital, said a forlorn goodbye, and I drove us (myself, Dianne, and Carolyn) the 220 miles to Lemoore, CA, near Fresno. Mom had moved there, and we needed to bring her back to be in the home that was without Mildred, while I must be away to teach.

In the mountains of the "Grape Vine" of the Golden State Freeway just as we came down toward the flatlands stretching toward Bakersfield, the massive dark expanse below us was sprinkled by farm lights here and there. Dianne was old enough by then, at ten, to be my partner in a joke.

"Look at the sea out there," I visualized, "and all the ship's lights."

Dianne caught the tease right away. Carolyn, younger at seven, at first imagined that indeed it was a vast ocean and ships with lights. Dianne had a good laugh on her sister. Then we explained that it just appeared that way because of the darkness and the lights of homes that shined in that seeming "sea of darkness."

At Mom's home after that long drive, in Lemoore, I flicked on the radio to try to catch news of the Omaha title game, Arizona State versus USC. For by now it had ended. USC had won the first game in the finals to "stay alive" 4-3, forcing the next, this championship battle. Just as I turned on the radio, the sports announcer was reviewing after the title tilt. The two teams had gone 0-0, then USC had squeezed a run across from third on an errant pitch. Southern Cal stopped the uncanny ASU season, 1-0, grabbed the crown, and left the Devils with a 64-6 season record, best in the school history and one of the finest any Division I college baseball team ever assembled. A year later, in 1973, the same two teams clouted their way into the NCAA title game, and this time USC again won. This was after the Trojans fell behind the All-American Dave Winfield and Minnesota 7-0, then put on a late rally to stay alive in the tourney, 8-7.

But back to 1972.

We got back home. Mom helped, as she often did, and in a few days we all were glad when our dear Mildred had recovered enough to come home. A special sweetness seemed to be in the air when she was with us, and our hearts were thankful to God.

Many students went through my Talbot classes (1965–87). They went out to be college presidents, professors, pastors, Christian school teachers, youth leaders, home and foreign missionaries, counselors, writers, camp directors, lay people who could count for the Lord, and other occupations to glorify God. The daughters kept growing, and eventually both graduated from Biola, Dianne in 1984 and Carolyn in 1986.

Several times other schools invited me to join their faculties—so Northwest Baptist in Tacoma, Grace Theological Seminary in Winona Lake, IN., Liberty University in Lynchburg, VA, and Dallas Theological Seminary, my alma mater. In the Dallas case, the late Dr. Harold Hoehner phoned me after I had gone there to interview and speak and offered a position in either the New Testament Department or the Bible Department. I told him that I believed God would have me stay at Talbot for the sake of Mildred's health as we were uncertain of Dallas weather conditions, and because our daughters, as part of a faculty family, received more tuition help.

What was best for Mildred and the girls was all-important.

It was heart-rending at that time to say "no" to my Alma Mater. However, God kindly assured me to tough it out in that decision. In things to follow, as well, He would confirm the choice in many ways.

Dianne fell in love with and married Caleb Gutierrez, son of a very godly couple, Louie and Irma, who had devoted many years of their adult lives to Salvation Army ministry. Their impact on countless lives was vast. Carolyn married Randall Long, third son of Roy and Joey Long, members of Calvary Baptist Church, Whittier. Roy had sung in the famous, much-traveled "Calvarymen" Quartet of the 1950's–1970's with Verdon Mengel, Bill Webb, and Marvin Martin. The quartet had ministered in many churches.

Another result of staying in California would come in 1987. God opened the way for me to teach at The Master's Seminary north of Los Angeles. We could keep our home and I could drive the 40 miles to the different school. In countless blessings the Lord has verified that this was where His eye led us (Ps. 32:8). Oh, to be in the center of God's will!

One morning while driving to Talbot to teach, I got to Imperial Boulevard and was going west to the light at Telegraph Road about a mile from the school. Across from me to the right was the Carriage House Coffee Shop. I saw, to my surprise, that right ahead of me was Randy Long driving his car. I knew that he, too, was on his way to the Biola campus, for he was a student.

Thoughts flashed in my mind. I knew that Randy had just broken up with a girl who often had sat with him at Calvary Baptist Church, Whittier. It must be painful for him, I figured. I began to pray that in God's kindness this young man would meet the girl the Lord had for him. Little did I know. Some time later, Randy asked our daughter Carolyn for a date! Then one night they pledged their hearts to one another at their wedding (1986). Did not I read something about God going beyond what we ask or think (Eph. 3:20)?

He is our amazing God! He is our Lord who honors prayer! He is our Savior who in principle has plans to give us—as well as Israel which first is in view—a future and a hope (Jer. 29:10-14)!

The Rosscup Family

The Rosscup Family.

18

Our Venture in Bonnie Scotland

LOOK BACK WITH ME to pick up another phase of our lives.

In 1973, a dream of years burned like a candle flame in my heart. Mildred, a woman of faith, encouraged it, and we prayed to God. Would our Guide want us to go to Scotland for me to study for a Ph. D in New Testament so as to be a sharper instrument for Him?

We began to pray as part of our evening family devotions. Even Dianne and Carolyn got into this. They started saving pennies in their "piggy bank." God gave me an opening to have lunch with the famous Dr. I. Howard Marshall, lecturer in New Testament at the King's College in the University of Aberdeen, Scotland. This was at a conference of New Testament Scholars in Los Angeles. Marshall was encouraging, and I went on to correspond with him, he and the "the senatus academicus" accepted me for the doctorate, and with this prospering by the Lord our plans were well along.

But where to get enough money?

We kept praying. One day a Talbot student brought me back from lunch and handed me a check for $1,000. On another occasion Dr. Feinberg called me to his office and asked me to brace myself and sit down. Knowing his austerity, I wondered what I had done that I would be on the "hot seat" about. He brought forth an envelope and drew out a letter. I waited breathlessly, indeed bracing myself. The letter read something like this.

"News has come that Dr. Rosscup wants to go to Scotland to work on another doctorate. Here is $1,000 to help him."

God poured other gifts in. He answered prayers. We put our home up for a mortgage to finance part of the expenses, and would later pay off that mortgage.

Something else of a wonderful nature happened in 1973. I was teaching one Sunday morning at Calvary Baptist Church in a young couples' class. A new couple sat down near the front, and seemed to listen very intently. Afterward, as people were filing out, they introduced themselves. Stan and Kathy Edwards. They had just moved to La Mirada from Stan's studies at Los Angeles Baptist Seminary in

Newhall, CA, for Stan was to teach Old Testament at Talbot where I taught while faculty member Tom Finley was on leave doing his doctorate at UCLA.

Mildred was in the hospital, so she could not meet the Edwards that day. But they invited me to have lunch with them. We sat down to the Colonel's fried chicken and the fixin's at a Gardenhill Park table in La Mirada, near the Talbot campus. We talked as their young sons Steven and John played nearby.

A friendship of years sprang up. Kathy right away contacted Mildred after my wife was out of the hospital. Later the Edwards invited us to several meals, and we had them over. I did various things to help Stan as he struggled with Ford Mustang break-downs. I drove to UCLA to pick him up when his car quit on him, at another time went to an auto shop to get parts he needed for Mustang work in his driveway.

When my family got to the LAX airport to go to Scotland in July, 1974, the Edwards were among a group of friends gathered to send us off. Mildred was having severe problems breathing, but in her usual brave way was doing her best. A bomb had gone off in an airport locker and traffic had been stalled on arteries leading in to LAX. After losing valuable minutes, we hurried inside just in the nick of time to rush to our plane. Without even time's opportunity to say thanks to friends, we were rushed to the corridor into the plane. Mildred was desperately fighting for breath, especially due to the hurry, and I was praying with all my heart as we were swept along, Dianne and Carolyn also concerned for their mother.

I remember Bob and Rosemary Warren, Calvary Baptist Church's pastor and his wife from Whittier, were there. Bob was our pastor in two churches, the first earlier in Tempe, AZ. Stan and Kathy gave us their love send-off, and several others waved, clasped our hands, or yelled as airport personnel rushed us by. How precious it would have been to have had the time to hug each friend before we left them!

We flew to New York for a stop over to visit Mildred's retired Dad and Mom for a few days. There we stayed in their Pleasant Street two-story home in Oneonta. Then Dad Currey drove us to Syracuse to catch our plane on to New York City. As the plane in New York lifted off the ground I leaned back in the seat and was quite overcome with emotion as I prayed silently, amid tears. A TV program of those days gave me a theme.

"Lord, help us to return from 'Mission Impossible' with 'Mission Accomplished'." I also prayed that Mildred's breathing would ease up, and this dear one would feel relief. But all of us suffered, for the plane was packed like sardines, the air steamy, passengers and even stewardesses out of sorts. One man near me was consuming glass after glass of beer, and it was almost impossible to get to a rest room due to stewardesses and passengers constantly squeezing their ways along a narrow aisle.

Hours later we touched down at Prestwick Airport, in Glasgow, Scotland, showed our passports, and were urged to rush to a small plane flying on to Aberdeen. A brief crisis beset us. Airport personnel could not locate two of our Samsonite suitcases. So, as Mildred and the girls hurried to the plane I lingered behind, praying that this lost luggage would show up. I was nearly at my wits' end when, at the last minute, handlers came up with the cases, sped them to the Aberdeen craft, and I had to sprint as if in a hundred yard dash to get aboard with my loved ones.

The small plane was batted this way and that, violently, in the air, side to side and up and down as if the boisterous weather would slam it to the earth. Mildred in addition to her breathing problems got very sick in the stomach due to the turbulence, and was reduced to a state of helpless misery. Such a pitiful situation which she could not help was so unlike this woman who always found a way to overcome, no matter what. Her agony must have been horrendous. I prayed and prayed, as if my heart was in my throat, silently beseeching God to help her feel better (Ps. 34:8).

A young business man on that plane recommended a trucking firm to contact to move our box and barrels of goods from another city seaport to our new home. He handed me a card of that firm. God used him to give us help. Later I contacted the company, Lep Transport, which delivered our things to our rented cottage in the village, Muchalls, 10 miles from Aberdeen. That new home was on the terrace overlooking the usually boisterous North Sea.

Mildred was "out of it" at the Aberdeen airport. I scurried, trying to see things work out in a land strange to us where we did not know a soul. How thankful I was that we did know a God! And He was sufficient. I hired a taxi driver to take the four of us to the town, Stonehaven, which he told us had the Commodore Hotel, a few miles from Muchalls and our rental cottage soon to be available. At the hotel we could have lodging temporarily. He got us to the place, and we made it to our room, where Mildred fell into a bed in an awful state. I found crackers and drinks for the girls to help at the moment.

We had not thought ahead properly about the different electrical connection needed for the breathing machine Mildred used, a "Porta Bird." I asked the hotel receptionist if she knew who could help us, and the need was now! The lady kindly asked to look at the machine, for she knew quite a bit about electricity. In a short time, that nice person converted our American electrical set-up to the Scottish system. That was a gigantic, providential God-send, and I rushed the Porta Bird back to help Mildred get her breath.

The hotel was quite expensive, and we were careful about our budget.

I went out walking and praying, and scouted the town a half mile away, searching for a lower priced lodging, and food. God walked with me. After finding several "Bed and Breakfast" places with no confident decision, I spotted a sign, "Beachview," on the main street, and a kindly old lady met me at the door. She beamed that she was Mrs. Barkley. Oh, yes, she had a room on the second floor, and breakfast plus an evening treat besides. I got a taxi to bring Mildred, Dianne, Carolyn and me there. Mrs. Barkley proved to be not only a gracious hostess but a friend with whom we would correspond long after leaving Scotland. She made us feel at home, and seemed not to know where to stop helping us, as if she was a dear mother.

God, our Helper (Heb. 13:5-6), had gone ahead of us!

Mildred revived quickly from the stomach air sickness and, after using the Porta Bird, also the breathing crisis of the moment. How I found that God answers prayer even when we were reduced to total desperation and just did not know what to do. The lesson of Isaiah 41:10 became so vivid: "Fear Thou not, for I am with Thee. I will strengthen thee, and help Thee, and uphold Thee with the right hand of My righteousness." The assurance was true for Israel, and God made its profit likewise a reality sweet to us.

Two weeks passed at the dear Mrs. Barclay's as we waited for the village cottage to become vacant. When we went out for our first try at a restaurant, we found a kind of fast food place a few doors away that was packed. We took seats at a table, and others sat down at the same table, crammed together, as was the custom. Shortly after, in a grocery store, it was difficult to find food with which we were familiar. But we chose a few items to take back to our room.

A young lady, Kirsty, was engaged to the absent, traveling owner of our rental cottage, and was moving out of it. I phoned, and she told us the place was ready. She even drove over to give us a ride there, so we loaded our suitcases into her car and got to the cottage a few miles away. Muchalls lay close to the North Sea a quarter mile off the highway that runs from Montrose and Dundee to Aberdeen. When we looked out on the sea northward we were gazing toward Norway and Denmark.

Our new home was right on the row of eight cottages on Stranathro Terrace, parallel with and nearest the sea. We could watch the foaming waves a quarter of a mile or so away, down a green slope where cattle grazed. Down there, cliffs imposing their walls against the boisterous sea dropped off about a hundred feet to rebuff the turbulent onslaught of waves. Often the winds would whip up white sea foam to slap it against our windows, or drop it in the small yard across the driveway out front. At a small distance the foam looked like wadded up white paper.

Our quarters downstairs had a bathroom, small kitchen with a midget refrigerator, dwarfed dining room, one bedroom, and a living room with a fireplace. Up a steep, twisting flight of stairs was a bedroom for the girls, and a "wee" room I could use as a study, furnished with a sky light and desk. By placing the desk right under the sky light, on a clearer day I could have a focus of brightness. I would spend thousands of hours there, with light from God's heaven and an electric light.

Those were happy days from the heart of God. Being without many things so available in America, we all learned to "make do." Every little treat was a fun time of celebration. For we needed boosts, being far from home, family, friends, and usual enjoyments. A small village grocery store did sell Coca Cola, so we kept bottles of that on hand as well as sweets that helped in a land where much was "savory" and stirred up ferocious taste buds for something sugary.

Scotland was a culture of bus lines, and good ones. A bus ran from Montrose through Dundee, and on to Stonehaven (that was also on the sea about six miles from us). When I thought of Dundee, thoughts flashed back of reading Andrew Bonar's famous *Memoirs of Robert Murray M'Cheyne*, an unusually godly Dundee pastor and sweet man of prayer, who had died at 29. The work is one of the compelling classics on men God has shaped to bear "much fruit."

I would trudge to the bus stop carrying a big brief case, usually stuffed heavily with books I had studied. The bus took me another 10 miles into Aberdeen, where I got off on Union Street, the main artery, and walked to a que [line] to wait. Then I boarded another bus that carried me a couple of miles to within a block of the university library.

On the trip back to Muchalls from Aberdeen, I usually would stop at a market along Union Street, purchase a bag of groceries, and wait for the bus with that load in one hand and the lead weight brief case in the other. If I timed buses just right, I could be home before ice cream melted (it was colder in Scotland, so it kept longer). This was one treat our little family could enjoy.

Aberdeen was "the gray granite city." Workmen had quarried the stone from the area round about and many of the homes in a city of nearly 200,000 were made of it.

I would go to the King's College, one of the schools in the University of Aberdeen, and meet with my supervisor, Dr. I. Howard Marshall, one of the brightest scholarly lights in the British Isles, author of many books. His office was at the top of gray granite steps on the second floor. About a year later he moved to the ground floor in another building. I would spend all day finding books related to my subject, "The Christian's Future Reward According to Paul." I did this with special reference to Paul's longest passage on the subject, 1 Corinthians 3:10-15. I would pore over books to get an idea if they could help me, or spend time in the inter-library loan area filling out order cards to request key journal articles from other libraries to be secured and sent for me to pick up at a later visit.

By devoting several weeks and sometimes a few months to each chapter, I was able to "inch" my way forward in research and in writing. The daily grind presented a pressure that was almost more than I could bear at times. The early regimens all my life had "steeled" me to stay long at the hard labors. God gave me needed discipline to stay at the labors, and was answering the intercessory vigils many were keeping on our behalf. I believe that Mildred was lifting many a fragrant prayer to the Father (Ps. 141:2; Matt. 6:9-12). For she always lived very close to our God, and was a Christian of unshakable faith. She clung to what Keith L. Brooks has said, "It is impossible for faith to overdraw its account in God's bank" (*The Cream Book*, American Prophetic League, Inc., p. 23).

When I turned in the first chapter at the head of those granite steps to Dr. Marshall, I lived in fear from stories I had heard about how demanding he was. One Ph. D student had to write his dissertation six times, and never satisfied the standards of this scholarly professor. Another student had to return to the States and keep up his research work for a couple more years before he gained approval. So I submitted the work in deep awe of my mentor and high respect of God. Dr. Marshall took a week to go over the chapter. I came back, sat on the other side of his desk, and silently continued fervent prayer that God had prospered my work to meet his standards.

"Oh, God, help me!"

Prayer indeed was a key. Prayer, more prayer, and even much prayer. And I was keeping up frequent correspondence with friends back home, Talbot faculty and students, people who had helped us financially, and others. I gave these friends frequent up-to-date briefings on how things were going. We had a lot of people interceding. And new Christian friends even in Scotland were joining in beseeching God for us.

My supervisor, helping me in the chapter, went over small things page by page, suggesting changes which I could make rapidly. Finally he got to the end of the chapter. I looked across at him and asked, rather apprehensively, "What do I do next?"

"Go on to the next chapter," he replied. What a tremendous word of blessing that was. I would take it home to Mildred and our hearts would play a symphony in joyful celebration.

Later Dr. Marshall, after looking over each successive chapter, would do that same thing. Go over it with me page by page if need be, pointing out little things that could improve it. Almost all of these I could do quickly. When he finished each perusal in my presence, I would ask anew, "What do I do next?"

"You're ready for the next chapter."

Unbelievable! No, believable! Oh, praise God!

Those were his words after every chapter until the work was done. A thousand thanks! Mildred's sufferings and sacrifices had not been in vain. Friends' support had not gone for nothing. My own 16 or more hour a day vigils and painstaking labors, often so very difficult, were paying off. Proverbs 3:5-6 was a light so real, especially that last part, "He shall make smooth your paths (or clear away the obstacles)."

One day at the university some of us students walking back from lunch in the cobblestone street out front were comparing notes. It was a time when the weight and strain of studies was getting to me. The weariness that racked me was beyond words. The end seemed nowhere in sight, and my heart could use a strong dose of encouragement to dig in, and keep on keeping on. For one wonders, as the mounting mental pressure exacts its toll, if after all it really is worth the all-out, painstaking ordeal. Just when I needed it most, the Lord suddenly delivered a boost in quite an unexpected way.

"Dr. Marshall told me," one of the students confided, "that you have made the fastest progress of any student he's had, and he likes your work."

That lift came out of nowhere, a bolt of spiritual electricity. For I had had no idea that God would give me a "thumbs up" to keep on in the struggle. I did not understand how such a thing could be true of me. But my heart leaped away from nursing any illusion of self-pride to render the gratitude up to God to whom praise really belonged! Of Him had come the opportunity, the wife who was ever a help, the strength to cling to long vigils, the eyesight and wisdom to plod through many books, the patience to work my way through seemingly endless translations of German and French, and the insight to make decisions about diverse viewpoints. My Lord had made all these things possible, blessing with progress I did not deserve. To Him be all glory! Once again, thanks to Annie Johnson Flint and the God she exalted: "He giveth more grace when the burdens grow greater."

It was a joy once at home to share the encouragement with the woman I loved. She largely had made it possible for me to have the present opportunities. Her heart felt fresh elation and new courage as well. We had not come to this land so far from home in vain. Apparently God's prospering and the strenuous toil were reaping benefits. The encouragement laid on my spirit the distinct determination that when I would find one of my students working hard but needing an uplift, I would encourage him! We do need to encourage one another (1 Thess. 5:11).

Still another of God's encouragements blessed us in the land far from home.

A bit into my program, that is, after a few chapters' headway, Dr. Marshall looked at me one day. I had mentioned to him that our financial struggle was nip and tuck. "You have done well," he said. "I have asked for, and it was granted, to give you a scholarship. That will help."

And so this additional supply did. And in the mail from time to time letters would arrive with checks from supporters back in America—$300 here, $100 there, and others. Not only that, but during our two years in Scotland, the worth of the American dollar grew to our advantage in relation to the Scottish pound, so we gained some that way as God met our needs. We saw afresh that God stands behind what Paul says in Philippians 4:19, "But my God shall supply all your needs according to His riches in glory in Christ Jesus."

Often, too, we felt God picking us up when letters said, "we are praying for you."

At home, Mildred would do the cottage housework, visit with kindly Scottish neighbors who liked these Americans, gaze out across the sea at American oil rigs (barges) hugging the waters, write home, or walk slowly about the village as much as her breathing struggle would allow. A gracious young Christian couple in nearby Stonehaven, Hugh and Meg Duncan, had heard in the Christian "grape vine" about us and Meg had looked Mildred up. These were fairly well to do people, and they seemed not to feel they could do enough to serve the Lord in love. Meg would drive over and take Mildred with her to the "warehouse" where people could buy bulk groceries at lower prices, sort of like at our Costco.

Dear Hugh and Meg even insisted that we use one of their cars a couple of times to enjoy vacation tours through Scotland. We would stop several times for overnight stays at easy to find bed and breakfast delights along the routes.

On many a Sunday night, I caught a bus near Muchalls as it came from Aberdeen to go through Stonehaven and on to Dundee. Getting off at the Stonehaven station, I would walk to attend a large Christian gathering in the hillside home of the Hugh and Meg. In one Bible series, at the group's invitation, I taught Romans 6–8 to my precious spiritual brothers and sisters. An atmosphere of love and vital focus on walking with Christ fragranced those and other fellowships.

Dianne went to a school called an academy in Stonehaven, and had to wear the special dark blue apparel as other students did. A bus picked her up in our village and brought her back in the afternoons. Carolyn went to a Newtonhill School on the coast about two miles away toward Aberdeen. A bus came for her as well. A new trial came when Carolyn's juvenile rheumatoid arthritis bothered her so much that she had to stay home from school part of the time we were there. The school provided a kindly lady, Irene Reed, to come to our home to tutor Carolyn, who did well in studies.

God also graciously helped our daughters meet girls whose families invited these young people to their homes for children's parties. The mothers would drive over and get the girls, and bring them home later. God was watching over us even in this splendid hospitality.

When Mildred was able, all four of us would walk the quarter mile out to the highway on Sundays, and stand under the hut roof until the bus came on its way to Aberdeen. Sometimes a drizzle of rain pelted down and we were glad for heavy coats and head coverings to brace us against the sting of cold. Or the wind would whip rain into our faces. Once on the bus we could relax and let somebody do the driving for us.

Off to church we would go. God kindly made us aware of Gilcomston South Church of Scotland on the main artery, Union Street, in Aberdeen. There, a famous and very conservative, exceedingly dear evangelical Pastor Willie Still led the flock. He was a Bible expositor, mighty in the Word, rich and perceptive in his messages, obviously Spirit filled, and a single man tempered by much prayer. We loved to hear him make the Word so plain and plead for believers to lay hold of wealth God bestows in Christ. A few years after we returned to the States news came of Mr. Still "graduating" to his home in glory.

I invited Mr. Still to lunch in Aberdeen a number of times over those two years. We had a fellowship of kindred hearts. And I know that man of prayer pleaded to God for me. At times I was free to catch the bus and go into the city for the Gilcomston Saturday night prayer meeting. It was an "on fire" fellowship, people pleading with God, sometimes quite aroused as they felt so mightily moved, imploring with hearts aflame. I have never been in prayer meetings where I felt more the powerful Spirit, so soul-stirring, something like Acts 4:23-31. We interceded for Christians in various countries and for those at home in Scotland.

After we would leave the "Bonnie" land, I would for quite some time keep the prayer warriors informed of our prayer needs, and word would come back in their newsletters' personal sections about their intercessory pleadings.

For one occasion the prayer fellowship had invited me to give a message before the prayer session would begin. I found myself quite moved and lifted. I was so conscious of Spirit-tempered prayer freeing men at glorious liberty to speak boldly (Eph. 6:19-20). This unleashed the Word into its crystal clarity, in wonderful power (2 Thess. 3:1).

Willie Still was one pastor who stood for the truth of the Word. Many pastors of Church of Scotland congregations were "dead as a doornail" at that time. Pastor Still was quite burdened about this. Among other things, these church leaders focused on water baptism rather than the new birth. They did not seem to fathom at all what the new birth really was. But Willie Still knew, and he had through the years sent out many young men into other pastorates to shine as lights (Phil. 2:15-16). He was a kind of "dean" to these men scattered to pulpits in that land, and each year these shining pastors would meet for a conference, I think at Creif, to fan flames in one another. Mr. Still also would keep up an amazing volume of correspondence in counseling and encouraging these many who were "carrying the torch" throughout Scotland.

One day a pastor of another town's Church of Scotland visited us in our cottage. As we talked I became aware that he did not appear to know at all what the new birth was. He kept talking of baptism and church attendance. When I sought to explain being "born again," his dullness did not pick up on this, as if his heart was shrouded in a deep darkness.

Several families at Gilcomston invited us, different Sundays, to their homes for lunch. We sat at some amazing meals of these hospitable people, and felt their Christian friendship. Some would show us around on car rides after the meal, and the fellowship in their living rooms was splendidly uplifting. We will see in glory the William Leslies, the Alan Massons, the Harold Robbs, Erik and Mary Wood (of Stonehaven), and beloved C. B. Cornishcrest, a dear old lady who was so outrageously in love with her Lord.

On one occasion at the church I met a blond-headed young man, a newcomer, from America. He said he was working on a road crew building a pipeline. We arranged and had several meetings in which I discipled him. He wanted to please the Savior, but six days a week at his job he felt the torture of the vilest language from the raw crew. He felt that it was spewing its hot filth right out of hell. When we returned to the states, God so led that he lived in Newhall, CA about 50 miles from my teaching ministry at that time in Talbot Theological Seminary. He drove to our home, and later I was among those at his wedding, wishing him and his bride well. They moved out of the state, and I trust that they continued to live for the Lord.

God gave Mildred a good doctor not far away from our village. She would go, or we would go together, by bus, to a small village along the route to Aberdeen and visit a medical clinic. At home she used her "Porta Bird" breathing machine, with the electrical fixture adjusted to plug in to Scottish electricity.

Nights could plunge into a teeth-chattering iciness. We used very thick "comforters" as covers on beds. During the day, the wind whipping off the sea would sweep up the grassy slope and some of the biting cold would knife, head on, through the crack where our two front doors came together. In winter days we kept a coal blaze going in the small fireplace of the living room. We also used "fina" petroleum in the oil heater in that room; a truck would bring a new supply to our garage tank periodically. It took the heater, fireplace, and several layers of clothing to keep us warm.

On more sunny days if Mildred was up to it the two of us could go for a short stroll down along the "dry stone dyke" fences that separated fields, and cling to rocks while we gazed out at the tumultuous sea. Some lashing waves we saw and heard booming against the cliffs were gigantic, and we had to hang on for dear life so that the ferocious wind would not wrench us away. On some of the calm days of sunshine it was refreshing in the bracing air to eat our lunches sitting on a broad stone fence while gazing far away across the waters.

I was more able than Mildred, so I would break away from difficult studies, seek to keep my sanity, and stroll sometimes for miles. Out along the stone paths I would plod, following a dry stone dyke with its ribbon of yellow gorse blooms, cutting down another pathway, over the countryside, talking to God and enjoying the heather on the meadows as well as the yellow broom or golden gorse plants along the dykes. The chilly breeze would lay a sting on my cheeks and ears, but the padded Canadian coat and a thick skin cap helped me keep my bearings.

I would come back sharpened, refreshed, recharged, and renewed, have lunch with Mildred, and play card games with her like "Touring" or "Whot." Then I clambered up the stairs to "hit the books" once again in an all-out study of future reward.

"Whot" was a simple, quick Scottish game. One of us would win, then the other. Mildred was a sharp competitor, and won overall. She seemed to be adept at anything she did.

In one case, Dianne participated in a 16 mile "walk-a-thon" of a type at her school. She, with others in the village and the school, secured pledges from people to donate so much for every mile walked to support a program the school was behind. The day came. We wondered how our petite Dianne would do in a walk so long; since she had never walked that far. And the trudge was "over hill and dale."

That afternoon I was upstairs under the sky light studying. Window open, I heard Mildred calling along the terrace frontage street to Dianne who was just getting home, off the bus. I heard Dianne answer, "I walked the whole way."

My heart, and I could tell Mildred's too, leaped for joy. Our Dianne! What a great achievement of courage and stamina for this little "lass"!

Dianne led her village friend Norma Reid to the Lord. Norma used to come over in the evening and sit with us while we had our family devotions. I would read a portion from God's Word or a Christian book, we would exchange thoughts and then prayer needs, and pray. Norma rode with us as I drove Mildred and the girls to catch their plane to New York. This convert unfolded a long, broad banner of goodbye when Mildred and our daughters waved back from the steps to the plane, leaving Scotland.

"Goodbye, Rosscups. I'll love you forever." We were teary eyed then, and often in later years, after our arriving back in the States, when we again spread out that banner.

We had enjoyed driving the Duncans' car to several places in Scotland and stopping at a number of bed and breakfast places overnight. We also had a special trip in a rented car to see the famous woolen mill and the world-renowned golf course at St. Andrews. And we took a special trip by train to Shakespeare country, Stratford on Avon [the Avon River] where we visited Anne Hathaway's cottage, Shakespeare's home, and some other places. On that trip we went on to London to its famous railway center, King's Cross, and spent 10 joyous days using special passes on the subway system and on buses. We saw Trafalgar Square, Pickadilly Circus, Downing Street where the prime minister lives, and went to the famous All Souls Church, Langham Place, where the internationally known Bible expositor, John R. W. Stott, then preached.

We visited several people with whom our friends back in the states had put us in contact in the London area and in some other cities. In this way not only did we get treated royally as at meals, but the gracious hosts and hostesses took us on tours of ancient castles.

When I was almost finished personally typing my dissertation on a rented typewriter in 1976, Mildred read a telegram that her mother Harriet had fallen into a coma in New York. So Mildred and the girls were on a flight the next morning to hurry to Mom's bedside. I had to stay behind to complete the dissertation, pack, and make arrangements for our box and barrels of goods to be shipped back to Los Angeles.

Mom Currey never came out of the coma, but passed into heaven. A few days after Mildred's and the daughters' flight, I myself flew out for New York City, then to Syracuse. There I met Dad, who had driven over to pick me up. I was so sad that I had taken Mildred away those two years and she had not gotten to say goodbye to her mother. We spent several days with the family before flying on home to California.

Will Currrey, or Dad, would drive all across the country alone annually to visit us for several weeks from 1976 until his death at 84 in 1981.

Word came that Dad Currey had been helping his elder son Richard get a home ready, digging in a trench. The hard-working ex-farmer had apparently sat down to rest, leaned against the house wall, and God called him home. Mildred and her other brother Bob, who lived north of us in Citrus Heights, CA near Sacramento, flew back to help arrange the funeral and take care of possessions Dad had left. Then they drove a loaded rental truck to California.

But back to 1976 and our return from Scotland to home in Whittier, CA.

19

Back to the U.S. and Home

A THRONG OF FRIENDS gathered at the Los Angeles Airport (LAX) to welcome us back. Again Pastor Bob Warren and wife Rosemary were there to hug us, so were Stan and Kathy Edwards. My mother had come from Lemoore, and was among those catching us up in warm embraces.

We got home in August during a heat blast. It was quite a shock coming from the 50-60 degree weather in Scotland to about 105 in California. We found, upon arriving home and stepping inside, that the man on whom we relied to keep the place rented had taken advantage of a house that for a few days had been vacant. He had allowed some people to store a truck load of things piled so high and broad in our living room that we could barely squeeze our way around the "mountain" to the kitchen or bathroom. At the same time, the air conditioning had gone out, and a furnace of heat met us.

Difficulty of a new kind especially for Mildred beset us. I called the man, but it took a couple of days for those who had stored their things to remove the load. We stayed in a motel waiting for the place to be free and the air conditioning to be fixed. This all was very difficult for Mildred, added to her breathing pressures.

Another thing I found out soon enough. For September came on us suddenly.

I had thought a certain faculty member would keep things up to date in the Bible Department while I was gone those two years. Instead, I learned that his other duties had kept him swamped. So, in addition to the challenge of a heavy load, I had "catch up" things that had been neglected so as to "bring order out of chaos." The days were difficult ones, the times loaded with severe testing.

We also were getting some things back that we had stored at my sister Betty's garage in Pasadena, and meeting with friends who invited us, catching them up on our lives better than mail can do.

Some time later Dr. Marshall wrote me that he and an outside reader in another university, Nottingham, Dr. Steven Travis, had approved my dissertation. It was done quite carefully, covering bases, my mentor said. In light of this he saw no real reason why I should have to make a special, costly trip back over there to be examined in an oral defense. So I was done, and just had to wait for the degree.

What a God-send! All glory be to the Lord!

Mildred and I in faith's anticipation had ordered a Scottish graduation robe, cape, and John Knox cap in Aberdeen before leaving. These in due time came in the mail, and I have worn them to Talbot graduations (1977–1987) both mid-term and in May, and also in The Masters Seminary May ceremonies (1988 to the present).

The second doctorate helped me gain full professorship at Talbot and aided my salary. I continued to teach and help send men to the ends of the earth to serve the Lord.

Mildred later taught me some things about using a computer. She seemed to be versatile and perceptive at everything she did. She would come into my study and spend long times patiently showing me how to do different tasks so that I could type materials and run them off. She herself would become very proficient at her own computer in her room, and publish countless productions of material for the church Women's Missionary Fellowship meetings. And she kept up a good correspondence with some ladies via email. They exchanged news, words of cheer, items of humor, and love.

Mildred's patient investment to help me learn the computer was an invaluable key that opened the way to do some of my writings. One was updating and enlarging the commentaries book. Later, in Jan., 2008, still within Mildred's lifetime, she would rejoice with me to see my 2,900-page writing on every prayer passage in the Bible (except abbreviated in the Psalms part), in all the Scripture books, published digitally by Logos Bible Software. It is in their Libronix system which makes different biblical works available. It became one of Logos' top-selling works with a burst of interest during the first months it was out. The five-volume prayer work is entitled, *An Exposition on Prayer in the Bible*.

Now, with this writing (Nov., 2009), I continue to discuss the possibility, though it has not yet been accomplished, of finding the right outlet for a printed edition.

I am glad that Mildred lived to be excited about these things coming to pass. We rejoiced together, and when in February, 2008, the prayer work gave us the fattest check (not wealth, but big for us) we ever had from a publisher, Mildred felt sky high. For she kept our business records faithfully, and having some financial help was a boon to make her feel a sigh of relief. She was such a very great key to the works coming out, and always so interested out of a true and pure love.

At Talbot, Mildred and I saw students graduate and go to many of the world's countries. Many have written books—John MacArthur, R. Kent Hughes, Josh McDowell, Mark Saucy, Clint Arnold, Larry Helyer, Alan Gomes, Tom Finley,

James De Young, Don Ekstrand, Alex Montoya, Irven Busenitz, and many others. Several have become presidents of Bible colleges or seminaries, many are pastors, some professors, some editors, a few publishers, many missionaries, and scores of youth leaders.

In 1984 Dianne graduated from Biola. Carolyn received her diploma in 1986. I should have been "on the ball" in 1984 when it was Dianne's turn, but failed. But in 1986 when President Clyde Cook handed Carolyn her sheepskin, "something got into me." I leaped to my feet in the faculty section (unheard of!) and boomed out a cheer almost at the top of my lungs, "Way to go, Carolyn!" That got a rouse out of the crowd. A father's jubilation!

The daughters' graduations earlier from La Serna High School in Whittier, 1980 and 1982 respectively, were very notable celebrations in the kind providence of God. When Dianne was a baby at the outset of my doctoral program at Dallas Seminary, Mildred said to some of the young ladies in the Scofield Memorial Church co-uni-bus class I taught, "I pray that God will help me live 'til this little girl finishes high school."

God did. He even helped the mother to live nearly 28 years past Dianne's high school commencement, and 26 after Carolyn's! That seems, in principle, to be one way of God fulfilling Paul's prayer prospect in Ephesians 3:20. "God is able to do exceeding abundantly above all we ask or think, according to the power [probably the might of the Spirit] that works in us." Imagine the thrill in her God that Mildred felt.

Dianne would go into teaching in a secular elementary school. Though offered opportunity to lead in a Christian school, she made the public school her value choice. Pupils in Christian homes already had some help, but many children in a secular school have no spiritual help. With this in mind, she deliberately devoted her life to do what she could for these. In 1982, she married Caleb Gutierrez, graduate of Whittier Christian High, whose parents devoted a lifetime of ministry touching many lives in Salvation Army ministry. Often in classes Dianne has had special "Dr. Seuss" days, or C. S. Lewis Narnia exhibits. She has shown much love to children from homes sin has shattered.

Carolyn majored in computer science, worked at Hughes Aircraft and later at Fleetwood Enterprises (a company producing recreational vehicles), and married Randall Winslow Long in 1986. After sons Zachary (1995) and Benjamin (1996) came along, she was a stay at home mom for several years. Then she was selected as an analyst at a Christian credit union.

Both daughters and their husbands have continued to follow the Savior. Each couple is a part of a local church in their worship of Him.

20

The Years at The Master's Seminary

In 1986 John MacArthur and Irv Busenitz, both past students of my Talbot days, led the way in founding The Master's Seminary. By January of 1987, they had secured a few faculty and were mid-way through their first year of operation on the campus of Grace Community Church, Sun Valley, a few miles north of Los Angeles.

The school grew out of what was a Talbot Theological Seminary extension (1977–1986) in Sun Valley, 40 miles north from the Biola/Talbot campus. That extension had kept growing, with a man that we on the Talbot faculty had taught, Irven Busenitz, leading it. This ministry was after he completed his doctoral work at Grace Theological Seminary, Winona Lake, IN.

Things at Talbot in the mid-1980's were not going in a fashion with which I still felt my skills could best serve. Perspectives had changed under newer leadership. Restlessness gnawed at me. An increasing uneasiness and distress disturbed my life. I pleaded with God for direction, for I had never before felt this heavy burden. Previous years had been very fulfilling, and many students had told me I was one of their most impacting professors. I had wondered how a person would reliably know if God was guiding him to change—especially after so long, 22 years (1965–1987). I must be sure. I knew that I no longer felt really good about how my ministry fitted with new emphases.

I was aware that quite a number of the other professors, especially in the Bible and New Testament departments, were as disturbed as I was.

The new seminary made no move, no contact whatsoever, not in even a remote way, to "pirate" any faculty away from Talbot.

Finally I myself took the initiative and phoned Dr. Busenitz, the associate dean of the new seminary. I asked if we could meet. We did sit down at lunch in a Denney's Restaurant.

I poured out my heart to this man of God about how I was ready for a change if one at The Master's was open to me. I realized it might be too late, for the new school had been building its faculty, but was there any opening left? He said they were <u>still</u> adding teachers and that he would take my case up with his dean, Dr. Charles Smith, as well as the president, Dr. John MacArthur, and Dr. Robert Provost, the vice-president at The Master's College, a school that Pastor MacArthur also headed up.

Shortly after that Irv phoned and asked me to meet with the leaders in the president's room at The Master's College in Santa Clarita. On an afternoon when I had no Talbot classes I drove those 51 miles. We met in Dr. MacArthur's office, and with him were Dr. Provost, Dr. Smith, and Dr. Busenitz. These men cordially went over a number of matters about doctrine with me and felt me out as to my beliefs, goals and dreams. Finally, MacArthur spoke, highly in favor of me. He wanted me there.

I had made the first move. They had not contacted me to lure me away from Talbot. It was sad that a false claim of their doing this circulated later. Gossip can be misguided, in error, and a tool of the devil's work.

I confided in private to a friend on the Talbot faculty, Dr. Robert Thomas, that I was going to make the move. I also told Dr. W. Bingham Hunter. He had become the dean of the seminary after Dr. Feinberg left in 1976, and after his successor Glenn O'Neal's death while dean, and even after Wendell Johnston had been dean for three years. Dr. Johnston had resigned the year before, in 1986, to become Director of Training at Dallas Theological Seminary.

Dr. Thomas immediately also got in touch with Dr. Busenitz, had a similar interview. He, too, was received into the Master's Seminary faculty.

That summer, 1987, Dr. Thomas and I left Talbot. Several others also did—Paul Enns of the Bible Department, Alex Montoya of the preaching classes, Don McDougall of the New Testament, Dennis Hutchinson of the New Testament, and three or four others. Dr. Johnston, our dean, had preceded us by a short time, and Dr. Jim Christian of the church history department was retiring due to his age just as we left. McDougall had already been teaching part-time at the new school.

The Master's Seminary leaders welcomed newcomers Dr. Thomas and myself with loving warmth. Everybody was elated, support toward us was electric, and when we had social times leaders went out of their way, it seemed, to show that they appreciated us, and any of the faculty. We would always have a free luncheon before each faculty meeting, and joyous fellowship.

Faculty at TMS in those early days besides the two of us were: Dr. Busenitz who taught Old Testament and some Bible, Dave Deuel in Old Testament, Don McDougall who already had been part time in New Testament when the school was still a Talbot extension, Jim Stitzinger in directing the library and teaching computer methods as well as church history, Jim George in recruiting and placement, Dr. Charles Smith as dean and teaching theology, and Floyd Votaw, librarian.

A student body of about 95 greeted the faculty that Fall of 1987. The seminary by 2009 has grown until now it is not far from 400. Like Talbot, we have seen graduates go to many of the countries of the world—the former Soviet Union, Albania, the Czech Republic, Africa, Germany, France, England, Australia, New Zealand, Japan, Mexico, Spain, and others. Seminaries founded by our grads have sprung up in the former Soviet Union, Albania, England, Germany, Mexico, and some other countries.

In the years that would follow, at least into the Fall of 2009, this new seminary has grown from one to four degree programs, from four to 19 full-time faculty, from 95 to 375 students, and from a library of 10,000 books to a treasury of 250,000. It has 1,038 graduates, a 90 per cent placement rate, so far about 50 books by graduates, men ministering in 45 states, graduates serving in 40 countries, and alumni founding 20 schools in 16 other countries.

God has blessed me to teach pastors and others, several sets of two brothers, one set of three brothers (Talbot), fathers and sons, at Talbot husbands and wives, faculty members' sons, men who became university or seminary presidents, etc. Students have ranged in ages from their low 20's to their 80's. At Talbot, Dr. Wallace Emerson retired from teaching at Biola College, and enrolled in the seminary when past 80. He sat in my Daniel and Revelation classes, a true gentleman, his goatee almost touching his notebook as he wrote details from lectures. Years later he would publish commentaries he wrote on Daniel and Revelation. Dr. Fred Schelander, long-time missionary to India and in his 80's, was in some of my Talbot classes.

The focus now switches entirely to The Master's Seminary.

Faculty wives of TMS have visited Mildred several times at our home. 'B' Mayhue, wife of the senior vice-president, Karen Busenitz, wife of another vice-president, Teri White, wife of the financial leader, Pam Snider, wife of a professor of theology, and Missy Mehringer, wife of the director of placement, have been here.

In 2005 I retired from _full_-time teaching when my 40th year as a seminary leader approached its climax. The school devoted a special chapel as a memorial to me, and invited Mildred to say a few words. Others who led in talks were fellow faculty members Dr. Robert Thomas (The Master's), Dr. Richard Rigsby and Dr. Henry Holloman (both from Talbot School of Theology), Dr. Daniel Wong (The Master's College), Prof. Don McDougall and Dr. Busenitz (The Master's), and our president, Dr. John MacArthur. The dean, Dr. Dick Mayhue, held the "mike" as Mildred sat and shared her supporting words. Our daughters Dianne and Carolyn went to the podium together and each gave talks of appreciative remembrance. Carey Hardy, an excellent soloist and former student of mine at TMS, sang a song of tribute. Then it was my privilege to respond with a brief talk of celebration.

On several days that Mildred and I had sat down for patio breaks, we had discussed a possible change. I begged for her wisdom. In her typical way, she offered pros and cons, but kindly was sensitive lest she bring my teaching ministry to a close. She was delicate and tender not to commit herself, careful not to disappoint me, even though I earnestly probed. When I kept up insistent pressing, she finally conceded, "It's been a long time—maybe enough."

I said that for both our sakes I wanted to spend more time together. We did not know how few years we would have left. God already had done incredible things numerous times to extend her life, and bring her back from several lung collapses, perils of pneumonia, and other very serious threats when she was completely or virtually bedridden. I told her that I also longed for more time to do research and to write, now that the Lord had given me years of diligent study, in hopes of getting more books written while yet there was time. I would be at home, nearby, and we could have many more precious hours to be together.

Since 2005 at the seminary's invitation and with my desire and Mildred's support, I have taught part-time as an adjunct professor. This is one day a week in leading two classes each semester.

Dr. Busenitz issued a full page list around 2006 of TMS graduates who have since authored and published books. In addition, many also of Talbot have. And on the present Talbot faculty are at least eight men who were formerly in my classes there. Likewise The Master's Seminary's full-time faculty of 16 has 11 teachers who once were among students I myself and others taught. It has been a joy to have them in classes, then as faculty colleagues. In addition some men on a part-time teaching schedule were former students in courses I and other teachers led.

Often one of these fellow faculty men will instinctively say, "Hello, Dr. Rosscup." I often will reply, "Please, call me Jim. My name is Jim." Some do, others such as Dr. Alex Montoya say they just cannot bring themselves to do this. I feel unworthy of it as I look up to them, but they speak of their respect. That seems so out of place to me since my respect for them is so high. Take one example. Dr. Montoya since his Talbot graduation in the early 1970's has founded about 15 churches, is one of the country's most stirring and convicting preachers, and one of the most refined gold examples of pastoral fruitfulness I have known.

Jim Elliot put things so aptly when he spoke of himself and other servants of God in his book *The Shadow of the Almighty:* "We are just a bunch of nobodies seeking to exalt Somebody."

Teaching at The Master's Seminary

Top left: Professor profile picture; Top right: Jim and Mildred (1988).

Bottom left: Jim with Mike Chandler (student); Bottom right: Jim and Mildred (~2000).

21

Our 50th Wedding Anniversary

SECRETS CAN BE PURE and sweet. When our 50th anniversary, December 16, 2006, was a week away I kept mum about my drive to a nearby city, Fullerton. There I drove up a hill to the famous, classy "Summit House" restaurant. Inside, I "staked out" a reservation for Mildred and me on the memorable night to celebrate the union our hearts shared.

The night came. I had asked Mildred for a "date" that evening, so we got into the car, destination unknown to her as I told her it was my surprise. I drove to the restaurant entrance, climbed the curving slope upward for nearly a half mile, and we saw cars parked even on both sides of the road. The place must be packed as I had heard was the usual thing at this popular attraction. When we reached the parking lot on top, I saw cars and more cars. It was like the line of "The Ancient Mariner" that ran "water water everywhere, but not a drop to drink." Here, though, it was automobiles, automobiles everywhere, but not a place to park. Concern touched my heart. I had wanted to walk in and stay with Mildred, but it looked as if I would need to help her go inside, then go far down the hill to park, trudge back up the hill, and join her a while later.

An "S.O.S." of prayer went up to the God who hears. It was just as real as Nehemiah's quick prayer before King Artaxerxes (Neh. 2), and Peter's instant cry to Jesus to keep him from sinking into the sea (Matt. 14).

I worked our way from lane to lane of cars. No place was open. Then I turned in to the lane nearest the restaurant. There my anxious eyes spotted the answer! And it was the best. Right at the end, in the first spot, the one closest to the door and but a few yards away, was a parking place "with our name on it." That, at least, is what God said. Elated by overwhelming emotions of thanks, I pulled in. How God cares (1 Pet. 5:7)!

We walked in, and I gave our names to the girl at the guest registry. She found our reservation, and told me an usher would seat us in just a few minutes. She showed us to a waiting room with a cozy fireplace, warming and cheerful in the cool of December.

Sure enough, an usher soon guided us into a large room that featured a broad, windowed panorama of Fullerton's sprinkled lights below the hilltop jubilation. Once at the table, I presented a new ring for our 50th, and Mildred, eyes sparkling, slipped it on her finger. We were two glad people, God's work of being "one" in marriage, now celebrating afresh the wonder of it all (Gen. 2:24). Oh, happy night!

We had a feast fit for a king—and a queen.

God had kept Mildred alive through many trials, and gifted us with all those years of so many fulfilling things. In so many situations, in very difficult trials amid the joys, it had not seemed like Mildred could possibly live to our fifth anniversary, or our 10th, or 20th, or 30th, or 40th. And now God had kindly given us the 50th! Our hearts exulted as we bonded even in dearer jubilation and an emotional, special gratitude to our Lord. He "does great things and unsearchable, marvelous things without number" (Job 5:8-9).

In that same anniversary season, right after our family's Christmas joys, the entire family went to the Island Palms Motel in San Diego. By our daughter Carolyn's arrangement, we were there to remember together our half century of marriage. Dianne and Carolyn had made sure we had a king-sized bed, a spacious living room, and a full kitchen. The refrigerator was loaded with soft drinks and ice cream, and the counter welcomed us with plenty of "goodies." Both our bedroom and living room windows overlooked the bay where many boats and other sea vessels docked.

Our daughters had decorated a Christmas tree in the living room. We had a sliding door view of the harbor. With our daughters and sons in law Caleb and Randy, and our grandsons Zachary and Benjamin we enjoyed trips out to eat, such as to a very nice Mexican restaurant and an Italian feast.

Ahhhh! What a run of 50 years with their heart-satisfying memories. The bright things of God's goodness completely cast into the distant shadows the frightening struggles. God never promised to give us flowery beds of ease or a smooth road; but He did give us good shock absorbers (Isa. 26:3; Phil. 4:6-7)! "The pathway of the just is like a shining light that shines more and more unto the perfect day" (Prov. 4:18).

Thanks upon thanks to our Father is recounted as a review of our lives in the final chapter.

22

One Glad Morning Mildred "Flew Away"

I AROSE AT 4 a.m. that Tuesday, April 15, 2008. It was just as I had always done since switching to part-time teaching in 2005. Get ready, and drive the 40 miles that one day of the week to teach. I could have no inkling of God's secret counsels, and what the day would bring forth (Prov. 27:1). Neither could my dear Mildred.

After showering and getting dressed, I came as usual to sit on the bed beside Mildred and talk. She always wanted to awaken and see me off. We chatted briefly, then I kissed her, got to my feet, said "Bye bye, Dumplin'," and stepped toward the door. I had not turned the light on so as not to disturb her unduly.

"Do you have enough money?" she asked. How lovingly like her. She always was considerate about anything that might help me. Another example was listening to the radio traffic report to give me tips if I needed to drive a different route. She also helped on things I might have forgotten.

"Yes," I replied back over my shoulder, "somebody very precious to me left some on the top of the dresser. I have it." She chuckled, so did I. Neither of us realized what was before us, and that these would be our last words together in this life. Then I went out and softly closed the door. My expectation was, as weekly, to phone her during the day, and see her when I came home that evening. My second class would end at 4:50 p.m. and sometime after that I would drive the long way back.

I met with two students, Zachary Drake and Jon Peppers, for a discipleship hour very early. Then I went to breakfast and to exult in a time in the Word and in prayer. I came back to my office at 8:15. Hardly had I sat down when the faculty secretary, Dana Hilborn, stood in the doorway.

"Did you get the call from your daughter?"

"No. Tell me about it." I had forgotten to turn on my cell phone.

"She wanted you to call her." I wondered if the call was from Dianne or Carolyn. I dialed Dianne immediately. She and her husband Caleb were residing with us while a contractor was adding rooms to their own home a few miles from our home in Whittier. How gracious of God, in His providence, to have them there!

Dianne's voice was heavy with alarm. "Dad, I'm with Mom at the hospital. Mom's not responding."

A stunning shock. I sat there, thoughts spinning, my world reeling and crashing upside down. This simply was very tough to take. With Mildred's breathing struggles, and so many rescues, was this, finally, what human fears told us might be inevitable? But when?

"I wondered why she hadn't come out of the bedroom," Dianne went on. "So, just before I was to leave at 7:30 [she had to go teach], I knocked, got no answer, looked in, and Mom lay halfway in the bed and halfway out. She was not able to respond to me. I called for an ambulance, and they're working with her here."

I could hardly think. My heart was pounding as I felt frozen in time, an awful heaviness was upon me. Fear was so real. Was this the last hospital visit of at least 20 for Mildred? How could it be? How . . . ? Oh, no!

As quickly as my dazed mind allowed it, I told the secretaries, Christine and Dana, asked them to cancel my classes, and began the 40-mile drive home. My heart seemed in my throat in a deep, sobbing trauma, an awesome dread. I was praying as the Taurus ate up the miles. At the Whittier Hospital, Dianne was waiting by the bedside in the emergency room, and Mildred was unconscious, hooked up to life supports. It was so very hard to bear. Thank God that His sufficiency bears us up (Isa. 40:31). He gives a strength that is heavenly, and "He cares for you" (1 Pet. 5:7).

Soon after that our younger daughter Carolyn and son in law Randy Long came to the bedside. Our grandsons Zachary and Ben were also there. Caleb, Dianne's husband, arrived from his job at Chevron. We prayed and kept our concerned vigil near this beloved one. All of us were in a kind of daze. A doctor came in, asked us to go to a waiting room, then returned and told us his analysis of the x-rays. He said high blood pressure apparently had caused a burst of an artery in the head and a massive spillage of blood that flooded into the brain. Mildred had become "brain dead." Could surgery succeed? He contacted a second specialist, and both were sure that even with an operation there was no possibility she ever could recover and be conscious again.

We sat in family oneness, in a numbed silence, shocked, shedding tears, and in an indescribable agony. Slowly we fumbled out thoughts of what to do. I fought against the trial of making a decision about one who was dearer than life. How could I? But I finally said that in our Living Trust Mildred and I had decided that should one of us be in this kind of situation and two doctors advise firmly that there was no hope, the other partner would allow the life supports to be taken off. That is my dear one's own word on how she would want it. It felt like a shot put had dropped into my heart, but I had to face the situation. My heart wanted with all its desperation to hang on to my bride of 51 years.

One by one around the glum circle, each agreed. We were losing our wife, mother, mother in law, grandmother, friend, and greatest close-up example. Sobs of heartbreak punctuated the silence and made the words almost unintelligible. The difficulty was beyond articulation. What right did we have to stop another's life? For Mildred still was breathing.

Our Pastor John Ploog of the Calvary Baptist Church came, gave us solace, and prayed with us. He said later that standing there and witnessing how peacefully we were handling this (how could that have been?) he felt "a holy moment." Youth Pastor Israel Gomez and layman Bill Basham from the church came into the hallway and talked softly with some of us. Dr. Richard Rigsby from the nearby Talbot School of Theology and his wife Donna, close friends, hurried to the bedside in minutes. They consoled us, and prayed.

I phoned Kathy Edwards in Tucson. This was such an incredibly difficult thing. For I knew the news would hurt her deeply. Mildred had counted Kathy exceedingly precious as a friend since 1973, and the two ladies seemed to have a particularly deep heart oneness that only God can create in understanding one another, as He knitted the friendship of David and Jonathan. As I expected, the news came as a stunning wound to Kathy. Her voice was low, like one crushed, as if out of a daze. I could tell over the phone that her heart was shattered. I tried gently to ask her at such a difficult moment if she would consider coming to the memorial service and giving a four-minute tribute to the lady she had loved so faithfully. She bravely and kindly managed words through tears, agreeing to do this.

Mildred's body fought so well. She had always been tiger tough. But that night at 11:58 they took off the life supports, and Mildred then, in President Reagan's words about astronauts, also applicable here, "slipped the surly bonds of earth and kissed the face of God." A daughter of the Lord, she had lived her whole life so triumphantly well, in a pristine godliness. Her life, fashioned after that of her Savior, was a pageant of love, "a living sacrifice" (Rom. 12:1-2) offered up to God as "a sweet-smelling fragrance" (Eph. 5:2). Now she had made her celestial flight (Ps. 90:10). God had taken her home!

Though our hearts were indescribably heavy, how could we but rejoice over the blessing that this meant to her? The reasons were several. One was her liberty of joy, released from suffering, for she was in God's fully comforting presence. Second, I thought of the confidence we had in her life which left unmistakably an aroma of victory, and so many pleasant memories! She had lived well, lived all out for her Savior, full of good fruit that lasts eternally (John 15:16). Third, as God was so considerate, He took her first, so that she would not be left alone had I preceded her. Fourth, God had given her a long life, defying medical predictions of an earlier death that seemed highly probable, and let her have rich fulfillments in her daughters being well along in Christ-centered marriages. Fifth, she had delightfully realized a longing to be a grandmother, and had seen two beloved grandsons up to their ages then of 13 and 12.

Truly, all was bright, gloriously bright. The words of Horatio Spafford at the death of his daughters in a ship's sinking came back to cheer:

> "When peace like a river attendeth my way,
> and sorrows like sea billows roll;
> whatever my lot Thou hast taught me to say,
> 'It is well, it is well with my soul.'"

We admired Mildred for countless things. She seemed to be so versatile and to do anything skillfully. She was a testimony of the purest love to me, our daughters, our sons in law, our grandsons, and all her larger family and mine. She was a living, open Bible in patience, pleasantness, positive spins on life, faith, kindness, long-suffering, peace, joy, gentleness, all "the fruit of the Spirit" (Gal. 5:22-23). Faithfulness to the ministry for God's sake was always her native breath. She constantly spoke well of me to others (she was very forgiving!), as I spoke of her. Her wise counsel helped me clear many a hurdle, and she was ever the good cook and the one who kept the house neat and inviting, above all "Home Sweet Home."

This woman of God exercised care over most of our business, keeping good records, filling out tax forms, paying bills, making many business phone calls, saving us money, skillfully showing frugality in getting things our home needed, re-arranging the furniture, and creatively thinking of new ways to surprise me with joy when I came home. She was always kind to people who phoned. When she was having trouble breathing, she tried to her utmost not to allow it unduly to show, and wanted to set others at ease. She never angled for pity or whined about her trial. She sacrificed in such a variety of ways to bring blessings to others.

Currey grit and God's grace helped her tackle hard things, as her father had found God's strength to endure the quick death of his first wife, a hurricane's destruction of his barn, a fire's demolishing of another, and their pastor dying in that inferno. She could take a clock apart, re-assemble all the parts, fix it, and it worked. She could make shirts and dresses, in fact she made Dianne's and Carolyn's wedding dresses. Amazingly, amid her breathing problems, she would put up new wallpaper and do it neatly, despite the toll on her arms lifting the paper and making sure it would fit. Her knitted afghans often beautified our divans. She produced sweaters for Christmas gifts. She was ever the lady to rise above her own hardships and send cards and notes of encouragement to others. Many have told me of her good cheer "that made my day."

In her later years, Mildred studied meticulously to become quite efficient at her computer. Persistent practice and trial and error sharpened her to use programs well. So she sent and received emails with a good sense of humor to spark laughs. Her monthly colorful leaflets for the church's Women's Missionary Fellowship always made a hit with the ladies. She always thought creatively of some good theme from her Bible to be the eye-catching keynote. She was a member of a prayer circle pleading to God about needs of seminary students and faculty wives. Her hands could wrap a gift, put on a ribbon, and make it meet the best of taste.

Mildred always caringly showed her concern for members of my family—Dad (d. 1965), Mom (d. 1997), any of my sisters or brothers—or her own parents, Dad and Mom until their deaths in 1976 (Mom) and Dad (1981), her brothers Richard of Norwich, New York and Bob of Citrus Heights, CA, and their families.

We got to visit Richard in his Norwich home in 1998 when we flew back for Mildred's 50-year Unadilla High School graduating class's reunion. In our time there, Mildred guided me on a heart-touching tour of the places where her family had lived during her growing up—Clinton Corners and the church down the road from small Schultzville, the one-room "Bear Market School" house not far from the first of the Curreys' farms, and the Unadilla home where we had enjoyed many pleasant hours.

When we stopped the rented car and sat gazing at these places, a powerful feeling ran like electricity through me. It was goose bump time. I was overwhelmed, simply in awe of God, and the mind-boggling way He had providentially orchestrated things to prepare the delightful girl He would present to be my wife. I felt I was the extraordinarily blessed one in being the beneficiary of so undeserved a privilege. What must it have been like for this girl to be playing earlier in these homes and farm yards? Then the wonder of it all pressed upon my mind. God had brought her from the Currey farm all the way across the country, and me from the Rosscup farm. He had arranged that we be in the same state, same college, same Shakespeare class, same church, and same home!

On at least five occasions we drove to Citrus Heights, CA to be with Mildred's younger brother, Bob, his wife Jeri, sons Philip and Steve, daughter Crissy, various foster children, and later the grown up children's marriage partners and their children.

One highlight for both Mildred and me at her brother Bob's came in Dec., 1971. Arizona State had an 11-1 regular season football record, having lost only to Oregon State in an upset, 24-18 on a sloppy rain-soaked field and nasty drizzle at Corvallis. So in the Fiesta Bowl the Sun Devils were pitted against a powerful Florida State

Seminole team led by All-America passing whiz Gary Huff. But ASU had Danny White handling the ball, and Woody Green at running back. White would in 1973 be selected to the All-America team, and Green to the 1972 and '73 teams. White would go on to replace the famous, retiring Roger Staubach as quarterback of the Dallas Cowboys pro team, and break several of Staubach's passing records.

Bob Currey set up a big TV screen so we could watch the bowl game in their living room off the kitchen. The game see-sawed back and forth. In the second half, Arizona State took a 31-24 lead, but Huff's passes moved the Seminoles right down to a touchdown for a 31-31 tie. White, Green and company pulled ahead again, 38-31. Back came FSU in a passing flurry to match it, 38-38. Then, with seconds ticking down to the end, White master-minded a Sun Devil drive with Green knifing over to score with seconds left for a 45-38 victory.

Mildred and I had hoped to have several more years. The breathing struggle grew more severe as years slipped by, and her general health more precarious. Yet Mildred received help from medicines, oxygen tanks, her latest breathing machine (Pulmo resuscitator), and her hand inhalers. We were a happy, constantly celebrating family. So with an indomitable spirit she rose to occasions such as family holiday fun, grandson Zachary's piano recitals, and Ben's Little League baseball games at first base. Besides these were other events such as speech contests in which the boys participated, and school Christmas dramas and musicals.

She had driven the 26 miles to daughter Carolyn's home many times alone to "baby sit" or later "boy sit" as a dearly loved "grammy." And we together had gone countless times to allow Randy and Carolyn to have a getaway, or for special occasions. God gave Mildred many fulfillments before He invited her to the greatest fulfillment.

Mildred and I had also driven to Caleb's and Dianne's home for Fall ASU football games that were on cable TV. This had gone on for several years due to the host's and hostess' graciousness.

In the weeks after I had said "goodbye" temporarily to my wife, the sting of death dealt a hurt that the dictionary has no adequate words to convey. The aching depth of loneliness was one of the severest trials I have ever felt, and in my own bleakness of loss, the fact that our dear daughters suffered deeply turned my heart to special prayers for their comfort. Times of study often turned into sobbing more than I had ever cried. Daily walks for miles were filled with indescribable ordeals of pain, streaming tears, not knowing how to get past this lingering shock, just being beyond my wits' end about how to move on without the human light of my life. I wanted her but had to learn to take it without her. Friends put their arms around me, and spoke kind words that briefly consoled. And my reciting Scriptures gave comfort in God's sure faithfulness. Another boost was in an insistent focusing on the joy beyond all joys this wife and mother now felt. The hope of eternal life, the certainty of seeing her again and celebrating with her, distilled a cheer such as I had never before felt grip me with such a crystal reality.

Now when any of the family get together, our loving thoughts turn to missing Mildred. Then God beckons our minds on to jubilation. She has gone ahead to the haven where we shall go, a place "far better" (Phil. 1:23-25).

23

Special Friends

WE AS A COUPLE had many special friends through the days of love that were God's gifts. As I mention some here, may the Lord console any whom I forget due to human frailties, for we cherished them as well! And who can list in a chapter all the dear ones who truly meant so much throughout the various stages, places, and scenes of life? Though memory slips, these people are precious.

I will give some names, not in any sense intending an order or a ranking.

Together, we counted as dear Ethel Kelley, Don and Pat Denind, Dave and Babs (later called Bobbie) Ifland, Cyril and Aldyth Barber, Doug and Jan Friederichsen, Dave and Sande Sunde, Henry and Shirley Holloman, Richard and Donna Rigsby, Bob and Joan Thomas, Bob and Nancy Saucy, Roy and Joey Long (Randy's folks), Louie and Irma Gutierrez (Caleb's parents), Leon and Jody Cooper, and Stan and Kathy Edwards. A number of Mildred's personal lady friends, all dear ones she tugged to her heart, appear later in women's tributes to her (Chapters 28-32).

God knitted us in an unusually close heart bond with the Edwards. They visited us time and time again, and we them. We exchanged letters and made phone calls or sent emails. Ethel Kelley had been the secretary of Donald Campbell, Registrar at Dallas Seminary, when we were there. Later she retired to Tustin, south a ways from Disneyland, and Mildred often drove down to take her shopping and to lunch.

The Edwards became loyal friends since God brought them to Talbot in 1973-77. The friendship grew even after they moved to Gresham, OR (1977–1988), and later to Tucson (1988ff). They often stopped to stay with us a night or two on their way from Tucson to Springville near Porterville, CA to see Kathy's parents. We also visited them in their Arizona desert home when Mildred was able, and when she could not go I was their guest a number of times, driving south from seeing family members in Peoria and Scottsdale near Phoenix. With the Edwards we had precious times of prayer. We remain, after Mildred's home-going, vital supporters daily in prayer for one another.

When we went to Scotland in 1974–1976, the Edwards were frequent in writing to us. When we departed and when we returned they were at the airport to be with us. Our home was their home, and their home ours. Stan taught at Talbot until 1977, when the man, Tom Finley, whom he had temporarily replaced, returned from UCLA doctoral studies. Then the Edwards moved to Gresham, OR so that Stan could teach at Western Conservative Baptist Seminary in nearby Portland.

In 1979, we made a long drive to visit these friends in Gresham, and later when Western down-sized due to financial concerns, Stan lost his position. He had no doctorate, so, to make a living, he went into Merrill Lynch finances and the family moved to Tucson, where in subsequent years he worked with this company, and later another Paine Webber which became UBS. Then he switched to a mortgage business, and has served as a church elder. Stan and Kathy have a lifeline going to God daily in prayer to uphold me.

Kathy was ever the considerate woman of God. Her letters came often to Mildred, and always brought a pinnacle of joy. Her phone calls were highlights of Mildred's days as the two would talk and laugh with such fun like young school girls for an hour or so. I knew that Kathy, a former nurse, was one person we could count on to pray for Mildred, really pray with understanding and empathy about her friend's health struggles, truly giving her the love of a heart's friendship.

Jody Cooper, Shirley Holloman, Donna Rigsby, Jackie Jenkins, and Lorraine Smotherman also were very bright friends in kind ways, especially in the later years of Mildred's life. And several ladies of the church's Women's Missionary Fellowship came to visit Mildred and show their love in her duress.

It was a special joy for Mildred to have Jody Cooper stop by on a bike jaunt to chat over coffee or tea and fruit cake or cookies. Other happy times were when Jackie Jenkins, former missionary to Japan, now a resident of Whittier, would phone and come bringing lunch for both, and fellowshipping in talk and prayer. My study was just in back of the living room, so I could hear Mildred praying aloud. Her talks with the Father poured from a pure heart, loving, mature, fervent, often showing deep empathy for people in her intercession. I grew as I heard her pray.

Mildred's closest friends from ABI, friends of a lifetime, were Margine Clark [married name Mercado], Janice Eagon [married name Ehrlich], Valeene Hayes, a long-time musical missionary to Haiti, and Pat Denind with whom she has met often. Her dearest, most frequently in touch Christian friends during our married years were Kathy Edwards, Jody Cooper, Donna Rigsby, Shirley Holloman, Jackie Jenkins, Joey Long, Lorraine Smotherman, and Pat Denind. And she kept up a lifetime correspondence with a faithful grade school, Clinton Corners friend, Lois Knapp Mosher, now of another New York town, Katonah.

My beloved's heart in her latter years was knitted in Christian love with ladies of the church's WMF. These women were Oleta Jones, Doris Peterson, Jody Cooper, Lorraine Smotherman, Barbara Hill, Wanda Hill, Jackie Jenkins, Terri Ortner, Alice and Ada Page, Joyce Webb, Betty Morris, Priscilla Wong, Beve Mengel, Beverly Bangs, and Faith Canedo. Another lady in the church thought the world of Mildred, and Mildred prized her friendship. She is Ila Barnhart.

Mildred felt high appreciation for Nancy Schultz, and after her Memorial Service Nancy and her husband Ron and their crew hosted a wonderful meal in Calvary Baptist's Fellowship Hall for the many guests.

High esteem was in Mildred's heart for Beve Mengel, who held several socials in her Whittier Hills home and graciously included us among her guests. And after our daughter Carolyn married Randy Long, Randy's mother Joey of the church became one of Mildred's intimate friends. As parents of the married couple, we shared many outings to family events.

We also had wonderful times with my sister Ethel and her husband Larry Wood of Garden Grove, CA, and with another of my sisters, Betty, and her husband Glen Waughan of Pasadena. And my sister Mary Ellen and her husband Jim Edwards were gracious, loving host and hostess in our visits and at family reunions.

Mildred also held as dear "B" Mayhue, wife of The Master Seminary's Senior Vice-President and Dean, Dick Mayhue; and Karen Busenitz, wife of TMS Vice-President Irven Busenitz.

Jane Hobgood often traveled from Anderson, CA, near Redding, to be a guest in our home. She had been a member of the co-uni-bus class I taught at Scofield Memorial Church, Dallas (1962–65). Jane for years has been a nurse.

Dorothy (Dottie) Chick was another beloved guest in our home during missionary furloughs. She served with TEAM in Africa, and we supported and I still support her in quarterly gifts. She gave us her baby grand piano, which, during her missions service, was in storage, and she asked us to move it and keep it. So Mildred and daughters Dianne and Carolyn have played many a tune on that piano. We also bought an organ, which Mildred loved to play as well.

Sweet music often would flow from living room to study as Mildred sat down to play the piano or the organ. Inspiration amid my study of the Scriptures came from hearing "He Giveth More Grace," "The Old Rugged Cross," "Great is Thy Faithfulness," "My Tribute," "Channels Only," "Day By Day," "Beyond the Sunset," "Jesus is All the World to Me," "Gone, Gone, Gone" and so many other uplifting songs.

I would sit at my desk perked up to rapt attention, feel a fresh elixir for study, break down and sob, or walk in and tell Mildred how wonderful the music sounded. Often as the words ran through my mind God would stimulate me to confess sins, exult in the dearness of His presence, praise Him, or pray for Mildred or another person. How many the rejuvenating times in hearing "Will Your Anchor Hold?", "Thou Wilt Keep Him in Perfect Peace," "Fight the Good Fight," "Be Still

My Soul," "Praise Him! Praise Him!," "I've Found a Friend, O Such a Friend," "He Leadeth Me," "Jesus, I am Resting, Resting," "May the Mind of Christ My Saviour," "I've Discovered the Way of Gladness," and "Jesus is Always There."

One musical message among many came in the words of "What a Friend We Have in Jesus." Words of the second stanza would bless Mildred's spirit, and waft to my ears, "Have we trials and temptations? Is there trouble anywhere? We should never be discouraged; take it to the Lord in prayer. Can we find a friend so faithful, Who will all our sorrows share? Jesus knows our every weakness; Take it to the Lord in prayer."

In her last few years Mildred enjoyed slow walks with a nearby neighbor, the elderly Eva Holloway, going around the block. When she lost her ability to walk that far, she would ride her battery run mechanical cart (M. C.) and Eva would walk along beside her. They would pause now and then for Eva to rest. Eva had been saved when young and helped in some Billy Graham meetings.

We were delighted when long-time friends from out of state came to visit. Among these were Austin and Nancy Robertson (Missouri), Jack and Carol Arnold (Florida), Neal and Bev Nichols (Kansas), and Dave and Sande Sunde (Colorado). In our earlier years we also got to see Rich Jonassen from Long Island when he would come out on one of his business trips. I have already mentioned him as an Arizona State baseball player who married Shirley Christophel, a Christ-filled girl I dated in college before Mildred drew my heart.

We had several family reunions through the years. Two were at Larry and Ethel Wood's in Garden Grove; several at Jim and Mary Ellen Edwards' in Peoria, AZ, some at brother Jerry's in Tempe, one at Jerry's daughter Robyn Bellerson's home in Chandler, AZ, and one put on by daughters Dianne and Carolyn at a park in southern California.

As already described, Mildred and I and our daughters traveled to Gresham, OR to see Stan and Kathy and sons Steve and John in 1979. We also visited my brother Frank and his family in the Forest Grove, OR area. They treated us to a boat ride up the Columbia River to a huge outcropping called "Rooster Rock." On that trip we visited Orville and Anne Swindler near Bend, OR. Orville was a good friend at Dallas Seminary, and the bond continues.

We made several trips to Madera, CA to visit Gene, sister Anna Mae and their family of five boys and Connie, a girl. And I have made several trips when Mildred was unable to go. Besides these, we traveled to Lemoore a number of times to visit Mom when she lived there in 1967–1979.

We had people stay long-term in our home. Diane Fraley and Becky White were with us for a semester when attending Biola College. My sister Catherine stayed with us about a year when at Biola. Kevin Fraley, son of my cousin Dave and his wife Laura, stayed a year to go to Biola, before a dorm room became available.

How can one recount the cordial friends of all the years even of our marriage? Bill and Vonette Bright, international leaders of Campus Crusade for Christ, were quite special and deeply godly examples. So were Dr. J. Dwight Pentecost and his wife Dorothy at Dallas Theological Seminary. Dr. Pentecost's Bible exposition set a powerful example to draw me to this kind of ministry. Many have been blessed by his books such as *Things to Come, The Works and Words of Jesus,* and commentaries on Jesus' parables, and the Epistle to the Hebrews. I wrote "Dr. P" an email thank-you, one of several letters to him, in Oct., 2007. Back came his words at his age then of 92 as he still was teaching part-time [he is 94 and still at his labors in late 2009]:

"Your letter was at the same time humbling and encouraging. Thank you for it. . . I have followed your ministry from those you taught . . . who ended up here at Dallas Theological Seminary. As you have found . . . the rewards of teaching are not found by looking at a grade book but by seeing what those you taught have been doing in ministry. And I have been rewarded . . . because of the way the Lord has used you in the lives of many. Thank you for being such an encouragement to me.

"I was glad for the word concerning Mildred. I can still remember (45 years later) the smile she greeted us with when we went to get mail [at the Dallas Seminary front office]. . . . And I know her smile has not left."

No, "Dr. P," that smile has not left. And it is brighter than ever now in heaven!

Dr. Charles L. Feinberg, dean at Talbot Theological Seminary, was a brilliant man who invited me to the privilege of teaching Bible on his faculty. And later, after I decided to seek a different school, Dr. John MacArthur spoke kind words to lead to my being invited to teach at The Master's Seminary. Then he set many an example of humility, love, and encouragement in gracious words to Mildred and me through the years. Dr. Dick Mayhue, Senior Vice-President and Dean of the seminary, has been a cordial friend and resourceful, highly informed leader to help the seminary spring forward.

One of the friends I highly admired in Dallas Seminary days and since was Harold Hoehner. He earned a doctorate there, then a second doctorate at Cambridge University in England. Before his sudden, stunning death at 74 in February, 2009, he saw publication of his monumental commentary on Ephesians, more than 900 pages, surely one of the richest all-around exegetical works ever written on that epistle. Harold and I had kept in touch, and at one time he phoned to invite Mildred and me to Dallas so that I could join the faculty as a professor in whichever department I chose, New Testament or Bible. I prayerfully decided to stay at that time at Talbot for the sake of Mildred's health in the California climate and our daughters receiving more tuition help at Biola University. God helped me never to second guess, and look back in regret, but thank Him for prompting the decision that He meant for our good.

Less than two months before Harold's home-going, he visited southern California and came to have lunch and spend a day with me. The fellowship was one of the most blessed highlights in all of life as we chatted about many things dear to our hearts.

God gave us gracious friends in Scotland whom want to hug in heaven. Some of these are the very dedicated Hugh and Meg Duncan, Erik and Mary Wood, Allan and Cath Masson, the Harold Robbs, a hospitality couple par excellence named William and Eleanor Leslie, the elderly model servant lady "C. B." Cornishcrest, and a very great example of a walk with the Savior and mighty teacher of the Christian life, Pastor Willie Still.

Faculty members both at Talbot and The Master's were very close in heart to both of us. And students of these schools, many now in far-flung countries holding forth Christ's name, have prayed for the health of the woman I exalted in classes. How many are the alumni whom I admire, respect, and rejoice over when I hear of things they have done in serving the Lord. How often I feel it just a miracle that, with Mildred's key helps, I could have been graced to have a part in lives that have so adorned the doctrine by sacrificial lives laid down at the feet of Jesus (Titus 2:10). These, in some measure, are to each of us faculty members a "crown of rejoicing" (1 Thess. 2:19-20).

How can I forget the diligent and faithful faculty secretaries, friends, who made the professors' ministries work? These were daughters of God, gracious, Spirit-led servants of God, who worked day after day with a freshness of joy. At Talbot, Dottie Howie, Fran Elder, Marilyn Hall, Shirley Shively, Karen Grassle, Doris Hakes, Joan Anderson, Irene Ganolis, and Karen Tarbell were superb helpers. And at The Master's Seminary, God will not forget the labor of love (Heb. 6:10) by a long succession of faculty secretaries, Karen Adamsen, Nancy Martin, Laura Murphy, Carole Milam, Pam Leopold, Teresa Smith, Jennifer Bright, Christine Dixon, Kim Archer, Angie Torres, Tracy Pickle, and Dana Hilborn. And other secretaries have greatly honored the name of Christ—Aimee Osmus, Cathy Wahler, Marcia Griffiths, Tanya ten Pas, Heidi Thomsen, Cathy Romero, and Holly Swanson.

How many things these secretaries and a long succession of gracious school receptionists did that made the ministry work and contributed to fruit God gave in many lands. The secretaries typed book-length syllabi, printed class handout materials, helped with student inquiries, typed letters, made phone calls, put graded exams back in student boxes, brought notes to classes, recorded grades, prayed for faculty members and their families, and so many other ministries. They counted in precious ways in service that will count eternally for their Lord.

Twice when international New Testament scholar and my Ph. D supervisor Dr. I. Howard Marshall came from Aberdeen, Scotland to Fuller Seminary in Pasadena, I took him out to lunch. On a third occasion I drove him from Pasadena to our home in Whittier and Mildred and I also had dear friends Dr. Cyril J. Barber and his wife Aldyth as dinner guests. Mildred as always prepared a delightful dinner and was a charming hostess.

Other visitors through the years were: Mildred's older brother Richard, her younger brother Bob and his wife Jeri Currey on several trips; and Dad and Mom Currey who lived with us in La Mirada for a while (1967–68). Dad at that time built a study for me in our garage. After Mom Currey's death in New York (1976), Dad came in annual drives in his "Ambassador" to California for a few weeks each year, until 1981. We also hosted Jim and Millie Currey [Jim was Richard's oldest son]; Ruthie [Richard's oldest daughter] and her family; Mark Currey, Richard's youngest son; Stephanie Harvey, her son Matthew, and sister Dottie Chick; and dozens upon dozens upon dozens of other people in the bond of love.

My own parents, Francis and Lola, and each of my brothers and sisters have been our dear guests.

Special to our hearts also are Doug and Jan Friederichsen of Orange, CA. As couples we enjoyed many sparkling times of fellowship while Doug, a Dallas Seminary graduate, taught at Biola, and after this while he has been a pastor in Fullerton and other cities.

One lifelong friend in an interchange of prayer is Milt Pope. Milt watched and overheard me praying and witnessing at the Arizona State dining room table. Hungry for things of God but not yet strong in the Lord, he stopped me as I started to the door. He told me God had spoken to him through my actions, and that he too was a Christian. A friendship sprang up, and this led on to his being active in Campus Crusade Bible studies, growing via a trip to Forest Home Christian Conference Grounds in California, and his keeping in touch with us as "Uncle Milt" during his Ph. D studies at Stanford. In recent years, this dear brother and his wife Sharon host a weekly Thursday night Bible study on the slopes of Glendale, CA. Milt says he carries encouragement notes I have written in his wallet, re-reads them for new springs of courage, and phones with matters we take to the Father. He is one of our country's aerospace "geniuses" and a man sold out to the Lord.

Dr. Cyril Barber and his wife Aldyth of nearby Hacienda Heights, CA are also friends, in this case since Dallas Seminary. Cyril and I meet often for breakfast fellowship, and he has graciously given me most of the books, around 40, that he has written. He has, for examples, authored these on all the Bible books from Joshua through Esther, and now has completed a book on Abraham and is laboring on one about Isaac and Jacob, with Joseph in the plans for a trilogy.

In our local church, very special friends are Dean and Terry Ortner of their Wonders of Science traveling ministry in leading hundreds to Christ. Then there are Jim and Lorraine Smotherman of long-time Wycliffe Bible Translators' work.

Mildred appreciated the Talbot Seminary and Master's Seminary faculty wives. It hurt her more deeply than anything she or I could ever describe when her breathing made her unable to go to the ladies' meetings. Still the friendships were a tonic giving new inspiration to her spirit. At Talbot we enjoyed faculty people Bob and Nancy Saucy, Bob and Joan Thomas, Henry and Shirley Holloman, Richard and Donna Rigsby, and Tom Finley. Then I transferred to teach at The Master's Seminary in 1987. In TMS years, Mildred felt a blessed cordiality with "B" Mayhue and Karen Busenitz, and again Joan Thomas [who died in 2008], as well as Favy Montoya. She was thrilled to get to know other faculty wives, authoress Liz George, as well as Pam Snider, Teri White, Louise Essex, Betsy Harris, and Missy Mehringer.

Elizabeth George, who has written a great number of books for ladies via Harvest House Publishers, often sent an autographed copy to Mildred with kind tributes for her example and her prayers. Her husband Jim was for many years a faculty member at The Master's Seminary and has authored about 10 books himself. Liz wrote on the title page of her book, *The Lord is My Shepherd* (Ps. 23), "For Mildred—What a joy to witness your walk with Him for so many years!" (7/2000). In November, 1999, Mildred sent a thank-you note to Liz for blessing she received from one of Liz's books. Liz came right back with, "I was so touched by your note—and the pains you took to write it. Your thoughts and encouragement greatly blessed me. I miss you... I love your thoughtful, beautiful, creative card" (Dec. 1, 1999).

A beloved faculty member whom I esteem is Dr. Alex Montoya. This humble, unassuming Christian teaches TMS men to preach and is one of our nation's most rousing, Elijah-like speakers himself. Alex and I for years have ridden together to the Fall "kick-off" faculty retreat in late August, and enjoyed sweet fellowship. He is one of the truest, model men of a godly life and pastor's heart I know.

Other faculty members of TMS I have known more closely are: Greg Harris and Keith Essex of the Bible Department, Trevor Craigen in Theology, and Ray Mehringer who directs recruitment and placement of the students. Ray, for example, is a humble, sweet Christian who is ever putting others above himself, as Philippians 2:3 exhorts.

Last but not least are the members of a "Lunch Bunch" I have attended nearly every Friday since 1976 in La Mirada. We share the Word, pray for one another, empathize in matters of life, share news, and crack jokes. Mildred was often a subject of our prayers there, or in the men's daily lives. Dr. Rigsby, our king of joke tellers and "Bob Hope of Talbot," has led the group, which began while my family was in Scotland. One "charter member" was Al Oliver, Talbot student who had come out of pro football with the Denver Broncos and Los Angeles Rams at 6-7 and 280 pounds. Another was Talbot student Len Crowley, who had left the Kansas City Chiefs where he was a wide receiver, and later has been a pastor and a key man in a ministry to help churches in financing ministries.

Ed White, a long-time pastor and Talbot graduate, retired to Pagosa Springs, CO. While living in the very area where artist/writer Fred Hartman originated the famous "Red Ryder" western comic books that led to several movies starring Wild Bill Elliott and Alan "Rocky" Lane, Ed remembered one of my illustrations from years before in class. I had mentioned that as a boy I had longed, like many lads, to "ride the west" with a "Red Ryder" air rifle having the famous "Red Ryder" insignia on the stock. But I never got one. So, one day at our men's Friday "Lunch Bunch," in walks one of the members who had visited Ed in Pagosa Springs. He hands me a long box, and when I open it out comes a "Red Ryder" BB gun and a huge box of BBs. Ed had sent this, and it "made my day." Now the air rifle is mounted on the 9 foot 2 inch top shelf of my study, a glad reminder of a boyhood longing fulfilled, and a godly brother's kindness.

Then the early "Lunch Bunch" drew other Talbot students. One was R. Kent Hughes, who was to distinguish himself as one of the prolific commentary writers of our nation while pastor of the Wheaton College Church and afterward. Jerry Root, a member, went on to gain the C. S. Lewis chair at Wheaton College. Another "Lunch Buncher" was David MacDonald, a decal salesman and very dedicated layman. David's wife Judy read my book on John 15, *Abiding in Christ* (1973). This couple was in a Big Bear mountain retreat seminar I led on the vine and the branches before the book came out (winter, 1968). Judy wrote me recently about the book, "I loved reading it again, and it brought back wonderful memories of you sharing so much scripture and answering my many questions until late in the night [several couples stayed up, eagerly pumping me for answers]. My life was never the same when I finally realized, 'without Me you can do nothing at all.' I will always be grateful for your excellent words of wisdom" (card from Tehachapi, CA, May 15, 2009).

Besides these at Lunch Bunch, attendees in later years, are: Frank Lagorborg, who spent many years as a Moody Press book salesman; David Cox, key man in an insurance firm; Virgil Kleinsasser and Vern Hurlburt, long-time missionaries to Africa; Robert Seelye, insurance salesman who is one of the most successful laymen in leading people to Christ I have ever known; Tom Finley, Professor of Old Testament at Talbot; John McNichols, a retired missionary and exemplary layman;

and David Gray, a night watchman who was a member of a Bible class I taught in the Church of the Open Door, Los Angeles, in 1966–1972.

Mildred, I, and these friends and others have enriched one another. The fellowship is bright even in this life. But we shall also meet at Jesus' feet in the future city of light (Rev. 21:24-26).

24

Homes Sweet Homes During Our Marriage

MANY WERE OUR EARTHLY homes in the 51 years we shared. But beyond these we were seeking the city which is to come (Heb. 13:14). Mildred has gone into the heavenly presence of her Savior to be among the "welcoming committee" for others of God's dear children. Homes we shared were, in some measure, a little bit of heaven before heaven.

One of my meditations was on what a home meant to us. Here are samples of the blessings. Home for children of God can be a place where Christ is the chief inhabitant, the most prized guest. When this is true, home is a haven of rejuvenation and of rest. It is a refuge of privacy to give our hearts to one another, pray, meditate, and study apart from the world's busy blast. It is a resort of peace, of service, of learning godliness from the flow of situations and responding to them.

Home is a venue of joy with children God gave, and later grandchildren. It is a place for planning and for producing good things to enrich others. It is, at times, a crucible of sufferings in ways and vigils that even friends know little or nothing about. It is a center for welcoming others in hospitable love, a chamber of counseling the needy who visit. Be it ever so humble, home can be a "castle" of beauty and a venue where faithfulness grows—in praying, being sensitive, listening to the hearts of others, and fixing upon new ways to be a blessing to them.

Home is a base for the practice of things Christ's church is all about, a bit of heaven away from heaven. It is a vista of cleanliness where we dust, wash clothes, and bathe our bodies but more importantly our spirits to be cleansed from sins. Home is a scene where we may re-enact what a Christian Dad or Mom should be, when we are right, pure, good, truthful, and an example of what to be like. It is a place where, as the psalm writer cast it, one can "walk within my house with a perfect heart." When this is not so, it is the chief location for taking unrighteousness to Jesus and seeing His blood make us pure from all sin.

Home is a residence where we can learn to empathize with those who hurt, who need our thoughtful love and understanding. It is the center where we can learn news of our world and react wisely to be the citizens God wants us to be to touch those out beyond the sheltering walls, and, if we have the vision, to the ends of the earth.

Home is the most special, immediate resort that can focus our vision to the beauties God has given—in flowers, grass, the melody of birds, the warmth of sunshine, the cheering foods, the changes of clothing, and above all the loveliness of those who are closest and care the most.

Home is the spot where we look forward to what we yearn to be, finally, as God's family in our eternal home. Then we shall "go no more out" (Rev. 3:12). On the other hand, tragically, home is a hell ahead of hell for those who neglectfully allow themselves to live in that dark, hateful state.

Home is a consolation from the whirl and the flash of life going fast, and the pressure of our work outside. It can offer a quiet nook to renew ourselves, to rethink, to try again, to do things better, to offer ourselves up to God to be what He wants.

Home is a place where we have the right of way to make new and responsible choices. So let us choose well, for the choices may bless or blast. Home is a haven apart where we can build relations with those for whom we care the most and who, often, care most deeply for us.

Home is a sanctuary where the clothes washer can remind us of the greater washing, the kitchen of putting our priorities on the greater spiritual food, and the dining room of tasting the food that satisfies our hunger in a more lasting way. It is a place where the bedroom can hint of the final rest from our labors (Rev. 14:11-12), and the living room of all the facets God gives us in spiritual life. It is a venue where the study illustrates the treasures of knowledge in Christ (Col. 2:9), and the stove pilot or fireplace the flame the Spirit can live in us.

Home is a location where the pictures on the mantle and the tables can remind us of the dearest Person of all—the face of God that shall fill our vision forever (Rev. 22:4-5). Home is a scene where the garage can be, even if faintly, an example of all we have stored up that means the most to us to reward us eternally (1 Cor. 3:12-15). It is a dwelling where cups in the kitchen shelves or china cabinet can call our attention to the "cup of salvation" filled with joy that forever quenches our thirst.

Home is a scene where the clothes closets can picture the fine linen we shall wear always in the future presence of Christ (Rev. 19:7-8). It is a situation where the medicine chest can suggest God's healing of our malady of sin (1 Pet. 2:24) and physical diseases now (Exod. 15:26), and His ultimate giving of eternal health (Rev. 22:2). Home's workshop may suggest our doing the works that will last forever (John 15:16; Eph. 6:8).

Home is a scene where the letters, cards and emails can speak to us of friends by whom God has made us rich in fellowship, as well as people who need the Savior.

Home is a haven where the garden, flower beds, and pots of blossoms can point our hearts on to the lush flora in the New Earth and the New Jerusalem.

Here, then, are places that were our homes while passing through this world on our way to the future "Home Sweet Home."

A little green cottage. This, our first home after the wedding, was in the Max McKinley courts on McAllister Ave., Tempe, then about four blocks east of the Arizona State campus. The cottage offered us a kitchen/living room, bedroom, and bathroom. This was our abode after our return from a New York honeymoon in Jan., 1957 to June of that year. Then, after graduation, we journeyed to Dallas to begin seminary.

One of our cherished joys during nights of these months in young marriage was relishing successive readings out of the Moody Bible Institute teacher Kenneth Wuest's books. He commented richly on Greek word meanings out of the New Testament. We savored his colorful word pictures for the English reader, such as *Bypaths in the Greek New Testament, Untranslatable Riches from the Greek New Testament,* and *Golden Nuggets from the Greek New Testament.* At that early stage of our lives, these were good food to satisfy our spiritual "taste buds" and encourage us in Christ.

Another vivid memory during that stay was the landlord's wife's strong insistence to Mildred. If she would drink carrot juice several times daily, and limit her intake to this, it would cure her breathing problems. Mildred did try this for a short while, it almost did end her breathing problems (that would have been in death), and we stopped the juice "cure all" rather quickly. We saw in this a lesson. People may mean well with their pet, home remedies, but they can be quite narrow minded, lack humility, and be very uninformed and unkind by insisting on treatments they foolishly fancy cover all cases. They rate their remedies as wiser than doctors' prescriptions on how to relieve the suffering!

A Dallas Seminary apartment. This residence was on the second floor of the school's Carroll Avenue House of eight apartments.. It was so named because it was at the corner of Carroll Ave. and Sycamore Street, about eight blocks north of the seminary, 1957–58. I was a student constantly pushed in Bible studies and the job as sports editor of *The Garland Daily News.* Mildred was a receptionist at the seminary.

We had an interesting experience with an elderly couple who lived in the house next door to the apartments. They were of a certain Baptist background and rigidly strict in their legalistic notions. One Sunday Mildred's breathing struggle required a refill of special medicine, so I hurried to a pharmacy to get the help for her. When I walked back carrying a prescription package in my hands, indicating that I had shopped on a Sunday, we would learn that these "straight-laced" neighbors were offended. The so-called Christians living next to them—Mildred and me—were hypocrites, not true to the Bible.

From then on, we were careful, if such a need came up on a Sunday, not to offend this couple again by letting them see us committing what they construed as "sin." But we thought of a scripture principle that if an ox is in a ditch on the sabbath, help it out, and felt Mildred was so much more important to God.

Another green cottage. This was on the Dallas Seminary campus, north side, on Apple Street. I recounted earlier how fellow seminarian Ralph Braun and his wife Dorothy decided in sacrificial love to make this cottage available as our home in 1958–1961. Here, Mildred needed only to walk a hundred yards to her work at the office.

Apartment on Ford Street in Pasadena. This was just across from the campus of Fuller Seminary, Pasadena, CA. We had traveled to Pasadena for me to be managing editor of Campus Crusade's *The Collegiate Challenge*, 1961. We lived there about five months, then the land lord "dropped a bomb shell." He was selling the place, so we had to "pull up stakes."

This home was where God began to fashion what appeared to us to be a miracle after Mildred's doctor had told her she could not live through having a child. Our daughter Dianne was on the way. God would bring her into the world a few months later.

A second Pasadena apartment. Here we were just off El Molino Ave., near Orange Grove Blvd., the street where the annual Rose Parade begins. This home served us the rest of our year in Pasadena (1961–62). Dianne was born at Huntington Park Hospital, south of Pasadena, in 1962. Her birth marked God's kind rejoinder to Mildred's Dallas doctor's prediction that her breathing dilemma would not allow her to have a child and live. As in Isaiah 55, as the heavens are high above the earth, so God's thoughts are above our thoughts.

Back to the Dallas campus. Here we lived in one of several two-story apartments of Dallas Seminary along Apple Street which then flanked the campus (1962–63). I drove home one dark day in 1963 from *The Texas Mesquiter* news office where I was the sports editor, heard on the car radio the shocking news flash that President John Kennedy had been shot in Dallas. I felt a terrible thud in my heart. I hurried inside our home, alone since Mildred was away at the office, and fell down to cry out to God. Never before had I heard of our national head being gunned down.

News soon came that Lee Harvey Oswald had killed Mr. Kennedy from a high ambush perch at a window of the Texas Depository School Book Building where he looked down on the car cavalcade. That structure, up town, was about two miles from our home. Shortly after Oswald's evil deed, we were sitting in Scofield

Memorial Church a few blocks from the seminary during a Sunday morning service. An usher rushed a note to Pastor Harlin J. Roper and whispered urgent words to him as he paused from his message. Dr. Roper gravely opened the note and read stunning words to the congregation. A man named Jack Ruby had waited in a crowd of bystanders as police were moving Oswald the assassin. Suddenly Ruby whipped a pistol from concealment, jabbed the barrel at Oswald, and shot the prisoner to death.

House in Casa View, TX. The city was an outskirt community east of Dallas. Mildred was no longer working at the seminary office, and this home allowed me to be near my sports editor job while I continued work on a doctorate degree in Bible (1963–65). Our second daughter, Carolyn, was born at Baylor Hospital in Dallas while this was our home in 1964.

Our home was a frequent meeting place for dear people of my "Co-uni-bus" Bible class. In the residence's bedroom "study," I put together my doctoral dissertation.

Guest stay with the Sundes. This was a three day visit with David and Sande Sunde, Southgate, California, while waiting to find a regular home as I was to teach at Talbot Seminary (Aug., 1965). The Sunde's hearts and ours always seemed in sync, in "the unity of the Spirit in the bond of peace" (Eph. 4:3).

Guest days at the Saucy Home. Here we lived while Dr. Bob and Mrs. Nancy Saucy of the Talbot Seminary faculty were away on a vacation. The house was in Anaheim, and it was comfortable while we searched to locate a more permanent dwelling. The Saucys permitted us to stow a trailer load of belongings temporarily in their garage. At Talbot I would have many happy and stimulating lunch hours talking about things of the Bible with Bob.

Little red house on Pecos Street. This rental was in Norwalk, CA. and our home during my first year teaching at Talbot, 1965–66. A theme song on awaking many a morning was *"Blessed Be the Name"!* While we still lived here, we made a flight to Dallas Seminary at the end of the school year, May, 1966, for me to receive my doctoral degree. For I had completed the dissertation in the summer of '65, too late to march in the commencement ending that school year.

Our La Mirada Home. We bought a three bedroom home at 2519 Stanbrook Dr., La Mirada, a mile and half from Talbot, 1966–69. Our joy here would include having Dad and Mom Currey come from New York to live with us a few months before they found their own temporary apartment in nearby Whittier. Later they continued their retirement back in Oneonta, New York.

One evening in my garage study I was desperately "wiped out" from teaching a double load, six courses, but struggling to prepare for the next day's classes. I felt dreadfully weak, and did not know how I could be ready to face these. I sat on a narrow "cot" (like a bunk bed) praying, but discouraged. Our daughter Carolyn, then only about three, rode her tricycle in front of the garage and sang "Jesus loves me, this I know, for the Bible tells me so. Little ones to Him belong, they are weak but He is strong."

Out of the mouth of a babe, God spoke to me. I was weak, too, and quite a little one before His majestic greatness. He is strong! I got up, freshened from a new shot of courage, and went in the strength of "Jesus loves me . . . He is strong!" My Lord who is Sufficient carried me through the day I feared, and many a day (Isa. 40:31; 2 Cor. 12:9)!

The present home. It is at 10909 Grovedale Dr., Whittier, CA, and our home from Aug., 1969 forward. We bought it from a man whose wife had died, and who had decided to invite in special guests, many pigeons that shared the house with him. Our move there required a lot of cleaning up and removals, such as curtains where the birds had perched. After that was done, the residence became a lovely place, and smelled better too!

When I left Talbot in 1987 and became a professor at The Master's Seminary, we decided to stay at this address. This meant a 40-mile drive to the latter school.

In 1990 we had a 21 by 16 study built with shelves nine feet and two inches high. This addition became my haven of meditation. It replaced a cramped, "cracker box" study walled off in a quarter of the garage. For the new study with its old west motif, Mildred put up an entrance sign, "The OK Corral." The name came from the famous wild west Tombstone, AZ where Wyatt Earp, his brothers, and "Doc" Holliday had a fast shooting corral gun fight with the Clanton gang. But Mildred used that episode as a take-off for her better idea. With my interest in old west things, too, my study was "OK" in the service of the Lord, an offering to the King.

Mildred's own room featured her computer, various "kitty cat" pictures, a radio with its music and Angel baseball games, her Christian books, missionary prayer letters and calendars, business files, and a nook for her computer savvy missionary productions as well as "cheer up" cards she sent to people.

Now think back a few years.

Mrs. Barclay's "Bed and Breakfast" Refuge. This two-story apartment on the main street of Stonehaven, Scotland, was our home for two weeks when we first landed in that country. It was 16 mi. from Aberdeen, and there we waited for a pre-arranged cottage to become vacant in the village of Muchalls six miles away (Aug., 1974). Both homes were on the lip of the North Sea. While waiting for our cottage to become available, I translated much of a German book, with many a glance out at the restless sea. Mildred and the girls delighted in frequent short walks to the seashore.

A Small Cottage in Muchalls. This Scottish place was owned by Ian Main (1974–1976). There, under an upstairs "sky light" window, I wrote most of my doctoral dissertation on the reward God promises for believers. And there we hosted many a party or special Scottish guests such as our beloved pastor, Willie Still, and other new, dear friends of that Bonnie land. Our home, too, was often the fun meeting place of our American friends who, with me, were enrolled at the University of Aberdeen.

House in the Gray Granite City. This spacious dwelling was on Osborne Place in Aberdeen, our residence for a few months (1976) when Ian Main returned from a long trip and had to have his Muchalls cottage back. We had two stories and a back garden. Nearby bus service could hurry us to wherever in Aberdeen we wanted to go.

Home Again in America. Now we were back on Grovedale Dr., Whittier, Aug. 1976, and since. Mildred's time here would end in April, 2008 when God said "come up here."

Glorious Accommodations on High. These began for Mildred that night at 11:58 o'clock. She is now a "receptionist" in the office of the greatest "President" of all! And our daughters and I go on living in this present world for the values that Mildred and we cherish. They are more valuable than gold (Ps. 19:7-10).

25

Trips We Enjoyed

GOD HAS PREPARED FOR the trip and the haven that is the epitome—the perfect and the final one, the rapture and the home par excellence (1 Thess. 4:13-18; John 14:1-3). Mildred has already "checked into" heaven. We who have received the Christ she loved will join her in that wondrous grandeur. There, awaiting us after the trip that tops all trips, is the time of our lives! No, let me correct that; time then will be no more; ours will be eternal life in its finest sense.

Memory helps recall past good trips and respites, but years have caused some to slip from the mind. The vacations point up how a family can enjoy special diversions free from the heavy toil. In our case, journeys we took together, or when I went out alone or Mildred traveled without me, are a testimony to God's faithfulness to help Mildred be able to share in such joys. They also are, even if faintly so, earthly examples as temporary trips before the eternal TRIP and THE BEST REFUGE OF ALL.

When Mildred could go on journeys, God lifted and freed her to triumph even when she suffered from breathing tightness. Often she was really struggling, yet she rallied courageously to make these times enjoyable. She loved to celebrate being away and having fun. Besides, she selflessly sought God's help even when hurting. She tried so hard not to keep the rest of us from being there. Even in trips when I went without her, her heart peaked in a special joy at <u>my</u> being able to go. Upon my return she usually had had done some extra, springing some joyous surprise as her "welcome home, Jim." And it was my joy to see her again, exude over the sparkle in her eyes as she opened special gifts, and have a good time in our glad reunion.

Now, samplings of the trips come back like video scenes from those fond venues. In quite a number, God enriched us with very special blessings.

Carlsbad Caverns. In a Spring break away from Dallas Seminary rigors, we drove in 1959 to the famous Carlsbad Caverns in New Mexico. We packed into our sky blue '56 Plymouth the two of us, and two other couples, John and Pat Kramer (he was the bookkeeper at the seminary) and Alf and Eileen Nieuwoudt from South

Africa. The Nieuwoudts would, after graduation, count greatly in God's work in their home country.

We were amazed by the stalagmites and other ice formations God had formed far into the earth's depths. And standing in early evening near the lips of the caverns, it was awe-inspiring to see thousands of bats, each with a God-endowed instinct to know its own tiny "parking place" in the deep, dark, vast interior, spiral up out of the cave's mouth. Like a thick cloud, they winged out on a flight over the desert to devour tons of insects during the night. Then in uncanny fashion, each one would find its way back "home" to its very own exact niche. How fascinating are the wonders our God has made, and how great the tributes that belong to such an incredible God (cf. Ps. 148).

The New York farm. In the summer of 1959 Mildred and I drove to New York to visit her family. When the time came for our return to Dallas, Mildred's breathing struggle was so intense I called John Kramer (cf. 1. above) at the-seminary, and asked if he and his wife could meet Mildred at the Dallas airport, "Love Field," and drive her to a hospital. John conferred with Dr. C. Fred Lincoln, the school's treasurer and a professor of Bible, who insisted that the seminary air mail the $85 that paid for the flight then. Our hearts exulted at this gracious gift, and seminary friends' prayers.

On August 5, I drove Mildred to Binghamton to get on a flight Tourist Class Rate via Mohawk Airlines and later Braniff to reach Dallas. Her breathing would ease up in a few days, and this period gave me time to drive back on that long journey and take her home from the hospital. After getting her on her flight, I drove our Plymouth back to Unadilla, said goodbye to Dad and Mom Currey, and the next day started my four-day cross country drive alone to Dallas and a reunion with Mildred at the hospital. The trip gave me much time to trust God in a special way to cope with this new trial, and pour forth to Him my cries out of the depths (Ps. 130:1). Tears spilled down my checks as I sought my dear one's recovery over the long miles.

I believe that such very difficult times were among God's gracious means of helping us grow. As spiritual muscles become stronger by exercise on weights, so God makes our spiritual lives tougher by trials. The tests are God's kind invitations to us to trust Him and exult in His sufficiency. He is the God who is there! We both felt the pains of trial, received solace from the God of all comfort, and later would be, in His crafting hands, sensitive to comfort others also in their hard times (2 Cor. 1:3-4).

One special blessing to me during the New York stay was reading much of George N. H. Peters' old, famous, massive, 3-vol. defense of a premillennial perspective on Scripture, around 3,000 pp. The set is called *The Theocratic Kingdom*.

Abilene, Texas. In 1960 we drove some dear friends, David and Sande Sunde, from Dallas to Abilene to stay in a Sands' Motel and root for Arizona State vs. Hardin Simmons in the football clash which I mentioned earlier. Sande, as seen before, worked in the Dallas Seminary office with Mildred.

Dave, in his love for us, would fly, so many years later, from Louisville, CO to read Scripture (Lam. 3:22-23) on God's faithfulness at Mildred's memorial service April 19, 2008. And Sande, who was also set to offer a tribute at that memorial but became ill, would send her memories honoring Mildred that are in a chapter toward the close of this book.

Pasadena, CA. In the early summer of 1961 after I received my Th. M degree at Dallas, Mildred and I drove to Pasadena. There I became Managing Editor of Campus Crusade's *The Collegiate Challenge.* The move had a kind of vacation atmosphere for us after the tough seminary push. We lived in an apartment on what then was called Ford Street, immediately across from Fuller Theological Seminary.

Dr. Wilbur Smith, who taught Bible at Fuller and served as a special, constant resource for the magazine, became an admired friend. Though gruff at times, he also had many gracious moments. He often was in our office a few blocks from the Fuller campus, dictating letters to Christian scholars from various disciplines whom he knew in the world, inviting them to send testimonies of their faith in Christ to put in the magazine. Governor Mark Hatfield of Oregon was one who contributed.

Since Dr. Smith was a world renowned scholar, popular at prophetic conferences, with an uncanny breadth of knowledge about Christian books, it was a special privilege to "pick his brains." Here is one example of the treasures this gave me. I asked him if he knew a good one on godly traits for men. He was instant: "Young man, come with me." I followed him to the elevator, and we went down four stories, then out to his car. He drove me to the Fuller campus and led me upstairs to a door. Turning the key in the lock, he opened a room and I found myself in his personal, vast library of nearly 28,000 vols. He walked past several long, towering rows of shelves, then in a military sort of spin, wheeled to his right and led me to the end of a row. To my surprise, he plopped himself on the floor and plucked a book out of the bottom shelf.

"Young man," he invited, "read this." I found in my hands Robert Speer's book, *The Marks of a Man.* The chapters were lectures Speer had delivered to young men on such themes as truth, purity, and service. Dr. Smith made that copy a gift to me, and right away I was riveted to it as a treasure. The chapter that impacted me most was on "Freedom, the Necessity of a Margin." It was about not living as close to the edge of sin as we half-heartedly might fancy we can dare, but keeping as far from falling into sin as we can get. I have often pulled that old book off my shelf, despite its falling apart, and re-read parts of it as one of the volumes that have been the biggest spiritual stimulants to me.

Lake Minnetonka near Minneapolis. Shortly after getting settled in Pasadena, Mildred and I drove to this lake for the summer Campus Crusade for Christ Institute. All staff members were to train there for two weeks. Mildred's breathing became perilous, so I drove her to the Minneapolis airport and she flew home early. We had phoned a couple back in California to meet her, drive her home, and take her to the hospital if need be. I remained at the lake and drove back home when the training ended, taking a car load of Campus Crusaders back to the Phoenix area in our '56 Plymouth. That car had succeeded our dear Willys.

I dropped friends off at their Phoenix residences. Then I pushed on to reach Pasadena by night, eager to get home to Mildred. In the bone weariness of a long trip with little sleep, I kept dozing. I pinched myself, slapped a wet towel to my face and neck, and summoned every bit of youth and grit to fight off sleep. Fatigue overwhelmed me, and my dead head slumped over the wheel as I sped through the desert.

A blasting terror of noise snapped me back. My heavy, half opened eyes glimpsed a mountain of lights bearing down on me. It was a huge truck, and the driver was on his horn desperately trying to warn me as I raced toward him head-on, errant, over in his lane. By some instinct of panic and speed in the providence of the God who rescues, I whipped the wheel to the right. The Plymouth swerved, the tires squealed protest, death stalked me on the pavement, and I shot off the highway, plowing roadside sand. I had missed the truck, it must have been by inches!

By now I was wide awake. Trembling with great fright, I climbed out of the Plymouth into the desert's biting night air. As I walked around, I felt goose pimples, my heart was thumping, and I was trying to get my wits back. The deep impression chided me that I had played the fool, big-time. I had veered precariously on the sliver edge of death, and cheated it by a fraction of a second. I kept saying, "Thank you." The merciful God had spared my life. Mildred would not be a widow hearing of a desert wreck, and we could fulfill other plans. Still shaking, I slid back into the car, and drove resolutely to a filling station. There I cut the engine, locked my doors, and fell almost instantly into a deep sleep.

In the morning I drove on to greet Mildred. I had learned a lesson. Now I was again thanking God that I was still alive, not a bloody corpse, dismembered and splattered in mangled wreckage out in the lonely wastes.

God delivered me. And after this would come my work on the magazine, doctoral studies at Dallas, then teaching at Talbot and The Master's Seminary. Just as importantly He would give us 51 years, daughters Dianne and Carolyn, sons in law Caleb and Randy, and grandsons Zachary and Benjamin. Our lives sometimes flirt at the gateway into the shadowed zone of death, but thank God that His plans are good in contrast to disaster that stalks us in our mistakes.

After the year launching the magazine in Pasadena, we drove back to Dallas in 1962 so that I could enter the doctoral program in Bible.

Home to Buckeye, AZ. In Dec. 1964, we drove from Dallas to Buckeye to join my family for Christmas and let them see our two little girls, Dianne who was two and a half, and Carolyn two months old. Near El Paso, the two-lane highway was treacherously slippery from winter ice, and every slow mile challenged us with extreme hazard. We faced the peril of slipping off the pavement at any second and being stuck in a winter freeze miles on the back side of nowhere. God let us be at wits' end corner, but graciously helped us reach a small town, check into a motel room, and sleep a few hours. Then in the early morning we drove around a curve into El Paso, glorying in the welcoming morning sun and giving thanks to our Lord for keeping us safe.

Home for Dad's funeral. In Feb. 1965 my brother in law Larry Wood phoned at supper time to tell me my father had suddenly dropped dead of a heart attack. The family's "rock" was gone. I drove for 22 hours to Buckeye to be with my numb mother and the rest of the family. A very large crowd of people came to the funeral, since Dad had won many friends through his long-time kindnesses. And once he had retired from his 80 acre farm/ranch (1958) he had run a basement recreation hall that youth frequented as they liked playing pool, snooker, billiards and eating confections he sold. Dad had a way of looking around, spotting a kid who held back because he did not have money for ice cream or a soft drink, and handing him one on the sly. The youths loved "Pop" as they called him.

California to teach. In July 1965 with doctoral studies done, we packed all our things and pulled a trailer to California. This was a kind of brief vacation after the pressuring classes. I was to teach Bible at Talbot Seminary in La Mirada. We found a rental home in Norwalk six miles from the school. That was our abode for a year.

Fellowship with the godly Anna Mae. We took several vacation trips north to visit my Christ-filled older sister, Anna Mae, husband Gene, and the Arter family in Madera, CA. We also drove various times to visit family in the Phoenix/Tempe/Scottsdale area, or attend summer family reunions.

For a few years Anna Mae alone was saved in the Arter farming family. We pleaded to God for the salvation of her husband, five sons and one daughter. Anna Mae was a tenacious "prayer warrior." One by one as years went by, most of the family came to Christ. Gene held out for a long time, but finally put his trust in the Savior, and today is a very committed, tender, humble, praying son of God.

A San Clemente weekend. Doug and Jan Friederichsen invited us to spend a weekend in a time share with them. Doug was a pastor in Fullerton, and previously at Dallas Seminary had been chosen as the best graduating preacher of the year. He taught Bible at Biola University for several years.

When Mildred and I took our daughters to Scotland for my Ph. D studies, we felt the pain of being so far from home and separation from loved ones. We also were in a life of depending on the Lord to supply our needs. Every day it was a special excitement to wait for the mail truck to pass our cottage and hope to hear the driver drop mail from home into our box at the front door. One day we opened a letter from Doug and Jan and out fell a check for several hundred dollars. Their friendship, love, and the gift were such a boost to our spirits.

Uplifts like this said something to our hearts. They taught so loudly, so insistently, "You, too—when others are in need and you have what can help them, be willing to give" (Jas. 2:15-16; 1 John 3:17). And we are not just giving to them; we are doing it to Christ (Matt. 25:35-40). A sad reality is in not being able to give to all who have real needs; that sadness can be overcome by praying to the One who IS ABLE.

The towering Sequoias. We traveled to Sequoia National Park in two different summers, once with my sister Joyce who had returned from Peace Corps service in Ecuador, and another time to take Ethel Kelley. Ethel had served many years as secretary to the registrar Donald Campbell at Dallas Seminary, then retired and lived in Tustin, CA. On that second trip, we went on to visit uncle J. T. Fraley and his wife Louise in Fresno. At that time J. T. ran a filling station on one of the main arteries, Blackstone Highway.

In an earlier year, J. T. and his brother Gennis invited me on a fishing trip and sat beside a campfire for hours trying to convince me to "get it right" spiritually for my eternal salvation by baptism in the Church of Christ. They turned to passages in the Book of Acts, one after another, to persuade me of baptism as one of their ways to gain eternal life, which at that time they felt was only in their church. God helped me winsomely answer their ideas on each passage (Acts 2:38; 10:33ff; 22:16, etc.). Finally, God opened their eyes to see that they were skewing the verses, and later they realized the way of faith through grace's gift was right. After that, "Jay" as we called him wrote me often, depending on me for help on passages that were growing him as a believer and a lay preacher.

Jay and Aunt Louise lived a sweet Christian life. This man had not had formal Bible training, but spent much time meditating in God's Word. When we were stunned by his death in his early 50's of a heart attack, his family asked me to lead at his graveside memorial service. And he and Louise have always wanted to get any book I wrote and devour it. Some years after Jay's home-going, his brother Gennis married Louise, for his own wife Patsy also had gone to heaven.

To God be all glory for being willing to work through us, His channels, to bear witness that His Word, correctly interpreted, is the answer.

Now a leap further back.

Grandma's funeral. When Grandma Bertha Fraley, my mother's mother, died in 1967, we drove northward to Lemoore, CA to join in celebrating her life. This dear, believing woman, born in 1892, had raised twelve children, eight sons and four daughters in penny-pinching trials. This family had begun in Oklahoma after her folks rumbled over the long trail from Tennessee in a covered wagon shortly after 1900. She married James Thomas Fraley. James died after a slow toll of stomach cancer at 45 in 1933, and Grandma was left, in great difficulty, to take care of the family. She put her trust in God, and led her household by "grit," by grace, and a whole lot of love.

Permit another flashback, this time far back into my childhood.

One Christmas around 1937 when Grandma then lived briefly in Liberty, AZ not far from our farm, we all met at her home to open gifts. I was very small then. After the gifts were distributed, my own family was getting ready to go home, and Grandma said to me, "Bye now, Pat [my nickname]. I won't see you any more this year." As a child, my mind was boggled as I thought she meant a whole, long year. I could not stand that, so I cried out, "No, Gramma, I can't wait that long!" She broke out in a hearty laugh, for it was but a few days to the end of "this year," and the start of the new year!

A tour through America. In the summer of 1969 Mildred, I, and our two daughters went on a month-long vacation touring many states from California to New York. We enjoyed visits with several Dallas Seminary alumni friends, and spent many days with her Dad and Mom in their place of retirement in Oneonta, New York. On the journey home we went to Washington, D. C. to visit the Library of Congress, sat in on the Senate, and even went to Gettysburg, Williamsburg, Mount Vernon, Valley Forge, and other historic sites.

A trailer park weekend. While in Muchalls, Scotland, in 1974, we went on about a three hour drive with Jan Woodward and family to a trailer park for a weekend getaway. Jan's husband Steve was working as I was on a New Testament doctorate at the King's College, in the University of Aberdeen, but had left on a trip to talk with scholars who might help on his dissertation.

When we had first arrived in Aberdeen, we did not know a soul. I rode the bus to the university, and heavy with loneliness walked into the King's College office where Jean, the secretary, welcomed me. She knowingly took out a phone list, and called one of the current American students, Steve Woodward. Then she handed me the phone. Steve welcomed me heartily, and invited me to come right over and have lunch with him, Nan, and their children. Jean told me where to catch the right bus, and I soon found myself with the Woodwards, new friends who were warmly gracious. They invited my entire family over, and we all became close friends. I marveled at God's faithfulness in leading, even far from home. How He is able to put a kindred love in His people.

Two years later I was with Steve in his apartment as he put finishing touches on his dissertation, and we prayed. He had just opened a letter from Winnipeg Bible College offering him a teaching position. Overcome with emotion, he exclaimed, "It's just fantastic. I get to teach the Bible, which I so enjoy—and they'll even pay me to do it!"

That has amazed me, too, through my years of teaching.

Other vacations in Scotland. In Scotland [1974–1976], we made two vacation drives around the country to Bampf, Inverness, and other places. All the family enjoyed our overnight stays at bed and breakfast nooks we easily found as we motored in heather beauty.

A seminary reunion. Still in Scotland in the summer of 1975, we drove to St. Andrews and stayed in a bed and breakfast place. Our main aim was to attend, with several others, a Dallas Seminary alumni dinner. We had a banquet at a restaurant, and later got to see the world-touted golf course and famous, colorful Woolen Mill. In the latter we saw, for example, the many Scottish clans' plaids, even the McDonald design and beauty that much earlier Curreys in Mildred's ancestry had known.

When we were going into a restaurant we looked out and caught sight of men braving pelting snow to stick with their golf. Then we drove around Scotland, stopping at delightful bed and breakfast places, and finally back to our cottage in the village Muchalls overlooking the North Sea.

Our search for the Loch Ness Monster. Another Scotland venture was our family's bus ride to Loch Ness, where we did our utmost to catch sight of the elusive "Nessie" the monster. To our chagrin, the storied lake creature did not show her face.

Nine days in London. Also in Scotland, in the Spring of 1976, the four of us rode a train from Aberdeen to Edinburgh, where we visited the hill fortress, caught buses along the main street, took a special bus tour to key sites in and around the city, and even went to see the castle. Displays in the John Knox House, some under glass, drew me as a magnet, for I had read of Knox who prayed, "God, give me Scotland, or I die."

God wonderfully sustained Mildred. The trip involved walking to see certain attractions, and though she had to stop often to catch her breath, she insisted on being right with us. There it was again—true grit, no, sufficient grace in action (2 Cor. 12:9).

From Edinburgh we caught the train on to Stratford-on-Avon (a river), Shakespeare country, and stayed in an upstairs motel room before a next day sight-seeing of the famous Anne Hathaway Cottage where Shakespeare courted Anne, and other scenic spots. The first night we were aghast at crackling ice when I pulled back the thick comforter so we could get into bed. It was too late to do anything about it, so we had to "tough it" for a while to allow our bodies' heat to warm the bed into a comfortable state.

A nine-day excursion in London followed our leaving the train at the King's Crossing. At that strategic center, rail lines of England converge. We bought four tickets for unlimited train and bus rides in the city. At underground railway tunnels, different colored lines on walls directed passengers to trains zipping to other places. So our young daughters Dianne and Carolyn caught on quickly and were our proud "scouts," leading our way in an intriguing game of pursuing the colors.

Just off the train upon getting to London, we saw a teenager leaning against a building with a Kentucky Fried Chicken box in his hands. Since we were far from home and its old familiar culinary delights, the sight of that Colonel's box caused our taste buds to go wild. The young man told us that the place was just around a corner. We were overjoyed at a "taste of home." But we, too, had to stand on the street while satisfying our aroused appetites with an American treat.

In the days at London, we saw the Tower of London, Pickadilly Circus, Trafalgar Square, Downing Street where the prime minister lives, "The Old Curiosity Shop" about which Charles Dickens wrote, and a famous tea room that was a delight to Mildred. We ate at nice restaurants. Another lure was the famous Madam Toussaud's Wax Museum. It was rather fascinating to see several of our American presidents in wax but looking so real. None of them waxed eloquent that day.

We stayed in a Bed and Breakfast place near the All-Souls Church of Langham Place where the famous expositor John R. W. Stott was pastor, and went that Sunday to visit there. I had read Stott's books, and we had heard him preach in a town near Aberdeen. To our disappointment in this London trip, Stott was away on vacation. We also enjoyed walking through a tunnel beneath the Thames River.

A quick flight to New York. In mid July, 1976 Mildred received a startling telegram. Her mother Harriet lay in a coma, so the next morning I took Mildred and the daughters to the Aberdeen airport to catch a plane to New York.

I remained behind in Aberdeen. A Christian couple had loaned us a gray granite apartment for our final months in Scotland. In very long days, I finished typing my doctoral dissertation and also arranged at a dock company for all our goods—in two barrels and a huge crate—to be shipped back to California. I hosted parties for some of our American and Scottish friends to say reluctant "goodbyes."

Two weeks later I too caught a flight to New York. As the final plane's wheels touched down at New York's Kennedy Airport, my heart sobbed in thanks, "Mission Accomplished" after Mildred's struggles and my hard study those two years.

The sting of death for her beloved mother was difficult for Mildred to bear, and a painful hurt to me. I felt a sharp grief because I had taken her away to another country, causing her not to see her mother again when she could talk with her in this life. I will always cherish and appreciate Mildred's love and courage to undertake all the packing, travel, other hardships, and her trusting God for ways to cope despite frequent, critical breathing struggles. I credit the faithfulness she showed ultimately to the Lord for giving her supplies of sweet grace, and her refuge in Him (Ps. 91:1). She knew by faith how to "take" as God "undertakes." And she found Him constantly adequate (2 Cor 3:5). He was the El Shaddai of Genesis 17:1, the Sufficient One, "The God who is Enough."

North to see loved ones. In July of 1979 we drove to Gresham, OR to visit Stan and Kathy Edwards. For Stan had finished Talbot teaching and joined the Western Conservative Baptist Seminary faculty in 1977. We spent several days of heart-exulting fellowship, our lives knitted with these friends, and also went to Forest Grove to have a good time with Frank, one of my two brothers, and his family.

At a motel along the route home, I was packing overnight things in the car trunk one morning. Suddenly Dianne, a teenager, ran out crying in great fear that Mom was caught up in an awful struggle in the room. I dashed in and found Mildred heaving in a desperate battle to get her breath. An "S.O.S." shot to God, and He helped her get her bearings. When she felt some relief, we continued homeward. The quick answer to prayer in a crisis was similar to Peter's when he walked on the sea to meet Jesus, began to sink, and Jesus instantly held him up (Matt. 14:22-31).

Honoring great youth sponsors. Ca. 1991 Mildred and I drove to Pine, AZ for the special tribute a church was giving for Carlton (Pop) and Ethel (Mom) Nason. They had been our dear youth sponsors at First Baptist Church, Tempe, when we were dating at Arizona State. They were people who had borne "much fruit" in heaps of love to the collegians and high schoolers. We esteemed them as prime examples of how lay folk can do big-time, eternal things if they give their lives over, sold out to Christ.

Mildred's high school reunion. In the summer of 1998 Mildred and I flew to Sydney, New York, for the 50th anniversary of her 1948 Unadilla High School class. The highlight for us was her tour pointing out to me the scenes of her childhood. God put burning sensations of thanksgiving in my heart that I could see where this lovely girl had walked. I exulted that, in His entrusting her with illness, He had brought her all the way across America to me. And He had always been her Faithful One. Each site she pointed out to me left me in a breathless awe.

Now to back track a bit.

Excursions to write western novels. I went alone on several western research trips during 1983–1987. One was to Albuquerque for a week, during which I drove a rental north to Cimarron in the same state to see the area I would write about in my novel *Treachery at Cimarron* and also two other novels, *Ambush at Vermejo* (a creek northeast of Cimarron), and *Longhorns North*. Another jaunt was to Walsenburg and La Veta, CO, and on another drive to Pueblo, where I was guest of my Talbot student Rod Schon and his mother Trudy.

Dallas and San Angelo, TX. In 1988, I flew to Dallas to spend a week researching in the Dallas Seminary library. Then I caught a plane on to San Angelo for a Western Writers of America conclave at a Holiday Inn. How did that trip come about? I just mentioned to Lance Quinn, at that time John MacArthur's assistant, that I did not plan to go because we did not have the money. The next day, a letter came from Pastor MacArthur. He said, "Don't even consider saying 'no'." And with his note he enclosed a check for $500, bidding me to go and enjoy the convention. I was grateful to my leader and to God for fashioning people whose motto is considerate love.

A flight for a football showdown. On an earlier trip (1981), I had flown from L. A. to Dallas with the Talbot Seminary flag football team which was to play the Dallas Seminary team. Both squads were studded with ex-pro players, and an undefeated Talbot team lost, 7-6.

The clash was the final game played in the famous P. C. Cobb Stadium there before work men demolished it. We watched as our receiver, Keith McKinney, known as "Mr. Clutch" since he never dropped the ball, angled to the goal line as his brother Dan rifled the ball right into his hands. A sure thing. No, the oval slipped through Keith's outstretched fingers and flopped on the turf. So we fell short of tying the game as seconds ticked to the end.

A seminary mountain retreat. While at Talbot, Mildred and I went to an annual Fall New Student/Faculty retreat in the mountains at Forest Home, CA. She stayed in a women's cabin with the women students, and I in a cabin with some of the men. An interesting thing happened. One male student refused to part from his wife for the night, insisting that they must be together to keep a marriage vow never to be separated. Student body officers scrambled to find a separate cabin just for them. We wondered how practical, mature, realistic, and considerate of others such a vow was.

South of the border, down Mexico way. We drove as a family to San Diego to visit Jim and Mary Ellen Edwards and sons Brent and Michael. Jim, in the Air Force, was stationed there for a time. Mary Ellen one of my sisters, gives her tribute at the end of this book. The Edwards took us south into Mexico, where we bought several colorful pots that held plants in our patio for years. One of them still houses a fern these many decades later. Mildred and I often took patio breaks amid our plants to have fellowship that was a prelude to the never ceasing fellowship in heaven's lush, eternal beauty.

A drive amid wild animals. As a family we drove south of Santa Ana and Tustin to what was called "Wild Country Safari," a vast drive-through an area where we saw lions, elephants, zebras, etc. We viewed the beasts from our car, in scenic panoramas, especially to our wide-eyed little daughters.

Back to Bethel. On about six occasions, we enjoyed a week in a Big Bear mountain cabin that Philip and Iris Chan of South Pasadena invited us to use. The refuge was named "Bethel," and was a two-story, spacious lodging with a kitchen and very large living room. Philip invited me to speak on several Saturday nights to a Chinese collegiate gathering in Pasadena, and also be guest speaker many times at Sunday morning Chinese services in the same city. In the latter meetings, I spoke via an interpreter, sometimes called an "interrupter" so the messages lasted about twice as long.

On one of our early visits to "Bethel," Philip and Iris drove up and asked me to lead in prayer to dedicate the cabin to God's glory. We joined hands in a circle in the living room and presented the haven to the Lord. Chinese youth stayed there many times for spiritual retreats.

A Wrightwood cabin and a western novel. Pat and Pat Murphy of our church invited us to use their Wrightwood vacation home in the hills for a week as a family (1985), and also in a later year their renovated place (ca. 1990). Then, too, they had let me use their cabin another summer for a week during which I wrote my third western novel, *Longhorns North*. I pounded the typewriter for around 16 hours a day, typing fast, and got the quick-moving tale done in six days. Tyndale published it under the pen name "Jim Ross" in 1987. The story featured a Texas boy of 17 who proved his manly grit on a trail drive north over the Ratton Mountains out of New Mexico and north beyond Pueblo, CO.

Incidentally, none of my three cowboy novels are still in print. I have even run out of copies and so cannot send any. People tell me that copies sometimes surface in used book stores.

Our entire family had spent a week at the "Bethel" cabin in Big Bear the same summer as that novel, so we drove from there to Wrightwood. Mildred and the girls left me at the cabin to work on the western, and Mildred drove on home. They returned late on the Saturday of that week, and I drove us back home, the rough draft of the wild west story done.

Guest lectures at Grace Seminary. I went alone two summers (1981 and 1982) to Grace Theological Seminary, Winona Lake in Indiana as a guest lecturer in their doctoral program. Each stint was for two weeks. The first was on biblical reward and the second on prophecy in Matthew 13 and 24-25. The school assigned me a guest room in a vacated girls' dorm both years. Special fellowship meals with President Homer Kent and several of the professors such as John A. Sproule, John Davis, and John Whitcomb, Jr. were delightful.

When I got back home, my dear Mildred greeted me with a refreshing summer surprise. For my home-coming, despite her breathing struggle, she had put up new wall paper in our bedroom—a snow-capped mountain, forest trees in winter, and an icy creek winding its way down hill, splashing over stones. The cold scene was a treat in the heat and a work of love that blessed me for several years.

Two series at a Bible citadel. I flew to be guest lecturer at the Arizona Bible Institute on two occasions. One series was on Abraham's walk of faith, ca. 1968. The other was at the Arizona College of Bible which had grown out of the earlier school. This time my exposition was on the Spirit-filled life in Eph 5:18-21. This was in the 1980's.

Fellowship in Arizona. I made several trips to Arizona (1988–2008) when Mildred's health did not permit her to go. Fellowship was blessed with my sister Mary Ellen and her husband Jim in Peoria, near Phoenix, with another sister, Joyce and her family in Scottsdale, and also with friends Stan and Kathy Edwards in Tucson.

Mildred's trips to New York. She went on two flights when I could not go. She took our two daughters, Dianne four and Carolyn not quite two, in 1966 when she went to help her mother Harriet who was ill. We had flown from L. A. to Dallas for me to receive my doctoral degree in May, and had arranged with a graduating couple from New York that Mildred and the girls could ride in their car with them to drive back home. Later, Mildred and the girls returned to California via the Greyhound Bus Lines.

On the other trip, in 1981, Mildred went to New York for her father's funeral, and helped her brothers Richard and Bob decide what to do with things left from the marriage. She and Bob drove back to California in a rental truck, hauling a lot of treasured things. Most of these they decided Bob should take to his home in Citrus Heights, CA since his health would permit him to work more at sorting them out.

Dad Currey, like the daughter he raised, was mighty in his God.

Sleeping Beauty. In the late 1970's, our family of four drove to Hemet, CA for a Spring break. We saw "Sleeping Beauty," which is our daughter Dianne's favorite Disney movie.

Into "Big Blue" Country. A nice highlight came in my flight to Ann Arbor, MI in the mid 1990's to serve on the ordination council of a TMS alumnus. I also spoke in his installation as the new pastor. The church put me up in a nice hotel, took me to wonderful feasts, and showed me a Barnes and Noble Book Store display of cook books that an elder's wife had written. Her husband took me on a tour of the University of Michigan campus, bragged about the "Big Blue" football teams, and we spent a happy time at the campus coffee and gift shop on a snowy day.

50 Big Ones. Our 50th Anniversary trip lasted four days in "The Island Palms" resort, San Diego, Dec. 26–29, 2006 (cf. Chapter 21).

Now Mildred has taken the greatest of all trips—a flight into heaven. We who also know the Christ who is preparing a place there for us expect to see her again. And our hearts shall rejoice.

26

My Tribute to My Godly Wife

WHAT CAN A PERSON say that will be sufficient to honor the Lord for His faithfulness? And how would he adequately extol a wife of such shining godliness? Here is an attempt at the impossible.

When breathing pressure very often kept Mildred from going to socials of the seminaries or the church, we both felt the hurt. She took the disappointments with a fine courage and a quiet, resolute submission. She knew how to make the most of each situation, content in her Lord, as Paul (Phil. 4:10-12). She missed the banquets, but she will be there at the greatest banquet, "the marriage supper of the Lamb" (Rev. 19:9)!

I would come home from a banquet, party, speaking engagement, or commencement, sit by the bed or on it, and share with Mildred things I could recall, or words that people said. She would drink it all in. Sometimes a hostess would give me a special plate of food to take home for Mildred, or brownies or cookies we could enjoy.

We thanked the Lord that Mildred did get to some parties. Not always breathing the best, she would try as quietly as she could to keep "on an even keel." Conversations with loving ladies long desiring to see her and asking natural questions would "wear her to a frazzle." This also happened at church. Pressure to get enough breath would mount, and Mildred would be at a point of desperation. She was possessed of a fine spirit to be gracious and brave to cope, though on the way home or once at home she would have greater difficulty breathing. Often after special outings she would be bedfast for several days. I wished that I could relieve her, and do the breathing for us both! For God gave me good health and strength to make a living. Mildred, bless her heart, knew best how to "make a life."

I cherish her sacrificial faithfulness to me. Words just cannot even come close to what should be said. One of her lady friends, in a card on which I can find no name, said "Mildred, I'm very sorry you're not getting the media coverage Liz Taylor is with the same diagnosis. But you no doubt have more friends who pray." She did!

To back track, we as a family had prayed that if God willed it we could go to Scotland for me to work on a doctorate in New Testament. This would help me be a better teacher. In the heavy, hectic days of preparation in 1974 just before leaving for New York and Scotland, Mildred's toils to get things at home ready and to pack for the trip had worsened her breathing struggle. She was having a tortuous time getting her breath. She confided to her friend Kathy Edwards, who told me this after Mildred's home-going, that she felt she "just must be brave and hold up. I don't want to let Jim down."

When Kathy told me that, tears began to trickle from my eyes. Mildred would never have let me down! Love is so many thousand times more important than a trip to Scotland and working on a doctoral degree. I told Kathy this, and mentioned how sorrowful I was that I had not been even more sensitive at that time to Mildred who had been so valiant for me. Kathy was gracious with wise words, "Jim, God has that covered." And the God who comforts those who are cast down consoled my heart to soften the deep ache of "Oh, if only I had . . . !"

How my spirit exults in God for helping my sweetheart bounce back from those severe trials many a time, and feel more zip. Even as she breathed, some obstruction lurked there, yet her breath came a bit more freely. And I would breathe easier too. For one suffers beyond words too, when a partner he or she loves is hurting. He or she feels sharply the desperation, the groping to seize on what to do. I marveled at how, with less strength of good health than most ladies, whenever my darling felt any relief of new strength she was up and about, doing so many wonderful things for me, Dianne, Carolyn and others. We could not keep her down. That indomitable spirit continued to assert itself in her as it did when, as a high school girl, her power slams in softball earned her the fond tag name, "Slugger Millie." She made many "home runs" later that were not on the ball diamond, and at last made a "home run" that crossed home plate into heaven!

Mildred's life was one of much suffering, yet an example of the poem she tucked away in a folder to review at times. It is called "The Valley," and the Faith, Prayer & Tract League of Grand Rapids published it as a leaflet in her childhood. Some of the seven stanzas are as follows:

> I have been through the valley of weeping,
> The valley of sorrow and pain;
> But the "God of all comfort" was with me,
> At hand to uphold and sustain.

When He leads through some valley of trouble,
His powerful hand we can trace;
For the trials and sorrows He sends us
Are part of His lessons of grace.

Oft we shrink from the purging and pruning,
Forgetting the Husbandman knows
The deeper the cutting and pruning,
The richer the cluster that grows.

As we travel through life's shadowed valley,
Fresh springs of His love ever rise;
And we learn that our sorrows and losses
Are blessings just sent in disguise.

So we'll follow wherever He leadeth,
Though pathways be dreary or bright;
For we've proof that our God can give comfort,
Our God can give songs in the night.
– Author Unknown

This astounding lady also must have been one of God's finest "showcases" in putting others at ease. She had quality, charm, and grace to bear up courageously in her struggles. I believe that in principle Mildred will have great consolation in 2 Corinthians 4:17 being true for her. The present struggles all of us Christians bear in faith's patience are not worthy to be compared with the eternal weight of glory. That is in the reward God keeps in store for us. As the old song phrases the reality, "It will be worth it all when we see Jesus!"

Lines from another song I often repeat express the idea. "He giveth more grace when the burdens grow heavy . . . For out of His infinite riches in Jesus, He giveth, and giveth, and giveth again." God gave Mildred much (Gal. 2:20), and by His living in her she gave Him much—"much fruit" (John 15:4-8).

She longed so much to act as normally as she was able! She wanted to invest the most into each situation for her own enjoyment and helping others feel some surge of joy. She never desired that people feel sorry for her. In fact, she was a victor in ways that I can gaze back upon with awe. I think Mildred knew how to "mount up with wings as an eagle" (Isa. 40:31). She was better at living this than I ever was even in teaching it.

Her "true grit" that was better than John Wayne's when he played "Rooster Cogburn" in a movie, "True Grit", and her "pluck" to fight the good fight were marvels. No wonder her softball teammates tabbed her quite early as their "Slugger." She could belt the ball and drive runs home to score. Then later in life she hit a lot of "grand slams" with life's "bases" loaded in spiritual ways.

I am emphatically sure that the degree of her future special reward will be a large capacity. She must be one of the "ten cities" people in Luke 19:11-27. Let me say it in outright candidness and objective truth. She was one of the most consistently godly, "true blue," and "real deal" people it has ever been my joy to know. A woman of rare excellence was Mildred, sincere, no put on, gracious, considerate, showing interest in others, patient, speaking well of people, leaving judgment to the Lord, praying, loving God's Word and drawing verses from it to cherish in her heart.

The verse we chose for her graveside memorial marker really sums it up after her overcoming life. It is Matthew 25:21, "well done, good and faithful servant; you have been faithful over a few things; enter into the joy of your Lord."

Among many other verses that stood out to her were: Dan. 12:2 on the future resurrection of believers; 12:9 on how many do wickedness but the righteous understand. The thoughts sank deeply into Mildred's heart, and are marked in special ways in her Bible.

One has to wonder. If she could be such a quality woman despite her breathing distress, what kind of dynamo might she have been if sprung free into normal health? God's equity to reward will be in wisdom that takes every detail into appraisal. He will get everything just right. Having been true, surely my "Dumplin'" will be one of the fairest of the fair in eternity as she was in life with us. Hers was a witness of worth, a testimony of triumph, indeed a life well-lived.

Besides, she always took care of our daughters with wisdom, love, and truthfulness. She seemed to know a lot about children. Was it from her study to teach Child Psychology and Pedagogy at ABI, just plain wisdom from being a keen observer, or the special endowing grace of God to fashion her as the precious mother she was? I believe she was available to God, who put it all together in her life. My heart holds the very highest esteem for her. Even now I take new courage from her character to bend my own efforts after an inward fire to be what the Lord wants me to be. How a great life can speak its volumes to us!

In earlier days, at times when I felt so down it would take a stepladder to climb up to a gnat's belly, so discouraged, Mildred's soothing words would rally me to look and find fresh courage in the Lord. Our Savior always found a way even when it seemed there was no way. Mildred had an indomitable drive of loving care to help my eyes fix on the path of God's way, to catch the light shining to illumine that way (Prov. 4:18).

Permit me an example.

Deep dejection beset me one night in my first year at Dallas Seminary, in 1957. I came home from sports editor work at *The Garland Daily News* (outside Dallas). I was dog tired from burning my eyes out on news copy, and faced possibly an all night, "last ditch effort" to study much and get ready for oral reading of Greek at 7:30 in the morning and exams in other classes later that day. I lingered in spending time with Mildred at supper and following, yet after this how could I get through the reading of an impossible night, let alone the semester?

"I think I'll have to drop out of seminary," I moaned to her. "I just have to face it. I can't keep up with everything, and my eyes hurt like they're going out. There's no way . . . ."

My darling sat on the couch, took my head in her lap, soothed my face with her gentle fingers, and let me feel the love of her heart pouring down into my heart.

"Jim, don't give up our dream," she pleaded. "God's faithful. He must have a way. He'll help us see it through." Then she remembered Dr. Harold Lovett, a Christian optometrist who was a special friend of the seminary. He gave turkeys to students every Thanksgiving and Christmas. "Let's get you an appointment with him."

How timely! How life-changing where two ways part: the way of making it, and the way to the dumps in failure. God did put fresh grace in me that night to study. He gave my eyes the strength, and I got through the next day's seeming "great tribulation."

This godly man, Dr. Lovett, told me things. God had made my eyes. And God would make them feel okay. Ah, it sounded like what the Lord told Moses—that He made his mouth (Exod. 4:11). This optometrist lovingly asked me to use the lens he had made to suit me, trust the Lord with all my heart (Prov. 3:5-6), and keep on keeping on. Sure enough, for how sure is God, He strengthened my heart and my eyes (Ps. 138:3). I kept up in studies, got good grades, and that year also stayed on target as a sports editor, "bringing home the bacon."

God, Mildred, and Dr. Lovett were the keys. My wife's faithfulness, maturity, devout refusal to "throw in the towel," and counting on the Lord made it possible for a discouraged young man to stay in the battle. Out of this poured nearly 50 years of touching lives that are exalting Christ in scores of countries. What might have happened if a woman of God had not been there that night?

This dear woman herself once was lost, and then was saved. From testimonies of people at various stages of her life (cf. Chapters 28-32), as well as watching her for nearly 54 years in all sorts of situations, I can say that she never lost her love, joy, patience, or heart to bless others. The only things she lost, at times, were her breath, and one other thing. An old news item in *The Unadilla Star* has the heading, "Lost Pocketbook Returned to Owner." The story reads: "Miss Mildred Currey, Unadilla RD 1, Tuesday got back the pocketbook containing $5 which she lost. Raymond J. Hayes, 24 East St., found the purse Saturday on Chestnut near Spring and took it to the police station. Ownership was established through a 'lost' want ad in the *Star* Monday."

Mildred was my lighted candle, a human example of a story I heard. It was a little train that was trying to climb a mountain. The way up was a tough chug. As the train labored to ascend the steep slope, it purportedly said, "I think I can . . . I think I can . . . I think I can." At times it slowed to a bare crawl, and it seemed it could not make it. But at last it edged its way to the summit, and shouted, "I knew I could!" Mildred knew she could even before the summit. "If you can believe, all things are possible to him who believes" (Mk. 9:23). Jesus had it right.

This wife had a God-honed skill as a counselor. Other ladies would sit and listen and go away very different, enabled to face up to life head on. God knows, all told, the varied and amazing fruit Mildred bore as a "branch" in Christ, the "vine" (John 15:1-6), fruit that will last forever (v. 16; Phil. 4:17). I wrote a book on fruit, *Abiding in Christ* (Zondervan, 1973; now Wipf and Stock), but Mildred was one of the most compelling examples of living the life in "Christ, who is our life" (Col. 3:4a).

We shall see Mildred again. Our hearts shall rejoice. It will be in the land that is fairer than light. We will join her, see her no longer in weakness but at perfect liberty to bound like an antelope on the streets of the city, the New Jerusalem. We shall stand with her there, on the bank, gazing in ecstasy at our Christ (1 John 3:1-3) and at the river of life. We shall eat of fruit from the tree of life with her and others who trusted Jesus.

And for now, the summons is clear. Live each day for Jesus. Live all-out, as this daughter of God did (2 Cor. 5:14-15). Soon after God took her home, those verses burned like a hearth fire in my heart. God spoke deeply, and I rededicated myself to be what had meant so much to Mildred and me, and what she had exemplified in a rare beauty before me. The verses spell this out. So, until then! That wonderful day of the future draws nearer.

Glad day! Glad day!

27

Mildred's Fruit as a Faithful Servant

THE MINISTRY GOD LED me to enter was a ministry that was Mildred's as well. We were "one" (Gen. 2:24), a team, two people who wanted to do the will of God, and devote our lives for His sake who gave His life for us. So whatever spiritual "fruit" (John 15:4-8; Phil. 4:17) God fostered in <u>my</u> life was very often in some linked way also partly <u>Mildred's</u> fruit, and vice versa.

It is like a child who has success largely because of things a faithful father and mother have done. And it is like a pilot who keeps his plane in the air because a tail gunner takes care of gunners below trying to shoot them down. And it is like a halfback who runs for a touchdown largely because a teammate has thrown the key block that springs him free into the end zone.

The labors <u>we shared</u> together those 51 years and 4 months bore their fruits that the Holy Spirit gave (Gal. 5:22-23). Several perspectives point this out. These follow.

Fruit in Students She Affected

The hundreds of students in the 22 years at Talbot Theological Seminary, later called Talbot School of Theology, and then the 22 years to 2009 at The Master's Seminary were of different ages. Mildred and I, just as other faculty people, had the privilege of impacting these lives. I often praised Mildred to my students, asking prayer or sharing how much she meant to me. And in the computer age I sent out frequent emails to all our alumni telling of things such as my dear one's faithfulness.

Many in classes or among alumni later have told me that Mildred's faithful coping with suffering and standing behind me had a profound affect to shape their own thinking and what they did. Much of what God was pleased to do through me, I owed to a very huge degree to the dear wife at home who made so many things possible. So she had a share in the fruit.

It was rare, but I even had students in their 80's. One example is amiable Fred Schelander, who came to Talbot from had many years as a missionary in India. He looked very much like the famous "Colonel Sanders" who originated the recipe for the Kentucky Fried Chicken. One day Fred brought me a gift. It was a little box that I still have containing "elephant seeds" made where he served the Lord. Craftsmen of India had meticulously carved tiny elephant shapes out of ivory, some the size of a fly, others nearly as small as a gnat, yet their elephant shapes were distinct. It was an amazing work of precision skill. The elephants were housed in pinto bean sized, maroon colored, hollowed shells, with tiny ivory caps (lids) that held them in their "pen." How often I have displayed these before the wondering eyes of adults and children.

But most of the students have been just out of college, young, around 21-24. And men and women who enrolled at Talbot were of all ages in between 21 and the 80's. One couple came from their very successful pecan ranch in California, hungry for the Word in their 50's. Often men who had been pastors for years sat in my classes and those of other professors, and limited as we were they told us they learned new things.

Whatever God helped me contribute to these students, Mildred had a strategic hand in. And how? She counted by praying for me, encouraging me, investing love in meals for me and washing and ironing shirts for me, doing the business matters that set me free to study and pray, and on and on. God knows. God keeps the records.

Fruit Related to People Of Various Backgrounds

Any fruit of impact I had on others I quickly attribute in some measure as also Mildred's. It was a team effort, and her faithfulness made many things of ministry work. God knows all she was and did, and God will reward her for her part in helping the students. How many students and alumni have shared with me how Mildred was a light of inspiration reflecting bright rays from the "Sun of righteousness" (cf. Mal. 4:2).

A Volvo dealer sold his Santa Rosa, CA enterprise, and came to The Master's. He hungered to steep himself in the Scriptures. He was Bob White. Before his move, Bob's wife became ill with cancer after several years of their marriage, and with three children, a son and two daughters. In a short time cancer would claim Mrs. White's young life.

The weekend before God called this dear one home on a Monday, she rallied in a courageous surge of love, got up, and went out shopping. Her heart led her to buy gifts to put into a trunk to be opened at various times long after her departure. In this treasury she placed birthday gifts and future wedding presents for her children, should they marry. Then overcome by weakness she sank down to rest, and God took her a few hours later. Bob, left single, in due time remarried, again to a godly woman, Teri. This fair lady accompanied him to his classes at The Master's Seminary, gave rapt attention, and drank in truths of the Word as I taught. Her tribute to Mildred appears in Chapter 29 in the Master's Seminary part.

When I heard the story of the Whites' background, I felt quite unworthy. Yet I have been entrusted with a very high privilege to teach people on fire for God like these.

Today Bob is the Vice-President for Development and Operations at the seminary, a key man assisting Dick Mayhue, Senior Vice-President and Dean. A more joyous, engaging couple than Bob and Teri White one never meets. Their home is, for us at the seminary, "The White House."

Students in both seminaries have come from a great variety of main occupations. Some of these were artists, editors, painters, archers, military men, a baseball talent scout, a man who set the national land speed record in auto racing, cowboys, even bronco busters, dentists, doctors, a heart surgeon, mathematicians, engineers, farmers, All-Americans in baseball, football, basketball, tennis, and swimming, chiropractors, therapists, ocean surfers, lawyers, a President's body guard, a yo yo champion who could snuff out a cigarette at eight feet, magicians, a former pick-pocket artist whom Christ transformed, soloists, pastors, youth directors, and church Bible teachers. And how many more one could add.

One buster of wild broncos told me he had stayed on one famous bucker that could leap very high and be gone from earth a long time. This rider said he had to send a telegram down to let his boss know what day he would be back to the ground!

Other students were former "hippies," auto mechanics, a heavy equipment mechanic, university presidents, college professors, coaches, authors, track stars, a pro football place kicker, a wide receiver, and a lineman, a starter on the UCLA basketball team, missionaries to many countries, restaurant managers and waiters, pilots of jets and bombers, house building contractors, cabinet makers, movie actors, airport shuttle drivers, and band performers.

The most published author who was at one time a student in a class I taught (Galatians) is John MacArthur of 1966–67. R. Kent Hughes is another from the 1966–1970 period.

One of my students, Paul Felix, a very diligent faculty member now at The Master's Seminary, is the father of Allyson Felix, a USC graduate, who set the world record for an 18-year old in the women's 200 meter sprint, and later won the silver medal at this distance in the 2004 and 2008 Olympic Games.

A former cowboy from the range in Wyoming, Tony Arnds, told me how he came to know Christ. He was lost, and had a Christian rancher as a boss. One day the boss took Tony in a pick-up to a remote line shack on a snowy day, and gave him his sack of lunch and a Bible with the words, "Just spend the day here, read this book, and I'll be back to get you tonight." All Tony had to occupy his time was keep poking wood into the stove to maintain a fire and reading. God got hold of his heart, and a few days later the Father drew him to know the Savior (John 6:44). Then the cowpoke went to Bible School, and eventually showed up in classes at The Master's Seminary. Today he is the Pastor of Potter Valley Bible Church in California.

Ralph Drollinger was the UCLA basketball star. At 7-1, he played four years for the Bruins (1972-75) when they won three national titles (1972, 1973, 1975). These were parts of 11 in their history. Two of Ralph's playing years were during an incredible UCLA run of winning seven national titles in a row (1967–73)! Later, he was a pro player on the Athletes in Action touring team. Today he heads up Capitol Ministries. This work is leading many politicians and family members to Christ as the ministry expands in putting full-time workers in state capitols. Ralph, a very godly example, jokes about his height, "With me, you [at The Master's Seminary] have the largest seminary student body in America!"

One brilliant student of law at Harvard climbed to the attic of the house where he was staying. His studies done, he remembered a pile of books up there. Rummaging through these, he came across a Bible. The thought struck him that he never had read this, so he took it downstairs to know something about this phase of literature. The Spirit of God put a burning desire in his life to know Christ personally (John 6:44), and he found himself telling the Savior he wanted Him to come in. This was Bill Bjork, who came across the country to Talbot, and won the top awards for preaching, Bible, Hebrew, and all-around student.

Bill became pastor of a church in Capistrano Beach, CA, and invited me to preach at his installation. Later he was a pastor in Simi Valley, CA, and the church invited me to speak at his "This is Your Life" night. Bill went on to pastor one of the three largest churches in Phoenix, Bethany Bible Church, and asked me to preach when he was in-. stalled. Today, years later, he is Pastor of Grace Bible Church for senior citizens in Sun City near Phoenix.

Bill was my grader for several years at Talbot. In an incredible way he seemed to know just what to say in the margins of papers. I would check these later, think how uncanny the wording was, and exclaim, "That's exactly what I would have said!"

David Hamner came from Phoenix to Talbot as a magician, a ministry in which he continued with "The Illusion Company" after graduating. His sister Mary also earned an M. A. in Bible under my supervision, finishing with her thesis on God's Kind of Woman in Proverbs 31. One day David sat in the Matthew/Romans class of about 70 students. Keeping his act hidden from me as I lectured, he was multiplying silver dollars in his clever fingers, causing nearby students to chuckle. Suddenly a coin slipped out of his nifty fingers, then rolled and rolled and rolled with a sound which, when I dropped into silence, was obvious throughout the room. Dave's face became "as red as a beet."

Another of my students, Bob Achilles, had been a band performer and so accomplished that he played in Carnegie Hall. He vaulted to the top of his profession but was in agony about his empty life. Then God saved him, he found fullness in Christ, and he came to Talbot, a man of voracious hunger for the Word. He pastored for many years in California, and two of his sons, Jim and David, later were my students in The Master's Seminary. Jim also became a pastor.

One Korean man had such difficulty with the English language that students confided to me that he was up many entire nights struggling to get assignments done in the dorm. Yet he turned his papers in on time. I felt so unworthy to be that man's teacher, and prayed hard for him. Whatever faithfulness I showed him was in part also from Mildred who was faithful to me. After he had graduated, I heard that he had become pastor of one of Australia's largest evangelical churches, a Korean ministry.

Again I thanked God for the indescribable privilege of ministering to a man of such motivation and zeal for his Lord. And Mildred's share in making this a reality was extremely conspicuous.

Fruit Expanding to the Nations (cf. below on Types of People)

Our ministry, made to fly in a profound measure by Mildred's faithful "helpmeet" services, reached out to touch the nations. Students have come from various countries and many have gone as missionaries to far away fields. An old song about this had as its theme, "a story to tell to the nations."

A tribute to this daughter of God came unexpectedly in a letter from her earliest pastor's wife, Orla Freer. I found it in a folder where Mildred had filed it. Orla's husband David was minister at the Schultzville, New York church (1932–1947) where Mildred's family were members in her early years. Orla suffered the shocking loss of David in the Currey silo during the 1949 fire (a story recounted early in this book). Then God helped her outlive her deceased husband by 47 years until 1996. Mildred often wrote her through all those years. Orla, near the end of her life, finished a book mentioned earlier, *Moments at the Manse* [minister's home], privately printed about 1994–1996. Late in life she said in a letter to Mildred as she recalled the children at Schultzville, "You were the only child I remember there who prayed for people's salvation."

God puts a child's Christ-centered prayers down as fruit.

In my Bible classes were men, and at Talbot even women, from America, even Alaska, Australia, Africa, Brazil, Canada, China, Croatia, the former Soviet Union, the Czeck Republic, England, France, Germany, Greenland, Haiti, India, Ireland, Japan, Mexico, New Zealand, the Philippines, Romania, Spain, Yugoslavia, and other countries.

Graduates from The Master's Seminary have founded area seminaries in several key spots in the world—three in Russia, one in Croatia, one in South Africa, one in Germany, one in Mexico City, and others. In addition, Robb Provost went to an Islamic country, Albania, with a passion he stated in the TMS chapel "to break the back of Islam." He won friends among certain government officials at the capital, started "The Lincoln Center" in a building that formerly had been a stronghold of an anti-god political dictator, and teaches people computer "savvy" as well as English. Hundreds have come to know Christ there. Robb's father, Bob, was vice-president of The Master's College at the time I began to teach at The Master's Seminary, and a few years later (1994) became president of the Slavic Gospel Association. Bob has distinguished himself as a key, beloved leader, selfless, apostle-like, a dynamo in reaching many for Christ in the former Soviet Union and other countries.

It peaks my joy to go to the annual March "Shepherd Conference" at Grace Community Church in Sun Valley, CA, where from 2,000 to 3,300 pastors and other Christian workers and laymen gather from the world to hear messages, receive training in seminars, secure books for ministry, and share experiences. For while milling through the vast crowd or sitting in the patio, I get to talk with scores of alumni Mildred's life touched through me. They have come back from their service in various venues of the globe. Some of the privilege is just in being inspired by what God has wrought in these places, as fruit of us faculty and our wives is expanded in fruit our students bear (2 Tim. 2:2). God knows.

Fruit in Writings

My writings are to a very great extent also Mildred's fruits. Her setting me free, her keeping me going, the spiritual atmosphere she fostered, and her frequent wise perspectives, were profound contributions to prosper these writings into fulfillment. She kept encouraging me to spend time faithfully, and so took care of household matters that she cleared my way. She also taught me to use a computer, which cleared the way for several of the writings.

I have listed earlier writings God let me do on John 15, appraisals of commentaries, five volumes on prayer that Logos Bible Software published digitally, and journal articles. Mildred's helps made these possible.

A stunning letter came to me in Scotland. It was from a man formerly in a couple's class I taught. He and his wife had moved to another state, and he, facing hard trials, had come to the end of himself. One night, he confessed, his wife left the house to go on a walk and he took her absence as an opportunity to get out his revolver, place it loaded on the couch beside him, and work up the nerve to blow his brains out. He had simply had all he could take, was utterly "fed up," and just could no longer cope. His eyes fell on a book his wife had left open on a table, and curiosity stirred him to wonder why it was open like that. He went over and found the book to be my work *Abiding in Christ*. His thumb was at the page where it had been open. He noticed it was at the start of the chapter on how the Vinedresser prunes His branches (John 15:2).

"I'll read just a few lines," he told himself. He simply had to know why the book was open at this point. Finishing the first page, interest peaked his mind to read a bit more, then even further. In a few minutes he had come to the end of the chapter. God spoke to him to see his trial in the light of His purpose to prune him and make his life more fruitfully usable. Hope's reason for living got hold of him. He broke down before the Lord, confessed his sin, put away his gun, and stood up to life. When his wife came back from her walk, he was delighted, not dead.

Much that Mildred did when I was writing that book (1973) early in my teaching career had its part in saving that man's life. He was set free to live out many years as a branch in the Christ who is the Vine.

Many of the technical points in computer expertise were never my skills. In a heavily busy teaching career, pushed hard, it was difficult to wrest free the time to learn, on my own. Mildred dedicated herself at home to develop my word processing computer "savvy." With her clear and workable pointers, I "got the hang of it"—but not nearly what our faculty secretary knew.

My precious companion's patient mentoring would make possible a lot of writing—some of around 50 book-length syllabi that were virtual commentaries, for classes, articles for journals, books, and even eventually the 2,900-page "encyclopedia" on prayer, *An Exposition on Prayer in the Bible*, Logos Bible Software, Nov., 2007 (cf. writings, Chapter 6). That work took me 15 years as it gave several pages of exposition on each prayer passage of the Bible and every reference to prayer (except that in the 150 Psalms, the great number of psalms caused me to select just 21 examples and incorporate with these key things from other psalms). All in all, expositions appear on more than 1,000 prayer passages.

Mildred's strategic fruit of love in this helped make possible a work that people are using for their spiritual lives and expounding of God's Word in many countries.

In addition to writings that Chapter 6 lists, God has helped me produce book-length syllabi on such subjects as Genesis, Exodus, Leviticus, Old Testament Survey (2 vols.), Matthew, The Parables of Jesus, The Pastoral Epistles, The Epistles of John, The General Epistles (James, 1 Peter, Jude), Revelation, Problem Passages, Manners and Customs of the Bible, Hermeneutics, Biblical Exposition of Prayer, and More Helps on Prayer.

Most of these syllabi—from different stagers in the 45 years of teaching—are on alumni study shelves or on desks, in hands, or in libraries of schools alumni have helped establish in the various countries. I have made them available only to my students, for themselves and their ministries.

Fruit of us faculty members and our wives begets other fruit.

At least 70 students whom we on the two seminary faculties had in classes have in turn published books themselves. Some examples are: Irven Busenitz, Nathan Busenitz, David Black, Mick Boersma, Murray Brett, Wallace Emerson, David Farnell, John Feinberg, Jim George, Greg Harris, Larry Helyer, James de Young, Alex Montoya, John MacArthur, David Nicolas, John Feinberg, Jack Hughes, R. Kent Hughes, Dawson McAllister, Mike Abendroth, Pat Abendroth, Philip de Courcy, Tom Finley, Alan Gomes, Clint Arnold, Tim Gombis, Jerry Root, Jim Walker, Daniel K. K. Wong, Michael Vlach, Matt Waymeyer, Rick Kress, Donald Ekstrand, David Turner [Grace Theological Seminary], and a host of others.

The topics these alumni books have covered deal with many key issues running the gamut of the faith. Examples are theology in general, salvation, the spiritual life, baptism, commentaries on Bible books, prayer, witnessing, hope, Christian amusements, the overcomer in Scripture, prophecy, preaching, exegetical method, suffering, Old and New Testament survey, how to interpret the Bible, defending the faith, introduction to Christianity, working with high school students, and so many other subjects with God at the center.

The more widely known among the authors are: John MacArthur, John Feinberg, Clint Arnold, Irven Busenitz, Alex Montoya, David Black, R. Kent Hughes, and David Turner. MacArthur has authored individual commentaries on most books of the New Testament, and issued *The MacArthur Study Bible* and *The MacArthur Bible Commentary*, both on the entire Bible. Kent Hughes' commentaries are on several New Testament books.

God keeps the records of what Mildred and other wives like her have done that bore fruit in the influence which shaped others' lives. He also keeps accounts of fruit in those who have given to us, prayed for us, or ministered to us in so many other loving ways.

Fruit in Types of People

As Mildred's life was fruitful for the Lord, her fruit profoundly helped contribute to any fruit the Lord gave me in leading others into fruitful lives.

God sent to my classes single men, single women (at Talbot), married men, married women (at Talbot; and some wives have sat in classes of both seminaries), several sets of two brothers, one set of three brothers, several fathers and sons, one father and two sons (Bob Achilles and sons Jim and David), several husbands and wives (at Talbot), a brother and sister (Dave and Mary Hamner at Talbot), and two sisters (Talbot).

The God of believers, whoever they are, has given Mildred and me and faculty couples like us, folk of all the colors of skin. These have come to classes, or been in other venues centering in the Word, in churches, retreats, homes, special meals, and other occasions. God has brought beloved ones of the various colors, the black, the brown, the red skinned, the yellow and the white. "Black and yellow, brown and white, they are precious in His sight." He who has a heart for the nations (Gen. 12:3; Ps. 67; Dan. 7:27) and taught Peter that His gospel is for all peoples (Acts 10) impressed on Mildred and me early that the message is for those of any hue. How many the precious brothers and sisters from so many lands with whom we have had fellowship.

Dear Daniel Wong, a Chinese student at Talbot who later earned his doctorate at Dallas Seminary (1995) and now teaches Bible at The Master's Seminary, came several times to our home. As was his Oriental custom, he would pause on the front porch, remove his shoes, then enter. Our hearts have always bonded in a treasure that only God could create. Daniel finished his degrees at Talbot, then invited me to lunch. To my surprise, he drove first to a men's clothing store and insisted that I choose a new suit, shirt, belt, and tie. Only after this did he take me to the lunch.

The Lord has extended to me the privilege of officiating in the marriages of several, even men and women who were in classes. Likewise, He granted me the joy of serving in many ordination councils and speaking at services for these, or installations of pastors, speaking in alumni-led churches, or giving series where they were pastors. I went from Mildred's loving presence and acts that shaped me to be, I hope, something like her with these people.

Then, when I would return home, I had the glad sense that Mildred had bathed my ministry in her prayers. Whatever fruit God bore through me was most certainly also in candid reality partly her fruit too. John 15:7-8 makes clear the intimate link between prayer while abiding in Christ and the multiplication this fosters—"much fruit."

Fruit in Several Schools

With Mildred's various helps, I have taught either full-time or in special days or weeks in many schools: Talbot, The Master's, Dallas Seminary, Grace Theological Seminary, Arizona Bible Institute (and later the Arizona College of Bible, still after that The Arizona Bible College), The Los Angeles Training School, and one summer (1968) a week's messages on John 15 in Campus Crusade for Christ's College Briefing Conference at Arrowhead Springs, San Bernardino, CA.

In the two summers of 1981 and 1982, I accepted invitations to be one of the guest lecturers in the doctoral program of Grace Theological Seminary, Winona Lake, IN. In the first summer the subject was the Christian's future reward, and in the second Jesus' prophetical teachings in Matthew 13 and 24–25.

Guess who was at home holding me up by intercession for God's blessing.

Fruit in Counseling

A ministry of teaching and preaching catapults into counseling people. I think that due to being on campus so many days a week I have counseled in more cases than many pastors. Countless are the hours. Whatever I was privileged to do, Mildred's making it work means that the fruit was in a substantial measure hers with whom God united me. Realistically, I believe that God will appraise her contribution as more. For I always held Mildred in high esteem as an example after whom I longed to model my life.

"Oh, to be like you, dear Savior" (1 John 2:6)! And "oh, to be like you, Mildred, in having Him live in me too" (Gal. 2:20)!

At Talbot, I had students come for counseling from the seminary, and also walk across campus from the larger Biola College student body. Add to these quite a number of Christians from off campus who would visit. Then at The Master's Seminary and in many church visits, as well, a number drew near for counsel. Then there were the mountain retreats, the times after ordination services, the phone calls, the "snail mail," and the emails. I have spent many thousands of hours pouring into people answers from God's Word. Through the years, too, it was a privilege to impact a great number of students in discipleship meetings. Quite a number gathered with me at Talbot, and others were a part of The Master's Seminary student registration each semester. In the latter, I would lead anywhere from four to eight each semester when in full-time teaching (1987–2005). Since then even in part-time, one day a week teaching I have had several students in discipleship "huddles."

Many, too, have sought me out in local church venues, or visited in my home. How often I have heard the words, "Dr. Rosscup, what is your interpretation of . . . ?" or "Can you explain so and so to me" or "What is your take on this?" With the advent of email, the volume of such cases has sky-rocketed.

They say "behind every good man [I hope I was] is a good woman, pushing." Mildred was always there. There for me—praying, encouraging, counseling, listening and humbly sharing her wisdom. She unselfishly allowed me to study and protected my study times, did things to put me at liberty, was always a plus and never a minus, did her great part to help our daughters follow the Savior, cheered us at meals, washed and ironed clothes in which we went out to serve God, and did innumerable other things. God knows all these gestures of service, and will be unerring to render the perfect assessment. His appraisal, no doubt, will highlight the greater fruit that abounds to Mildred's account (Phil. 4:17).

Several students of Talbot and later also a number at The Master's Seminary met often with me most of the years they were in school, talking about the Word, praying, and sharing meals together. One of these, Tony Capoccia of Talbot, a former Catholic altar boy, has for years since seminary carried on a ministry as an answer man in a Bible Billboard call-in work. After being an altar boy, he was a jet pilot, and came to Christ and then to seminary with an insatiable hunger for God's Word and a passion to lead people to Christ. Tony and I used to sit at a table in Mildred's and my back yard for prayer, and after a time Mildred would carry our lunch out to us.

Another student kept saying to me, "I want to be a man of God. Oh, that God will make me a man mighty in prayer! I want to preach His Word powerfully." And he kept coming to pump me on his lists of questions about different facets of the Christian life. How many the men who sat in meetings immersed in the unfathomable riches of Christ (Eph. 3:8), who now hold forth the Word in far-flung pulpits.

When a woman gives her life to Christ to count eternally with her husband, God sees the reality of fruit that is hers, and not just his.

Fruit in Hospitality

How amazing is God's enablement. What a God of making possible the impossibilities. Though often ill with severe breathing difficulty, Mildred also knew the

Lord's grace to lift her up and give her many times of some strength and a measure of freedom to welcome guests in our home. Her welcome was always fragranced with genuineness, her conversation delightful, her grace distinctive, her meals enjoyable.

In a life of much privation, stuck away, she dearly treasured those special moments to be with others. She even converted them into pageants of beautiful service.

Our hospitality in many of the earlier years drew a fairly steady stream of people from the Currey or Rosscup families. Often visitors were from the large Fraley family from which my mother Lola was one of twelve children. We had in our home uncles, aunts, and cousins, as well as my siblings and their families. Also frequent in the early Talbot years were area alumni of Dallas Seminary. We hosted several get-togethers. And from time to time we invited students who leaped to be at a "home away from home" for Friday night or Saturday parties.

Mildred had a "knack" of putting on the dining room table a pot of baked beans, along with buns, wieners, potato salad, coffee, tea, soft drinks, and brownies or chocolate chip cookies. I would help in ways she would let me. Sometimes we would munch on these good things and watch Saturday NCAA college football games, then play our own games and talk and laugh all afternoon.

If wearied, Mildred would finish all she needed to do. Then she would graciously excuse herself to rest, and the party would go on. Guests knowingly were sensitive to her kindness, yet her need, and felt her presence through the entire time.

When I have traveled to places and seen alumni, I often hear anew their joy at what these times of hospitality meant in their hearts. They have bragged about Mildred, and how she pleasantly made them feel happily at home. Did she bear fruit in those times? To me it is beyond question.

Fruit in Email Answers

Once computers came into vogue, an enormous email traffic began. People found this means of contact so quick and easy that faculty members like me started getting an incredible upsurge in mail. It was difficult logistically for teachers to handle. Here came more questions seeking counsel on what to do to resolve pastoral problems. Or what about the meaning of this Bible passage or that, for some lay person had stumped the pastor, and he was scurrying for his life. Or which books were good on this subject or the other?

Life is interesting. On a given day I may get an email from somebody I never met, or from a student, or a person a student has encouraged to contact me, or an alumnus, or a contact an alumnus counseled to write me. Many sorts of questions are put to me. Oh, if I had collected all those questions and answers! Would they not comprise many hefty volumes? And were they not among the wonderful joys of living? For as Robert Speer has as a chapter title in his book *The Marks of a Man*, service is the living use of life.

So also could be the volumes of "thank you" notes that poured back. And many "thank you" cards were as aptly to Mildred for the many-faceted influence her conspicuously servant life bore in the doing of these things.

Both Mildred (on her computer) and me on mine received a heavy traffic of digital letters from people, wherever they were in the world. Women prized Mildred's counsel, which was sage, practical, and homespun. Often in various places ladies would exude to me over their gratitude for Mildred. I myself wrote short and long answers to many sorts of biblical questions, and often asked the seminary faculty secretary to send attached material, or mail printed matter to people asking help.

Copies of faculty members' book-length class syllabi for classes found their way to various countries. Sometimes our dean would ask me to answer some query that had come to the school about a Scripture subject. In certain cases things God helped me put together were among the best materials I had done, and I could xerox these to do "double duty" as handouts for my current students. They could run into the same issues.

Shakespeare was right when he wrote: "All the world's a stage, the men and women merely players. They have their exits and their entrances, and one man in his life plays many parts." In a ministry to hundreds over the 51 years, Mildred and I played many parts, and thank God, in these He touched many lives. Of course many of the cases fade from our errant memories, but eternity will tell. For God is not unrighteous to forget our Christian work and labor of love in ministering to the saints (Heb. 6:10). And we know deeply that in whatever was wrought, "what do we have but what we received" (1 Cor. 4:7)? We owe it all to Him! To God be the glory!

Ministries that Mildred and I hope were fruit to last for eternity (John 15:16) came in many ways. There were our labors on the keyboard, screen, and printers, in the living room as hosts, in the kitchen, in gatherings of disciples, and so many other expressions.

Fruit in Family Devotions

Both Mildred and I kept up our individual, regular, personal, private devotions in the Word and in prayer. We also prayed together before meals wherever we were, and sat down after dinner to meditate heart linked with heart in family devotions. When our two daughters were growing up, they would be with us.

Various ways helped us through the years. In the earlier years we used books by Kenneth Wuest, which gave colorful word pictures in the New Testament (Philippians, 1 Peter, etc.), read a few paragraphs each night, then talked about what Wuest said. Then we prayed about pertinent concerns. Or we read a Bible passage, juiced its main ideas for a few minutes, then voiced our prayers to the Lord.

Other means were to focus on *Our Daily Bread*, a page each day, followed by our prayer. We always took a copy of this devotional from the tract rack at church for each quarter of the year. Sometimes I would read portions of a provocative Christian book, such as A. W. Tozer's *The Pursuit of God*, or E. M. Bounds' *Power Through Prayer*, or A. P. Gibbs' *Worship, the Christian's Highest Occupation*, or F. B. Meyer's *Abraham, the Obedience of Faith*, or Andrew Murray's *With Christ in the School of Prayer*, or a portion out of a Billy Graham book. One was his graphic chapter on the world of the future, heaven, in *World Aflame.*

Later, as our daughters were at different stages of their growth, I would read to them out of a book keyed to their level at the time. For example, in one long series, we used Kenneth Taylor's children's devotional book of doctrine in Romans, which put things in a simple fashion and used illustrations the girls could grasp. Later on, for instance, I read C. S. Lewis' *The Lion, the Witch, and the Wardrobe, Prince Caspian*, etc.

I sought, in leading prayers, to phrase things in words easy for our daughters to follow. And I would keep the prayers relatively brief, to the point (though even in this they sometimes felt they were too long). Later, when we had gotten the girls into bed, I read them a bedtime story, or told them some story I had heard, and prayed with them. I let them pray too, before tucking them in. Often when I could not be home at their bed-time, Mildred shared stories and talked to God with them.

Frequently we learned a prayer concern by phone, email, letter, word of mouth, radio, TV, somebody's visit, the church bulletin, or from one of the schools. I would say to Mildred, on the spot, "Let's pray." Then, if she felt a shortness of breath, I would lead us in an intercession. After this, we would go about our other labors.

I was aware that seminary wives' letters gave Mildred people and things to take to God at His throne. She was in one of the prayer groups the Master's Seminary wives set up, so she very often pleaded concerns of ladies when alone with God. If she mentioned a matter in our joint prayer vigil we took it to our heavenly Host, at His door, as He invited us to "knock, and it shall be opened" (Matt. 7:7-11). Or I would bring in a request I heard at the school or the church when Mildred had not been able to go.

A phone call might alert us to some believer's need. The two of us would sit down and usually, due to Mildred's problems getting her breath, I would lead the intercession. I was sure that she was into it also; and God knew.

Fruit in Music

I mentioned elsewhere that while studying I would often hear Mildred playing the piano or the organ in the adjoining living room. She was bearing fruit in worship. The music and messages of the words brought to us a fresh fragrance of God. Inspiration flowed with "Day by Day," "He Giveth More Grace," "Great is Thy Faithfulness," "Blessed be the Name," "My Jesus, I Love Thee," "Amazing Grace," "It Will be Worth it All," "Beyond the Sunset," "My Tribute," "Until Then," "That in All Things He Might Have the Preeminence," and other songs.

In earlier years of the marriage, the home was often permeated by the singing of George Beverly Shea, and in recent years a heart-moving Christmas album by the movie actor and singer, Burl Ives. And we always enjoyed Christmas songs by Bing Crosby. Piano numbers blessed our hearts from the skillful touches of keys by Pam Snider, wife of one of my students who has become an Associate Professor of Theology at The Master's Seminary. Pam grew up in New York later, but just a few miles from where Mildred had lived in her childhood and teen years.

Fruit in Leisure

In later years, Mildred and I enjoyed twice a day breaks relaxing in patio chairs just outside the French doors she loved. At 10 a.m. and at 3 p.m. our hearts would thrust us from whatever we were doing to sit, often with coffee or a cold drink, and gaze out across our back yard. Our feathered friends might be fluttering in the delight of our bird bath, or orchestrating their "concerts" from the Cypress trees, the huge rubber tree, or the high lines. Off in the distance was the purr of cars on one of Whittier's arteries. And at times a workman's hammer blows or the buzz of a saw were obvious in the air. Mildred loved to step out from the patio to let her eyes follow large planes flying to or coming from the huge airport, LAX.

Around us, her pots of many colored flowers lofted God's touches of beauty. A soft breeze could kiss our cheeks. A dove might become alarmed in its nest above and flutter away until it thought our departure from the patio haven left its home safe.

We chatted about this or that, or just sat in a heart understanding of silence, enjoying many things, such as the fragrance of nearby blossoms or the honeysuckle on the vines of the back fence. There might be a linnet's quest of bugs in the yard, a colorful butterfly's zig-zag antics, a trek of tiny ants like a wagon train cavalcade across the cement, or a bird winging to its nest deep in a cypress hide-out.

Occasionally I would get up to chase a stealthy killer cat away from its lurking place under cover of plants near the birds' bath.

Love and heart commitment were fruit in things dear to our kindred hearts. Another aspect of fruit was in thanking God for His uplifting things in the natural world (cf. Ps. 148).

Fruit in Giving

One commitment from the outset of our marriage was to give to God's cause. We always tithed, and at various times gave other gifts to meet some need of the moment. Our chief gifts were to Christ through the local church, and to certain missionaries.

The earlier days of youth in seminary found us just eking out an existence. But we kept up the giving. God always cared (1 Pet. 5:7) and supplied to meet our needs. We did watch our pennies responsibly at the grocery store, and were frugal as to which clothes we bought.

When seminary teaching began at Talbot in 1965, the salary was $2,700 a year. I took on extra teaching once the school had summer schools and January's "Winterim," for these extra teaching sessions helped provide what we needed to pay for medicines, clothing, furniture, and family trips. They also provided more to give to others.

Gradually we were able to donate more to missionaries, and took on contributions to several in different countries—Africa, Indonesia, Japan, the Philippines, and later Turkey, as well as the soul-winning "Wonders of Science" ministry of Dean and Terry Ortner to churches, military installations, schools, town halls, etc. When Moody discontinued the Ortners' ministry under the title, "Sermons from Science," Dean kept on, coming up with his own new name for such labors.

From time to time, God prompted giving special sums to encourage people. One joy was putting in a new garage door for an elderly lady who was fearful about safety. Another was a gift to help a Christian couple when he lost his job and was struggling in the first months of "learning the ropes" in a new field. A further one was a substantial amount to help a couple when the lady was battling breast cancer. She opened the envelope, took out the check, and simply went to pieces in sobs. Finally, regaining control of her voice, she said in a broken way, "I didn't know anybody loved us this way." A few weeks later, she was in glory. Another case was an alumnus who had been released from a teaching position due to a school's down-sizing, as he had come into dire need.

Mildred was sensitive and tender-hearted about giving to others and to Christ (Matt. 25:34-45). How I adored her for her vision. And when she told me of a longing to give, I realized her wisdom and heart. Once she brought to mind a retired missionary in need, so I quickly agreed, and off went the letter and check. On another occasion a former student mentioned in a letter his and his wife's very trying situation. We sent money, and he replied that it was a great tonic to their spirits and put food on the table.

It has been quite distinct that whenever we have opened our hearts to others' urgent needs, though we were not rich, Someone incredibly rich has acted very soon to give us a new supply (Phil. 4:19). This was usually in monies He sent to surprise us with joy. How encouraging are Jesus' true words, "Give, and it will be given to you, good measure, pressed down, shaken together, running over, they will pour into your lap. For whatever measure you deal out to others, it will be dealt to you in return" (Luke 6:38). He also said, "Freely you have received, freely give" (Matt. 10:8). We found that we could not out-give God. As Keith L. Brooks has said, "It is not what we take up but what we give up that makes us rich" (*Cream Book*, p. 30).

When I have met a person outside a restaurant hungry, I did not hand him or her money due to my uncertainty about motives. But often I would take that person inside and make sure he or she had a meal. I knew in this, too, that all the money belongs to God, and this, as well, was giving to Him. God has never forsaken us, nor permitted us to be hungry or begging bread (Ps. 37:25). As His pure Word says, He is unfailing in being our helper (Heb. 13:6). One of the fruits of the Spirit is love (Gal. 5:22-23), and faith works, for example, through countless expressions of love (Gal. 5:6).

Paul's words in 2 Cor. 8:9 tell us what is Christlike. "For you know the grace of our Lord Jesus Christ, that though He was rich, yet for your sake He became poor, that you through His poverty might become rich." He gave "His indescribable gift" (9:16). He wants us to be stewards, not stingy but responsibly generous yet careful with money, conscientious and caring, as is His own model to us.

Mildred was ever a sensitive giver. She picked this up from God. I learned much from Him and from her that blessed my spirit. How could I ever have been given such a companion? I know the answer in two words. God! Grace!

Fruit of Carefulness in Details

I tell my students it is important to take care of details. This is vital in pastoral work. It is important in anything in life.

Take an example. I was late getting home one evening, Mildred had eaten, and she was preparing tacos, just enough for me. She picked up the can of "Pam" to squirt some of its oil into the skillet before she laid the flour tortillas in. Ever alert, she suddenly stopped, blinked, and looked at the can more closely. It was not "Pam" after all. She gasped. It was ant spray! Somebody had negligently left this can where the "Pam" usually was, for we had had problems with ants on the counters. Mildred took the can of death into the garage, horrified at what she might have put into the taco skillet. She was shaking, very thankful for God protecting me, and keeping her from a sadness that would have dealt her incredible pain to the end of her days. She breathed a prayer of gratitude to God, and said:

"Satan must really hate Jim and what he's doing. He's after him, trying awfully hard to pull one of his tricks, and stop him!"

Her fruit in being careful about the details no doubt saved my life.

Jim Rickard, head of the Stewardship Services Foundation, our tax agent, and President of the Trustees at The Master's Seminary and The Master's College, can attest to her carefulness. She spent hours getting every detail right, rechecking, and being sure before we scrutinized and checked figures in a final time together. When we went to Jim, year after year, to get his official okay and file our final federal and state reports, Jim always remarked about her precision. She was a Wonder Woman even in this.

Fruit in Other Character Qualities

Scores of women have authored books to help ladies live for Christ and show forth beauties of His grace. Some of these writings are specifically on aspects in the fruit of the Spirit which Paul lists in Galatians 5:22-23, or how to be a minister's wife. I think that though Mildred never wrote a book on this, she was one of the most aggressive in putting the realities into a living book. She showed them in "shoe leather."

Mildred's life was a conspicuous example of reflecting "the fruit of the Spirit" (2 Pet. 1:5-7). All who knew her were aware of her consistent loving testimony. In her daily life what Paul exhorts stood out as a reality in her, "whatever you do, do all to the glory of God" (1 Cor. 10:31). Christ lived provocatively in her (Gal. 2:20), and His loveliness was easy to see. He was her life (Col. 3:4). She walked the talk, and the words of a youth song came to life in her, "Let the beauty of Jesus be seen in me, all His wonderful passion and purity."

In Mildred's frequent special pressures to breathe as a day of suffering followed a day of suffering, for years, she found consolation in meditating on God's Word.

One of her reflections is outlined in five points in her blue covered Bible on Daniel 12. Her meditations are:

1. Propagation (v. 2). She penciled in "waiting for Jesus," and underlined the words in v. 3, "they that be wise shall shine" and "they that turn many to righteousness [shall shine as the stars for ever and ever]."

2. Purification (v. 10a). She circled the words "Many shall be purified" and the words that follow are "and made white, and tried . . . ." Later in v. 10 she circled the words "wise" and "understand" in the phrase, "the wise shall understand."

3. Discrimination (end of v. 10). She drew a line from "understand" to the margin, where she wrote in "yes, it is wonderful," apparently in having a mind set on values God will vindicate.

4. Expectation (v. 12). She saw this theme as in her circled words "he that waiteth." From God's counsel to Daniel to "go thou thy way till the end" [of his life on earth] she drew a fifth principle, which she wrote in the margin.

5. Activation (v. 13). Mildred wrote in "Busy for Jesus." Evidently her idea was to keep occupied in serving the Lord until this life ends, and as the verse says, "for thou shalt rest and stand in thy lot [portion of reward] at the end of the days" [at the future reckoning God will have with His servants, and with all people].

Inside the blue cover of Mildred's Bible under her name, she wrote, "Do your neighbors know they have a Christian neighbor?"

This woman of God was always faithfully serving, as much as her health and strength gave liberty. She offered up a living sacrifice of worship (Rom. 12:1). To use an old saying, "there was not a lazy bone in her body." When God gave her any let-up from the breathing struggle and she felt a boost in energy, she sprang to action. Times set free to labor were special gifts of joy to her. She would be sewing, knitting, crocheting, cleaning the kitchen, preparing special dishes to freeze and get ahead, canning nectarines, hosing the patio, calling a person she could encourage, and the like. Or even if in pain she might be weeding her flower beds, painting, writing cards of cheer, or doing computer creations for missions. And she was praying, keeping tabs on business, hosting a lady at a tea or coffee fellowship, getting a hair-do to look her best, or shopping for a gift to lift somebody's spirit.

Mildred was a joyful person, a heap of fun. She kept up an attitude of cheer that even could express good humor about the oxygen tank that went with her when she had to go out. The usual, small tank was "Isabelle." A larger one was "Ichabod." And a tank at home was "R2D2." She nourished a spirit of "sweet reasonableness" (Phil. 4:5) in putting "the best spin" on things. When with others she sought to say things that would put them at ease though her breathing was often labored, a struggle was evident, and this could cause people to feel uncomfortable. She was on top of her days, and not brooding or downcast. One thing was true of us both. We always spoke well of one another to others, and we sincerely meant it.

I felt misgivings when Mildred first started using that tank on wheels and taking it to church. I feared she would feel inhibited. For it was so unusual, and it drew stares. It also was at times difficult to maneuver so that somebody did not step on it, or trip over it when a lot of people came together. But in walked Mildred, optimistic as she could be, not appearing in the least to be self-conscious. She was taking everything in stride, exuding in fellowship with others, just as if she had no tank to push or pull. What class acts!

I have heard the song, "My gal's a corker, she's a New Yorker, I buy her every-thing to keep her in style." This lady was a New Yorker, but she did not demand everything to keep her in style. Several times when checks came for my books, I gave the money to Mildred and asked her to buy something nice. Often she just never did. Our values went in another direction. But if I could rewrite those lines, they would go like this: "My gal's a corker, she's a New Yorker, I find her always joyful, riding the tide." Sometimes I would say, "What can I do for you?" She, ever the tease, would reply, "You can give me a million dollars." Both of us would chuckle. We both had God's riches that made a million in the bank mere "peanuts" (Phil. 4:19).

Peace was a radiance in Mildred's face. She was composed, content, and pleasant in the adequacy that the Lord was to her. And she was a testimony along the lines of the saying, "great saints are only great receivers." She exemplified the one-liner, "I take, He undertakes." She knew how to rest in her Savior, and not be out of sorts, of a morose spirit, or unpredictable in mood. In her experience of sufferings, God displayed His sufficiency in her life. In all frankness, she was more than a conqueror through Him who loved her.

She certainly was long-suffering. We took in a college-age girl to give her a temporary home when her desperate call came from a motel. She claimed to be a Christian. Her story was that she had had a falling out with her parents, whom she said would have nothing to do with Christ, and the father tried to molest her. We gave her a room, and Mildred was at home much of the time. About three weeks passed, and it kept getting clearer and clearer that the girl was an inveterate liar. She also let her room become a sort of "pig pen," and despite her agreeing with our request not to do so, she invited men to visit her when neither of us were at home. I walked in unexpectedly one afternoon and a bit after the "tip off" sound of the front door opening, a man startled me, coming out of her bedroom. Mildred was very long-suffering in trying to turn our guest to give her life over to the Lord in truth.

One Friday night a much older man, quite an unsavory fellow, came alone to pick Tara up. They told us this was to serve people in another city. Both were clear that she would be back the next day, then she did not show up until the next Wednesday, dragging in quite filthy, wasted, and evasive in eyes. Mildred and I had prayed and sensed that signs were adding up to immoral escapades, whether in our home when she caught us gone, or in times Tara was out overnight. On this occasion, when she came in the several days late, Mildred confronted her anew about her lying. She had no answer "that would fly" and was arrogant, evasive, flippant, and cutting. So Mildred asked her to pack her things and leave. She phoned a man to ask if she could move in with him.

The girl was haughty and "in a huff" of anger and hatefulness. She stalked stiffly toward her packed Volkswagen. Then she turned to sputter venom to me as I stood at the garage door. I felt compelled to speak [I have changed her name to guard her identity]:

"Tara, we tried so hard, and for a long time, to be kind to you. You yourself just kept misusing this." She later showed up at our home two times, quite unexpectedly, and threatened Mildred with boasts of how she could cut a person in two. But we trusted the Lord, our "shield" (Ps. 5:12). He kept us from any harm in carrying out her tough talk of how she could get even. And she never sought to make things right about her going against her promises, her glib lying, her spiteful spirit, and her lack of appreciation.

Mildred was gentle. She could speak softly and put people at rest. I never heard her say anything that was rough, abrasive, abusive, or inconsiderate. Other women were drawn to her sweet-tempered and gracious mood and her tender speaking that showed sincerity in a caring, sincere interest. She was good, meek in a way of not vaunting herself, and always respectful of others. Faithfulness was her disciplined tempering (1 Cor. 4:2). She was one of the best all-around Spirit-controlled Christians I have ever known. This is saying a lot since I have been with thousands, and because, with her breathing trials, she faced indescribable hardships many a time.

When she took her medications, she always was very disciplined (Gal. 5:23) and guarded to take only as much as the doctor had prescribed. Some people would take more if they were hurting, as she was, to try to gain more relief. She would not yield to misuse, but bore up bravely when the breathing was so great a struggle.

Another way she expressed self-control was in getting up to prepare meals rather than choosing what would make her life easier. She always insisted to take care of her Jim and her Dianne and Carolyn. It brought tears to my eyes, and we stood in awe and admired her!

"Mildred, I can get supper, you just rest," or "I'll go out and bring us something," I would say. Often she would reply with something like, "No, Jim, you need to study [or she would mention some other thing]. I can do this. Later I can rest." So she would take charge in getting a meal, I would set the table, and sometimes peel and later mash the potatoes, chop cabbage and make coleslaw, slice tomatoes, and set the table. After supper I often washed the dishes. But if she knew that I was under pressure due to a heavy schedule, she would push me aside gently and emphatically make it clear that she would do this work. She would wash dishes for a time, lean on the counter while waiting to get her breath, then get back to her task.

It was difficult even for me to awaken during the night, and find her no longer beside me. I would go into another room to find her seeking relief from her breathing machine. The pain I felt from her hurting was just about more than I could take. Or her medications would cause her not to be able to sleep, and she would be playing a card game to keep herself occupied, and as much as possible her mind off of her hardship. She would urge me to "go back to bed," for "I'll be alright. I'll get some rest later."

Now, after a life very well lived, she rests eternally (Rev. 14:12-13).

Other qualities her Lord weaved into her life were a very great wisdom, sub-mission, patience, and utter commitment to the ministry. She was always considerate to make sure that she sprang me free to study, write, spend vigils in private prayer, meet with people, take walks, go on trips, or make phone calls.

She treasured it as a great prize to be with any friend. In her later years the breathing struggle made it necessary for her to rest even far more and be confined more of the time at home. Even then, it was a special celebration, when she could summon even a bit of strength, to go out with ladies. She was jubilant over annual birthday lunches with Lorraine Smotherman, wife of a long-time Wycliffe Bible Translators leader. Other highlights were in lunches with Shirley Holloman, wife of a professor of theology at Talbot School of Theology; Donna Rigsby, wife of a professor of Old Testament at Talbot; Pat Denind, long-time friend from ABI student days; and Jackie Jenkins, retired missionary to Japan And the visits of Kathy Edwards from out of state brought her to a peak of joy in friendship's excitement.

Things she said showed me that it was always a joyous highlight when Kathy would come by, stay overnight, and visit. Kathy would drive from Tucson, AZ on her way to see her father and mother in Springville in the hills near Porterville, CA, and stop for fellowship both going and coming back. I would hear the ladies laughing in the living room, and sometimes would help Mildred by taking coffee and cookies or ice cream in to them. Or when Kathy would phone, or write a "snail mail" letter, I could tell by Mildred's rejuvenated face and her talk that this dear friend's thoughtfulness had "made her day."

Mildred was resourceful. If she took a notion to rearrange the furniture while I was away so as to surprise me with a fresh look, she moved the heaviest objects. She was ever the strong farm girl, and love found a way. And if I was having a hard time, as when my dean assigned me six classes, a double load, or at another time six committees, she would do whatever might lighten my life. Examples were washing the car, or taking my suits to the cleaners. When I or our daughters were sick, she was there for us with a thermometer, cough syrup, hot water and salt for gargling, pills, and a "mother hen" care.

In one long period what was required of me at Talbot Seminary was extremely heavy, with classes, committee meetings, counseling, and the like. It was "sink or swim." A couple was staying briefly in our home, and one morning when I returned from going to get breakfast donuts, the man and I looked out and saw Mildred in the back yard mowing the grass. I felt so horrified, sheepish and convicted over my delay to do that task, and hurried out to take over the mower. She could sit in the patio and rest. My heart kept rebuking me, "don't ever let this happen again!"

And how clever she was to provoke others to chuckle at funny things she said. So she could turn them from pity for her breathing struggles to bright optimism about things to which she could steer a conversation.

She was talented on the piano or organ. Her father's gifts of girlhood lessons paid huge dividends. When hurting, or having to be alone as I was away or at home but needing to prepare for a ministry, she would sit down and her fingers would perform magic on the keys. She would play some Christian song and hum the words about faith, or patience, or sufficiency, or prayer. She knew how to transform her suffering into glorifying the Lord.

Being considerate was one of this great lady's hallmarks. I would say, "I want to be with you when you go to the doctor." She usually would say, "That isn't necessary, Jim. I'll be all right. You go and study." She responded in servant concern even when another was also trying to be considerate.

Often when we were on vacations such as in the mountains at Big Bear, Mildred would set aside time to shop and find treats. These were to give to the neighbor children when we got home. Or it was fun for her to look for Christmas or birthday gifts far ahead of time.

Her being thoughtful was clear in another way too. Frequently just to keep herself looking neat for God, me, others, or for family celebrations, Mildred would phone and get an appointment with "Howard," her hair dresser. Sometimes I would go with her and get her breathing machine into and out of the car. I would sit in a Burger King restaurant studying where I could watch for her to come out, then go put the machine back into the car, and tell her how nice her hair looked.

I drive by that hair-do place after her home-going and instinctively my heart erupts. I find myself thanking God over and over again. How He helped her get ready to go there, walk to the car, drive, get out of the car, take her oxygen tank, and walk to get herself "dolled up." How bountiful are the things God does, and helps us do (Ps. 107:8)!

As Mildred grew older, and certain medicines to enable her to breathe dealt side effects of causing her to gain weight or have a puffy face, I realized she could not help this. She had to breathe. But being heavier troubled her. She did not think she looked nice anymore, and did not even want to give out recent pictures since she thought she did not look as nice as in her younger years. I would tell her that she was a very attractive lady, which she was, that I was always proud of her, and this was the truth. From what other women told me, they too thought she was a very nice looking person. And her inner beauty exuded its brightening adornment in her face, her speaking, and her actions (Titus 2:10).

Another thing I admired about Mildred was her superbly high moral standards. She was as pure as a lily. She always put on enough clothing so that she might not appear, in any suggestive way, to be unchaste. She felt disdain for women on TV who were lustfully bold and provocative with outrageously scanty clothing that deliberately showed off much of their bodies, was obviously planned to be titillating, or of downright indecency. Her language, too, was ever of a high, holy, and good taste. Once when a Christian friend passed on to her an email piece that was supposedly good to provoke a laugh, yet a bit off color, Mildred candidly wrote back a kind note saying that she did not want to receive things to count as funny if they might not please the Lord. The friend faced up to this discernment, thanked her for the soft rebuke, and learned something about being unquestionably careful to honor the Lord Christ (I Cor. 10:31; Phil. 4:8; Col. 3:17, 23). All should glorify God, nothing be off-color. Whatever is pure, think on this. Let your light shine, not be smudged with dirt (Matt. 5:16). Do not make sport of sin.

Was every thing in her life just right? None of us are perfect, and we all have our "feet of clay " To be candid, any bothersome things were few and far between. Yes, she could be hard headed occasionally, and insist on her opinion. Often she was right, but now and then she did not see the right spin on things. We all have been there. Her motives were kind even when we disagreed. She could sometimes choose neckties or shirts for me that to her taste were the greatest, but I felt were of drab colors. She could be a "pack rat," saving everything in a spirit that was frugal and resourceful. In earlier years, she would park the car so close to the garage door that several times I had to go back it up before I could get out and open the garage door to drive it inside. She did not think that was a problem, and I should have been more patient. Sometimes, too, she could put a painful misunderstanding on what I said, read something in that I never even remotely meant at all. But do not others, men and women, all imperfect, fail in such ways?

How few, actually, were the things that disturbed me. By comparison, I had so much to learn, and one lesson was patience. Her life was a continuing testimony in patience—in coping with her breathing, in waiting long on God for strength to do what her body often was not able to do but her heart prized, and so many other ways.

I have read many books on Christian suffering. Mildred's life itself was one of the finest "books," a veritable school of lessons that spoke to me.

In all her suffering, this lady never went to pieces, or angled for pity. She endured, I think as Moses, "as seeing Him who is unseen" (Heb. 11:27). How I ever could have been given the privilege of being her husband is of a sheer and wonderful bounty that only unfathomable grace can explain. I esteem her as one "of whom the world was not worthy" (Heb. 11:38). I have been around thousands of people who loved God in seminaries and churches in many states, and have read a great number of biographies or autobiographies about faithful believers. Without stretching anything, Mildred's consistent life for Christ, close up to me, was one of the fairest of the fair. It displayed being like Christ in countless living audios and videos, and it was a pageant of examples to see this drama enacted day by day.

How much light God has given for which He will hold me accountable!

Now that Mildred is in heaven, my desire is to live and strive to carry on the things that were precious to us both. One apt expression of this is in 2 Corinthians 5:14-15, the idea of God's love controlling us so that we live not for ourselves but for Him who died and rose again on our behalf. The essence of that is also up front in Galatians 2:20.

In our church patio a lady whose name I do not now recall shared with me what she said to our daughter Carolyn when Carolyn was small, "I heard some in the class complaining, but you spoke nicely." Carolyn replied with words like, "Mommy taught us to do what's right, and not complain." Reminds me of the person who asked a preacher what was the best translation of the Bible. The preacher gave her some possibilities, then ended by saying, "but the best translation is the translation into my daily life."

Mildred focused on listening courteously when people spoke. She never cut in, and was respectful to give others liberty to speak. Then she would respond in some apt, interested, uplifting way. And if it was a case of others needing counsel, many have told me that she could say what was down to earth, practical, sensible, where the rubber meets the road, and express much in a few words. In these times as in others what Jesus pictured was true, if one believes on Him, "out of his innermost being shall flow rivers of living water" (John 7:37-39).

She was ever kind and a "hit" with members of my family, and my friends. My mother always spoke in the highest admiration for her. My sisters each often told me of how she did something that helped when it really counted, or sent some thoughtful gift that "made my day." My friends would remark about what a nice person my wife was, and the boost it was to meet her. Whether in our home or with her out in public, I always felt confident of her poise, class, good taste, and congeniality.

Mildred made many 40-minute drives from Whittier to "baby sit" the grandsons Zachary and Benjamin. When they were a bit older she went to "boy sit." She or I would set two oxygen tanks, each good for six hours, behind the front seat. She then would breathe with the help of a tube that reached her as she drove.

The bottom line was that she, a branch in the vine, in union with Christ, bore "much fruit" (John 12:24; 15:4, 8), fruit that will last forever (v. 16). Fruit that her Savior lived through her as in Galatians 2:20 abounded to her account (Phil. 4:17).

She was my sweetheart wife, my best friend after Jesus, and my surest close-up model, consistently, of what I felt Christ would do. Life with her was a blessed seminar of growth. Oh, that I had learned better! In this good school, I saw Christ living in a person ever yielded to Him. Mildred's testimony helped me realize the truth of the slogan my eyes riveted on week after week on the back Sunday School wall in a church's little upper room before I ever came to know the Savior.

> "Just one life, 'twill soon be past,
> Only what's done for Christ will last."

Mildred with Her Grandchildren

Mildred with her grandsons on their porch in sweaters she made them. She fulfilled an ambition to be a beloved "grammy," as her own "grammy" Theda had been to her.

28

Ladies' Tributes to Mildred

Her Early Life and Bible Training (Up to 1954)

MEMORIES OF LADIES WHO knew Mildred at different stages of her life tell her story. It is a story of a heart in love with her Lord.

The first vignette, from childhood years, is from Lois Knapp (now Mosher), who lived on a farm just a quarter of a mile from the Curreys. The two girls often played together in the yards, or strolled through the woods at Clinton Corners, New York, before the Currey family moved far away to another farm near Oneonta, and even after that to land near Unadilla.

Lois Knapp Mosher

Lois later married and lived in Elmsford, New York, and after that until today in Katonah, still in that state. Mildred, I and our daughters visited Jay and Lois for a day in Elmsford in 1969 when we were on a month vacation trip driving from California to the eastern United States. Lois shares memories that come back to mind.

"Growing up on neighboring farms in the 1930's [after Mildred's birth in 1932] was a time of simpler things. Neighbors knew each other and were concerned for one another. We children attended a one room school, grades 1-8, which further bonded the rural community together.

"So it was that Mildred and I became friends and played together. She had her two brothers, but for nine years I was an only child. Our winters included sledding down snowy hills in the fields and on the dirt roads. Though we were cautious, very few cars interrupted our play. We did not have all the modern technology to distract us.

"Skating on thick ice of the farm ponds was another pastime, and later skiing. Inside, we listened to 'The Lone Ranger' or 'Captain Midnight.' In the summer, we swam and fished in the creek that ran through both of our farms. Another girl, Gertrude, who was a little older and from another nearby farm, often joined us.

"Since Mildred was about nine months older than I, she was always one grade ahead. All the students and sometimes the teacher would play baseball or 'Prisoner's Base' in the cow pasture bordering the Bear Market School yard. Other games were hop scotch, kick the can, and hide and seek.

"One school incident comes back. Mildred always excelled in academics and in behavior. But she decided to play a trick on her older brother Richard. Since he was larger, one desk seat had been unbolted and removed so that a captain's chair could be fitted in for him. When Richard was not aware of it, Mildred pulled the chair away as he stood up, and when he sat back down he fell on the floor. The teacher had to reprimand Mildred, but it also was a lesson for us all never to do that.

"Mildred's father taught her how to drive their John Deere tractor during the haying season. Her father gave her a pony which she named 'Star' because of the white marking on the pony's face. Mildred sometimes visited her grandparents, George and Theda, at Liberty, New York, in parts of the summer vacations.

"On Sundays, Mildred and her family would worship at a Congregational Church near tiny Schultzville. My family were members of a Congregational church in another town. Mildred invited me to her Daily Vacation Bible Schools.

"Shortly after Mildred became a teenager and a few years after her health became a problem [age 8], her family moved near Oneonta, later near Unadilla in foothills of the Catskills not far from Rip van Winkle country. I visited her there one summer day after her high school graduation [1948]. We took a stroll up a lane on the farm. We had to stop often for Mildred to catch her breath. I could see how difficult her breathing problem already was.

"That visit was the last that I saw Mildred until the year [summer, 1969] that you as a family stopped to visit in Elmsford. But over the years we kept in touch via our letters. As we grew older, we began sending birthday and anniversary cards. It has been rewarding to correspond with a childhood friend over the years of a lifetime.

"Mildred's marked faithfulness to Sunday School and church laid a solid foundation for the path her life's journey would take as she grew into a strong Christian."

Margaret Wright Blosser

Margaret is the daughter of the Wrights, members of the Unadilla Baptist Church with the Curreys. She married Leon Blosser, and they spent several years as missionaries in Egypt, and now for some years in pastoral ministry in the States. She was a bit younger than Mildred, and only recalls a little.

"I knew of Mildred's struggles with breathing even while she was in Unadilla and after she excelled at the Arizona Bible Institute and Arizona State. The two of us spent parts of summers leading Vacation Bible School in three or four towns. Your [Jim's] picture went with us to each new place, by the way" [so that had to be sometime in 1954–1956 when we were dating].

Valeene Hayes

Valeene directed the ABI sextet in which Mildred sang. She later served many years as a musical missionary in Haiti, then in Florida, and today lives in Indiana. Her memories are vivid.

"Mildred was the first person I met when I walked into the president's office to see Dr. V. C. Oltrogge in February or March of 1953. She was a secretary. Dr. Oltrogge had invited me to substitute for the choir director and music professor, who faced surgery. My father had become pastor of Capitol Christian Church, Phoenix, in January that year, and since Dr. Oltrogge attended there he had heard me at the organ and piano, and seen me direct the choir.

"I told the president I had not gone to college, and did not have a degree. He liked what he had heard and seen, and replied, 'You'll do very well.'

"From that day on I loved going into the office when I got to the campus, for Millie was the sweetest, most gracious person to meet. I don't believe I ever saw her without a smile, even though she was struggling with breathing. During our sextet rehearsals, or in the dining room, she had the cutest, most unique, infectious 'giggle.' She never bemoaned her fight to get her breath, and never had a negative word about anyone!

"The first day I came as the new choir director, Mildred just sweetly said, 'the male quartet has slipped out to practice in the dining room.' Within me something said, 'These fellows think they can get by because I'm new and young.' So I said, 'would one of you go tell them the choir is in session?' It wasn't long before the quartet arrived! I did notice that one of the fellows for a while tried to give me a hard time.

"I finished that year [1953] directing the choir and working with the male quartet. and ladies' sextet. These singing groups represented ABI in a beautiful way that changed some lives. We had so much fun singing, laughing, and sharing Christ, and God bonded our hearts. The testimony left a vibrant testimony in churches. Sometimes I felt the male quartet became a little jealous. Ha!"

Margine Clark Mercado

Margine was the daughter of Mr. and Mrs. Ercel Clark, members of the Unadilla church with Mildred's family. This girl, like Mildred, traveled across the country to be a student at ABI. She joined Mildred and other ladies in the sextet that toured the state. Margine later married Dick Mercado, who would eventually, after his father, become head of the Mexican Gospel Mission in Phoenix. People of that evangelistic center have led thousands to know Christ. Dick is an outstanding, rousing evangelist.

The Ercel Clarks moved from Unadilla to north Phoenix, so once I met Mildred we often drove over to visit them. To be in their home gave me an outstanding opportunity to witness how a Christian family acted. It also gave Mildred a fresh taste of friendships she had treasured from Unadilla days. Here are Margine's memories.

"What a joy to recall growing up as a school girl along the sleepy Susquehanna River, and counting as a dear friend Mildred Currey. Little did we know in those early years that even after high school, Mildred in '48 and I in '51, our friendship would continue and deepen since it pleased the Lord to lead us both all the way across the United States to ABI.

"Mildred was a beautiful testimony to me of one whose heart was fixed on the Lord. She was strong and steadfast in her faith. Her faithful witness for the Lord was rooted in a genuine Bible-based experience of God's saving mercy and grace. I saw the Lord's power shining through Mildred in so many ways. It was even conspicuous during her long illnesses. I was especially challenged when visiting her in the hospital after she had undergone a very serious surgery. I sensed that despite the heavy trial she was so unmistakably 'on the victory side.'

"Mildred and her family exhibited the grace of God during very grievous circumstances. I recall vividly the summer that their barn burned to the ground.

A dear brother in Christ, a minister, was trapped in the fire and died. God's grace saw the Curreys and the pastor's wife through that heartbreak.

"Mildred and I traveled together across the country by car three times [1951, 1952, and 1953 during ABI years]. One summer we taught Daily Vacation Bible School in three or four neighboring churches to the Unadilla fellowship [as Margaret Wright Blosser has recalled sharing in]. Millie was an excellent teacher with her heart all in it, and the Lord greatly used her in drawing children to Christ.

"I do not remember any time that she complained or was ill mannered toward anyone. Hers was the steadfast heart of Isaiah 26:3, 'Thou wilt keep him in perfect peace whose mind is stayed on Thee, because he trusts in Thee.'"

Janice Eagon Ehrlich

Janice sang in the sextet with Mildred, Margine and others. She, too, was greatly blessed in Dr. John Hubbard's ABI classes. When Mildred and I moved to the La Mirada/Whittier area in 1965, Janice also lived not far away, and she recommended her father George as an excellent mechanic. George worked out of his home garage, and did the work on our car. Janice for a long time has lived in Colorado with her farming husband, Bob. Her recall is sharp about all the ABI faculty and chapel speakers.

"We had fun singing together in the sextet. And we received much spiritual help, too, from speakers in chapel such as Dr. Vernon Grounds, who headed up the Denver Seminary [Conservative Baptist], Dr. Richard Beal, pastor for more than 50 years of the First Baptist Church in Tucson, many missionaries from foreign and home fields, as well as Reidar Kalland of Child Evangelism Fellowship, who brings fond memories. One speaker, too, was called 'The Walking Bible' because he had memorized so much of Scripture."

Pat Simpson Denind

Pat came to ABI from the Los Angeles area, and after graduation returned to California, where she married Don Denind and has lived in Bellflower, an outskirt of Los Angeles. In our earlier years in California, Mildred often met with Pat for lunch, or Pat would visit and they would chat over coffee or tea. In the earliest years, Janice Eagon (cf. above) sometimes joined them. Pat has remembrances of ABI days:

"Dr. Hubbard's spiritual life classes were a gold mine to me, as to Mildred and all of us. We used to go to cotton camps, gather children, and somebody would make the gospel vivid in a flannel graph display. We would explain the way of salvation to the children and sing together. Many professed Christ. We also had street gospel meetings, and people believed.

"One incident in the dorm stands out. Mildred had become ill and the dorm mother told us not to bother her so she could get lots of rest. She was ill for about a week. One day I just couldn't resist being with her, so I went in, sat down, and Mildred and I began to talk. She really longed for somebody with whom to talk. But the dorm mother caught me in the act. I thought I was in for discipline, but I didn't get into any trouble at all. Seeing Mildred's bright face sent me away feeling a deep blessing."

Memories now come from a lady originally from Douglas, AZ, who was a brain with straight A's at Arizona State. She for many years has served as a math expert in conferences across the country. Beverly Watkins was in the youth group with us at First Baptist Church, Tempe. She and her date, later her husband, Neal Nichols, took us on a ride after evening church, and to get ice cream sundaes, on our own second date.

Neal, president of Blue Key, the men's national honorary fraternity, was probably instrumental in getting me "tapped" as a freshman into Blue Key. One morning at East Hall, I answered a knock on my door and there stood a smiling Blue Key man holding out a blue sweater of induction and an invitation to their breakfast. Neal served as state president of the young people in our Baptist church, and it was my privilege to succeed him and serve two years in that office. He put out a newspaper called *The Stadium Hall Gazette* for several years at Arizona State. He and Beverly married and have lived many years in Overland Park, Kansas. Beverly writes her memories of Mildred.

Beverly Watkins Nichols

"Mildred came to Arizona State, leaving the cold New York weather behind because of her bronchial weaknesses. Most of us in our youth group vaguely knew that her health concerns were why she was in Arizona, but she never made it a big deal. Jim and Mildred and Neal and I double-dated. I can remember how excited Jim was when he came to my dorm in ecstatic to tell me that he had sold a calf and used the money to buy Mildred an engagement ring. After Neal and I married, and Jim and Mildred were still dating, they'd come to our apartment to play board games.

"My most poignant memory of Mildred comes from their visiting us in Clifton, Arizona, in late December of 1963. Neal was high school principal there. Jim and Mildred were en route between Buckeye [visiting his family] and Dallas [doctoral studies]. They stopped to spend a night with us. At that time their daughter Dianne and Bruce, our second child, were almost identical in age—18 or 19 months old. As Mildred and I visited while we watched the children, she said to me, 'My doctor tells me I must raise Dianne to be as independent as possible, as I won't live to see her grown.' Well, to paraphrase Paul Harvey, 'You know the rest of the story.' The Lord saw fit to keep Mildred on this earth much longer than that! And she saw Dianne, Carolyn as well, both grown into wonderful Christian women—and she saw her grandsons too!

"Many years have passed since we had such fun in that 1963 visit. And, while we've always exchanged Christmas cards and letters, the visits have been fairly infrequent. We've visited probably half a dozen times, but each visit has proved that true friendships—especially those based in Christ—last for eternity."

In the early 1990's, I went with several faculty of The Master's Seminary to a national Evangelical Theological Society conference in Kansas City, MO. Neal and Bev drove to the Holiday Inn Hotel, picked me up, and took me to dinner at a very nice Rembrandt Restaurant. Our hearts were refreshed in reliving happy times.

29

Ladies' Tributes in Our Lives at Schools

At Dallas Seminary (1957-1961; 1962-1965)

TWO LADIES SHARE. ONE is Dorothy Chick, a member of the co-uni-bus Bible Class I taught at Scofield Memorial Church a few blocks from the seminary. Later for several decades she was a missionary in Africa, and in retirement resides in Lawrence, KS.

The other woman is Sande Sunde, wife of David Sunde. This couple now live in Louisville, CO and have a ministry of helping men and women come to the Savior through Campus Crusade witness. They are in their 34th year of this (2009). The teams with which they serve are "Global Community Resources" and "Cities and Beyond." Dave and Sande equip CCC staff to reach business and professional people. So God has given them strength (Isa. 40:31) to labor in Abidjan, Sao Paulo, Johannesburg, Beijing, Budapest, Singapore, Manila, Almaty, Lagos, Cairo, and other cities. They have seen hundreds receive Christ, and led numerous couples in Saudi Arabia and other countries to build their marriages on Christ as "heirs together of the grace of life" (1 Pet. 3:7).

Sande is one of the most beautiful of ladies, and her life exhibits Christian graces that are a winsome testimony of what God can fashion. David towers at 6-5, looks a bit like the movie actor Jimmy Stewart, and is one of the most sweet-tempered gentlemen I have ever known.

Dorothy Chick

"Jim and Mildred were living in the married student housing at Dallas Seminary.

Jim was our teacher at church when I and my roommate Bernita Cooper first met this couple. We came in the backwash following the birth of Dianne [April, 1962] to help Mildred clean the apartment, for she had used up much of her reserve strength in bringing Dianne into the family. The thing that is especially poignant is my memory of her prayer, 'Please, Lord, may I live long enough to see this little girl graduate from high school.'

She pleaded, too, that she be allowed to see Dianne live independently and go on to serve the Lord.

"Having the singles from the church come to their home out in the suburbs [we moved a few miles east of Dallas to Casa View around 1963, until doctoral studies ended in 1965] was quite a scene. Mildred loved to be hostess to the young people in Jim's church class, and we loved going to their home. Mildred was a marvelous hostess even after expending her energy in caring for both Dianne and Carolyn [the latter came in 1964]. She always had goodies and was ever ready for a fun time. She thought it was such a good diversion for her man who had to be such a devoted 'student.'

"I fondly remember my victory over that student at a party when we played the game of 'Spoon.' To this day I exult in the thrill of beating the teacher [her clutch on the spoon was so tenacious, and she would not give up, so she wrenched the spoon free to win]. No way would I ever be able to understand, never mind explain, the Bible like he did, but I could get a spoon from him! I really think that Mildred relished witnessing that ferocious competition. Her Jim, her beloved husband, had to be occupied with hard studies, and rarely could relax in the luxury of just plain fun. When he did get such chances, Mildred enjoyed seeing him caught up in a frolic, and being the instigation of it.

"Mildred was a woman to whom we, as younger women, went with weighty matters of the heart. She was approachable, not as likely as others to be out about on errands. She took time to listen and really hear. She would meditate and only then advise Cleo in regard to her boyfriend Rip, Bonnie as to her boy friend Charlie, and all of us. Many of us were nurses, and Mildred seemed to understand the upheaval in our working lives. Had the Lord given her so many experiences with the medical profession just for those days when we needed to vent to someone who could give us the stab we needed to mature in the workaday world?

"I loved to hear Mildred play the piano! Such music she could bring forth! And with her skill it was so effortless. Realizing how little her reserve strength was, maybe the Lord gifted her in special measure so it wouldn't take so much effort. What a delightful home in which to make the 'storehouse' to place our baby grand piano when I went to the mission field and had to sell the house!

"What joy when Mildred could see both her girls complete high school and she was still there! Then a wedding and Caleb joined the family. I wonder how, too, Mildred managed to trap Randy for Carolyn? Now both girls are officially women. Words cannot truly express the gratitude Mildred had when she shared with me her wonder at God's answer to her prayers 20 years earlier! She now saw the girls not only mature, but she and Jim were grandparents of first one and then two grandsons! How much she looked forward to babysitting when her strength could manage it. And what joy she had to attend piano recitals and little league baseball games.

"On many of my furloughs, Mildred would make a haven for me in their home. She would get that brighter sparkle in her eye when the professor was coming home. She so enjoyed being able to serve him and to get him to enjoy people in the flesh as well as those who were between the covers of books. Arizona State football games and rooting at times for the 'wrong' team just to ruffle the waters were parts of her teasing, ornery fun.

"She was so fulfilled when she saw the completion of the 'western' or 'OK Corral' room [Jim's study, 1991]. Her joy was realized as she saw the joy of her loved one.

"She took on the challenge of being president of Calvary Baptist's Women's Missionary Fellowship for two years. Imagine this though her reserves of strength plunged so low. She was pleased to see her sisters in the Lord develop their support for the missionaries. Then when she simply did not have the strength to lead for another year, she was so sorry.

"I remember one experience when I as a guest with Jim and Mildred. We were all taken out to dinner by George and Alice Rutenbar [George, a former pro baseball scout, finished Dallas Seminary and was a pastor for many years]. Some days after that Mildred confessed to me how difficult it was to keep her mouth shut when Alice repeatedly called her 'Millie.' She was 'Mildred,'" and she said, 'I hated that name Millie!'

"The last furlough when I was in Whittier, I ran into all sorts of transportation problems. I had looked forward to the convenience of 'the Green line' [a transit train system], to which Mildred had introduced me. The airlines did not cooperate, and what should have taken me a couple hours' flight took all day and the early part of the night. Jim came in exhausted from teaching and fighting tortuous traffic that long way from the seminary only to have Mildred tell him that they had to go to the Los Angeles Airport to meet me at something like 9 p.m. She marshaled what strength was left after an already full day, and they drove across the city and back home to Whittier.

"Think of transportation. Mildred had real pride and happiness in the gift Jim gave her of a van equipped to meet her specific needs including her mobile oxygen chariot. Jim's gift made it possible for Mildred, Dianne, Carolyn and me to have a girls' birthday bash, and I got to take part in the fun tradition of shopping she shared with her daughters over the years. Jim delivered her mobile chariot [motor cart] and assembled it, and we ladies were off for the day. Mildred had saved up her energy as a priority to expend on her daughters.

"One other thing. It was her love/hate relationship with her positive pressure machine. She had regular trysts with it and spent much time cleaning it. The last time I was there she had graduated to three new household visitors [four foot oxygen tanks] parked by the kitchen door. And when she and Jim would go on a near carefree vacation, a company would deliver a tank there.

"Mildred's computer gave her a whole new world to explore while free to sit still and focus on getting her breath. Through her technology she could keep up on the prayer needs of her friends in far flung areas of the world.

"Heaven is richer and missions here have to do without her now that praying Mildred is spending her time bowing at the feet of the Savior. Be careful, professor! I'm sure that Mildred is busy today, planning for the extravaganza on the day when she welcomes you to join her in heaven. After all, now she is where she has all the energy in the world, and perfect freedom.

"Thanks for the joy to contribute and reminisce about so fine a woman of God!"

Sande Sunde

"Imagine me—a girl of 21, a senior at Western Michigan University and newly married! I traveled by train with my husband David to check out Dallas Theological Seminary. I had grown up in a small town in Michigan, and my greatest adventure after high school was going off to Hope College, a one hour drive. My dream and heart's desire was to meet and marry a man who would study to become a pastor.

"My dream came true. David and I married just prior to our senior year, and when it was time to choose a seminary I expected him to select the one connected with the college I attended. Much to my surprise, he wanted to look at a school in Dallas. Upon our arrival on that campus, a lovely woman greeted us; she was in charge of the switchboard, greeting visitors, and showing visitors around. Mildred welcomed us and led us in a tour. By the end of our time together I knew that I had discovered a wonderful new friend.

"Mildred was married to Jim, ready to begin his final of the four years for the Th. M. They invited us to their home on campus for dinner that evening. It was the beginning of a lifelong friendship, now nearly 50 years. When Dave and I arrived at the school the following Fall [1960] we were thankful to have new friends to welcome us.

"In the year that followed we spent countless evenings experiencing Mildred's wonderful hospitality and Jim's tutoring David in Greek and Hebrew. To this day,

David says, 'If it hadn't been for Jim, I never would have made it through the courses.' While the men were engrossed in study, Mildred taught me how to knit.

"I had been raised in a very difficult family. My father and mother had married young and without the blessing of their parents. They did not know how to manage or raise children. As a young girl I took on the impossible task of trying to make my dad and mom happy. Mildred, being more mature in her walk with God, modeled *kindness, humility, compassion,* and *perseverance.* She became a godly example and mentor to help me go forward in Christ.

"KINDNESS. Mildred was connecting and creative. She was gifted in creating a warm home environment, and was a gracious hostess. She excelled in hospitality. After finishing the seminary, both of us couples lived close enough to continue our special times together. No matter if it was a picnic in the back yard, a birthday party for one of the children, Thanksgiving, or some other special occasions, I never ceased to be amazed at Mildred's creativity.

"I also remember her kindness the time she invited my daughters and me to one of her daughters' birthday parties, and I completely forgot it. Mildred and the girls celebrated without us. She graciously forgave me. I know that was because Mildred spent time in God's presence—in prayer.

"Mildred was very resourceful. When we moved to California we had no furniture. Kind people from our church [Southgate] supplied us with some items. One piece of furniture in particular I remember. It was a very large, well-worn couch with a cushion that dipped down lower than the other two. When David and I were making our next move to Illinois [collegiate ministry with Campus Crusade] I decided that the couch would not go with us. When Mildred found out that we were leaving it, she asked if she could have it. I tried to discourage her from taking it, but she insisted. Later when we visited their home I could not believe it was the same couch. The broken spring had been fixed and it had a brand new velvet cover so that it looked like it was just out of the store.

"HUMILITY. Mildred modeled a mind that was set on the Spirit [Rom. 8:6b]. She demonstrated fruitfulness in consistency by living her life in the power of the Holy Spirit. The fruits of love, joy, peace, patience, gentleness, kindness, goodness, faithfulness, and self-control were provocative in her life. The reality of her inner life was very evident in her outward behavior.

"COMPASSION. My friend was caring and content. I could not help but see the tender loving care she showered on Jim and on Dianne and Carolyn. Jim had her 'helper design' stamped all over him. They modeled beautifully two people deeply in love with each other and their two children. A couple of verses in Proverbs 31 describe Mildred well, 'her children rise up and bless her,' and her husband also praises her saying 'you're the best.'

"PERSEVERANCE. Mildred suffered most of her life with a serious respiratory disease. Though all the difficulties she never stopped caring and loving life. She was a wonderful wife, mother, and friend to countless other women. She exemplified the saying, 'Even if God leads us to a desert, He continues to work through us.' Mildred fashioned for me the loveliness of feminine design. God created us to exhibit grace, strength, softness, and sensitivity. She had a heart God made beautiful, and its life flowed out into her creating a beautiful home environment that welcomed and blessed many people. She was the real thing, a *genuine, authentic masterpiece.*

"After David and I moved to Colorado 16 years ago [1993] we were able to see Jim and Mildred only a precious few times. Both of them were faithful to keep in touch with us, and Jim would update us on Mildred's worsening health condition. He was always full of praise for all she continued to do, not only for the family but for others. She continued to serve God with loving-kindness and grace. On a recent trip to California, David contacted them about our getting together. It worked out that we shared one of the most happy of times over a Marie Callender's lunch.

"Just a few months later we received the news that God had called Mildred home to her heavenly reward. But how thankful we were to have pictures of that special lunch, and the brief fellowship encapsulated the great years we had as cordial friends. And to think that someday we shall all be reunited to continue our special friendship in our precious Lord God Almighty!"

At Talbot Seminary (1965–1987)

Our ministry there was 22 years. I was the chairman of the Department of Bible Exposition, and saw the school grow from 99 to 719. Dr. Charles Feinberg was the dean from 1952 to 1975, so our years partly were during his leadership. After him, Dr. Glenn O'Neal, chairman of the preaching department, served as dean (1975–1983), then Dr. Wendell Johnston (1983–1986), and Dr. W. Bingham Hunter for one year while we were there (1986–1987), and for several years after we moved on.

Dr. O'Neal's wife Phoebe has contributed the first tribute to Mildred. Her life is a fragrance of Christ's lovely spirit.

Phoebe O'Neal

"It will not be difficult for me to share memories of such a dear friend. In spite of all her health struggles, she always had a beautiful, sweet smile—ever looking at the positive and sunshine side of things and praising God for His faithfulness! In every case it was a joy and a special lift to be with her.

"Do you [Jim] remember the time I was washing her hair at your home and broke the faucet? Oh, I felt so terrible, but Mildred just laughed! And you had to get a new faucet. [A lot of other temporal household things broke as years went by, but God's faithfulness never broke, and our love for one another never did. How good is God!].

"I still have the blue and white ceramic figurine Mildred gave me for helping out with one of the daughters' weddings. It sits on my kitchen counter all the time, so I think of Mildred in many fond memories during each day. She still is precious to me!

"The Lord blessed your family with two dear girls, and now you both have had the fulfillment of grandsons. I have heard Mildred exult in how she loved so much to be with them. I held Mildred to be more dear than I can put into words, and cherish the pleasant memories of times, such as fellowship for lunch, I spent with her."

Donna Rigsby

Donna is the wife of Dr. Richard Rigsby, Professor of Old Testament at Talbot and "the Bob Hope of humor" on that faculty. While Mildred, the girls, and I were away in Scotland, the Rigsbys came to the seminary [1975], and they were there to greet us as new friends when we returned to California in 1976. Richard and I, and Donna and Mildred became close friends. Donna and Mildred often went to lunch together, and all these times were highlights Mildred treasured.

"I think of a true lady, a lady in every sense of the word. She was a class act, in her demeanor and in her words. She never wavered in her loyalty to and love for her Lord and her Jim, and her Dianne and Carolyn, no matter how she felt physically. I never heard her complain about anything, though I knew that breathing was a constant, sometimes frightening struggle for her. She was so loyal to her church and her women's missionary fellowship and loved them so much that she sought ways to serve and become involved even if she could not attend the meetings. For Mildred's church activities and her family she was extremely creative and used her gifts in designing beautiful cards and programs, products of her self-taught computer skills.

"She made her family's house a home. She was very practical and wonderfully resourceful, always able to bring beauty and usefulness to everything she touched. This included tasks such as cooking healthy meals, sewing dresses for Dianne and Carolyn, painting the house, arranging furniture, choosing pictures to adorn the walls, cleaning (as long as she was able physically), and just being a general handy (wo)man. Her skills in making their house a home extended far beyond the tangible, visual matters. She loved making people feel special. She jumped at every chance to celebrate someone's birthday or put a happy touch on some special occasion. And she especially did her part in building and maintaining a Christian home. Loyalty, respect, order, discipline, trustworthiness, faithfulness, gratitude, dependence on God, prayer, and most of all love—these were the standards by which she lived and taught—for God and for each other.

"She knew and loved the neighborhood children. While observing her speaking with them, I've often thought, 'I bet she used to be a great school teacher.' Given her rapport with them, her creativity, and her sense of humor, she has been a winner.

"She loved her husband, her daughters, and her sons in law. She loved her grand-sons. She KNEW them, their likes and dislikes, their interests, their talents—and never ceased to share, with joy and pride, the latest news of the grandsons' ventures as they went through stages of growing up, whether their humorous comments or music or sports or school projects.

"And now I've saved what perhaps is what I enjoyed most about Mildred—her sense of humor! She loved life and loved to laugh. So many times I had to restrain myself because while just being together we would start laughing about something and this would make it harder for her to breathe. And I know that her sense of humor was still another attribute that contributed to their house being a 'home.'

"All of the family members of Mildred Rosscup may count themselves as blessed. God gave you a Proverbs 31 person in your lives. May the fruit of this be carried on through you to many future generations! I am Mildred's blessed friend."

Bobbie Ifland

Bobbie and her husband Dave introduced us to Dr. Charles Feinberg of Talbot during our one-year California ministry with Campus Crusade in 1961–1962. Dave sang on Dr. Feinberg's weekly radio program as they sought to win Jewish people to Christ. Bobbie writes:

"Our first meeting with you two was at the cabin above Lake Mears near Forest Home, a Campus Crusade mountain resort. God drew me to Mildred at once. She was so very sweet and friendly, a truly beautiful lady looking to build relationships. And she was wondering where your ministry was yet to lead you.

"We had tickets to the Cotton Bowl game in Dallas [early 1960's], contacted both of you, and planned to share the tickets with you. You made arrangements for us to stay in an apartment on campus near you when the couple living there had gone home for the holidays. Mildred, I, and both families' children decided to stay home from the bowl game after all to prepare dinner. We all were at supper that night in your home and listened to USC beat Wisconsin [42-39] in a see-saw thriller of a Rose Bowl game.

"When you later decided on ministry in California [at Talbot], it thrilled us. You had spent a Christmas with us before that [1961] in Burbank, but by the time you moved to the teaching at Talbot we were in a home in Huntington Beach. At times when you had a special event, you would bring your daughters to stay with us and play with our daughters Mamie and Lillian. Our girls loved them.

"I remember giving Dianne and Carolyn the pink (non-allergy) comforters for their beds.

"To me it was very hard to see Mildred's all-out grappling with her respiratory problem that just wore down all her strength. My heart went out to her. I truly understood and admired her for her ability to cope. Years later you and Mildred came to visit us at the Balboa Bay Club where I worked, and we had a delightful catching up time at lunch. It was so great to fellowship after a number of years when our lives had taken us in different directions. Mildred was struggling even more by then, but always with such a conquering attitude. She loved the Lord so much, and everyone loved her.

"I cherish the note she sent me a few months before God took her home. She was so proud of her grandsons and enjoyed every moment she could spend with them. A very proud Gramma!"

Shirley Holloman

Shirley, while going to the Dallas Bible College close by Dallas Theological Seminary, used to come and visit Mildred in our apartment on campus. She was always a bubbling personality who obviously had a deep love for the Savior. She married Henry Holloman, one of my seminary classmates, and several years after I came to Talbot Theological Seminary to teach, I phoned Henry who taught at Detroit Bible College to ask if he would be interested in teaching at Talbot. He came in 1974, the year our family left for doctoral studies in Scotland. We have been dear friends, living only a mile and a half apart.

"I first met Mildred in Dallas, and soon learned that she was the mother of two precious daughters, Dianne and Carolyn. Our paths crossed several times in Dallas, then God had designed to bring us together again in California.

"In the summer of 1974, Henry and I and our two sons moved west to La Mirada for Henry to begin teaching at Talbot. I was so pleased that I could renew my friendship with Mildred. This led to many times of joyful and blessed Christian fellowship.

"I will always remember Mildred as a faithful friend and confidante. Her commitment to her family and her church were quite evident. She viewed them as ministries for the Lord. Though her health challenges decreased her energy, she trusted God to give her the stamina to fulfill her biblical responsibilities as a wife, mother, grandmother, and faithful friend to so many.

"I have missed Mildred beyond what I can describe. I miss our telephone chats and our luncheons of precious time together. In every contact with her I always felt a closer bond with her and fellowship with the Lord. Truly, she was an example of the woman in Proverbs 31. Her testimony to the honor of the Lord Jesus by life and by lip was obvious to all who came in contact with her.

"I esteemed Mildred as a most cherished friend and precious sister in Christ. The three main things we shared in our many times of heart knitting were our spiritual bond in the Lord Jesus, our childhood experiences of farm life [Mildred's in New York and Shirley's in Powell, WY], and our husbands being seminary professors."

Jan Friederichsen

Jan is the wife of Doug Friederichsen, who earned his doctorate at Dallas Theological Seminary, won the seminary award as the best preacher among graduating men, pastored churches, and also taught Bible at Biola College for several years.

Doug and Jan, and Mildred and I have spent many evenings in precious fellowship at their home or ours, going to restaurants, shopping at a beach city, or strolling by the ocean. Our prayers for one another have arched the years of the friendship since 1965.

"We look through windows at a great walk with God. In the tapestry of life there are people who add a sparkling, colored thread by the things they do and contribute to our lives. Since I was a home economics teacher for 30 years, I was always aware of the importance of a beautifully set table. What a treat to enjoy eating on bone china and an Old Country Rose pattern. I cannot recall what food we had, but I remember the joy it was for me to sit down and eat in such style at Mildred's table.

"I knew the effort that it takes to get out a set of dishes and set a beautiful table, and then put it all away again. But Mildred was a gracious, giving person whose hospitality was a blessing to our hearts. She and Jim opened their lives to us as well as their home. How many the evenings when we just talked and laughed, or played games until it was quite late. I'm glad God let Mildred be a tangible expression of His love in my life!

"It was my privilege to have this special person as my friend."

Aldyth Barber

This lady is the wife of Dr. Cyril J. Barber, author of about 40 books, and former faculty member in Winnepeg Bible College, Trinity Evangelical Divinity School in Deerfield, IL, Simon Greenleaf School of Law, and Biola University.

We have spent several times as guests in the home of Cyril and Aldyth, and they have blessed us when visiting in our home. They had come from South Africa. We first met them at Dallas Theological Seminary. Since they in recent years have lived just over the mountain from Whittier in Hacienda Heights, we have had many times of splendid fellowship. Cyril and I often meet for breakfast.

"I shall always cherish the memories I have of Mildred. On several occasions, without pre-planning, Cyril and I would decide to have dinner at the Sizzler Restaurant in La Mirada. To our delight on a couple of occasions we found Jim and Mildred there as well. As we sat together we would notice a sparkle in Mildred's eyes, and before long her humor would spice up the conversation.

"I also remember how several years ago Jim and Mildred would come to our home on many a New Year's Day. We would enjoy lunch, then, often, Mildred and I would drive to see the 'Rose Bowl' floats after the parade in Pasadena, while Jim and Cyril watched the bowl games on TV.

"Mildred was in the hospital several times. Visiting her was a real treat to me. I came away with my spirit lifted—but I had gone to lift her spirit. Her disposition during all those extremely trying times with her breathing difficulties remains an inspiration to boost me. Never at any time did I hear her complain. She rather accepted the struggles she had to live with. I was always amused by the names she gave to her various pieces of equipment, 'Isabelle' and 'Ichabod,' etc. And we had great times together sharing about our grandchildren.

"Looking back over the years, beginning in the 60's, I can honestly say that I found Mildred to be unfailingly cheerful, showing the characteristics of a truly faithful servant of the Lord. I so miss her!"

At The Master's Seminary (1987–2008)

Mildred's health almost always left her unable to go with me to seminary dinners or banquets. She was able to rise to the occasions now and then, such as to one of the annual Spring banquets. But though the seminary faculty wives and student wives knew she was unable, they realized she dearly wished she could come. And they were aware of her being on one of the prayer groups, pleading needs of student wives at the mercy seat, before the Lord on His throne of grace (Heb. 4:16).

Several faculty wives tell of their memories here.

"B" Mayhue

"B" is the wife of the seminary Senior Vice-President and Dean, Dick Mayhue. She and Dick years ago were about to separate when they went to a couples conference to hear the famous speaker, Ken Pourer. God turned their lives around, set them on fire for the Lord, and led Dick to training at Grace Theological Seminary, several years as a pastor, and since 1990 being the Dean. "B" has always been one of the most gracious of ladies.

"The Lord brings some women into our lives who are so very special. Mildred was such a person. I could say many things, but when I try to put the words down they seem inadequate.

"Mildred was a joy. She radiated interest in others, love, and encouragement. I know that she was literally anchored by her oxygen tank, but she helped me hardly notice it when we were together. Her engaging, delightful sense of humor was always primed, and her complete dependence on God and His Word were ever evident.

"Although Mildred was not physically able to attend Seminary Wives Discipleship meetings, she was our faithful prayer partner. She took pleasure in presenting our praises and needs as she went into the throne room before the Lord's welcoming presence.

"Many passages of Scripture remind me of Mildred. One that stands out is Psalm 119:74-77: 'May those who fear Thee see me and be glad, because I wait for Thy word. I know, O Lord, that Thy judgments are righteous, and that in faithfulness Thou hast afflicted me. O may Thy loving kindness comfort me, according to Thy word to Thy servant. May Thy compassion come to me that I may live, for Thy law is my delight.'

"Mildred's example of godliness is one that I will treasure. I am thankful to God for allowing me to know her."

Karen Busenitz

Karen married Kansas farmer Irv Busenitz. Irv was a student of mine at Talbot in the late 1960's and early 1970's, and later gained his doctorate at Grace Theological Seminary. He became the director of the Talbot extension school in Sun Valley, meeting in facilities of the Grace Community Church that John MacArthur pastors. He led in this extension from 1977 to 1986, then was a key man, with MacArthur, in founding The Master's Seminary which opened its doors to 99 students in 1986. Now he is the Vice-President for Academic Administration. Their son Nathan is the personal assistant to John MacArthur, and starting in 2009 is a Master's Seminary teacher in theology.

The school has grown to around 370 students in 2009. It now has graduates serving in 45 states, and alumni have founded six schools in the U.S. In 40 other countries, 129 graduates serve, and 20 schools now operate in 16 of the countries, started by TMS men. With the 2009 graduation pushing the alumni close to 1,040, even more men from this seminary are pouring into U.S. and foreign ministries.

Karen is one of the most beautiful of women, prettier than many movie stars. But her main beauty is that of Christ glowing in a life given entirely to Him (Rom. 12:1-2; 1 Pet. 3:5-6). Here is what this woman of God says.

"Thank you for the privilege to write a tribute to your beloved wife. It has been a joy to remember her and her very sweet ways. What a legacy she leaves—one of joy in remembering! Her life, being an example in so many says, is one I hope to emulate with the Lord's help.

"She was a woman who exemplified the qualities of women as Paul describes these in 1 Timothy 3:11: 'women must likewise be dignified, not malicious gossips, but temperate, faithful in all things.' This was Mildred. She carried herself with poise, yet was not proud. Her words were wise and meaningful, yet her voice was soft. She loved to laugh, yet never was flippant. She was always proper, yet without pretense. She exuded a calming influence and in her presence one could relax and be herself.

"Not only was she a TMS professor's wife, she was also involved in the lives of the students. As a Prayer Partner for the Seminary Wives' discipleship program, she faithfully assisted with invaluable intercession. Who but God will ever know the extent of fruitfulness coming from her heartfelt entreaties?

"Our program today enjoys God's blessing because of women like Mildred. Although she could never be with us in person because of distance [40 mi.] and health issues, she was always with us in her prayers. How blessed I am because of her!"

Missy Mehringer

Missy is the wife of Ray Mehringer, a former student we faculty men taught at TMS, and now the Director of Recruitment for the seminary. She is a very lovely person with an infectious smile.

"Two years ago, shortly before God was to take Mildred home, I had the privilege of meeting her. I had heard so much about her from other seminary wives. I knew her to be a strong prayer warrior, especially for her husband's ministry. I met her in her beautiful home with some other faculty wives to take her to lunch. Her home was so welcoming, reflecting the love of people and hospitality. I was especially pleased to have her show me Jim's spacious home study. There I saw shelves nine feet high crammed with books, three desks, all sorts of gift mementos that were treasures from the years, file cabinets, and a huge bulletin board with pictures of many students.

"She seemed so enthused to be a ministry wife for all those years.

"I noticed that she was very gracious and did not complain about her perilous medical condition. She seemed really to enjoy the day out with friends. Even in just this one meeting, the Lord taught me some important lessons shining from her life. Mildred modeled for me the way I long to live my life as a senior saint. So often, it is easy to find grumbling and complaining even among Christian women when the aches, pains, and diseases come. Not so Mildred. Hers was a humble, gentle and quiet spirit which spoke loudly of her love for her Savior.

"It was obvious, too, that this lady loved her family and friends. She was a woman who seemed content to be behind the scenes, serving her husband primarily through prayer. I have always thought of her husband as a great prayer warrior, but I now suspect that she was just as involved in talking with God. She truly lived out Titus 2:3-5. For that, she was a great example to me, and I am sure that she glorified the Lord Jesus Christ."

Favy Montoya

Favy is the wife of Dr. Alex Montoya, who teaches preaching at The Master's Seminary, is a passionate and highly sought after speaker, and Hispanic pastor since around 1970. He leads the First Fundamental Church of Whittier, CA. Alex and Favy have been pacesetters even in founding about 15 other churches. Every year Alex and I drive together to the Fall faculty retreat that is a kick-off to the seminary year. I look upon this colleague as one of the truly great spiritual leaders and examples of down to earth, Christlike servanthood in our generation.

"I remember the first time I saw Mildred. I glimpsed her out of my living room window, and there she was, sitting in her car. She had driven over to wait for her husband Jim and my husband Alex to come back from a retreat. She arrived a half hour early. I went out and invited her to come into my home. But at first she was sensitive in saying that she did not want to bother me! I was impressed with this lovely and humbly unassuming lady.

"She talked in ways that highlighted her love for the Lord. Her eyes lit up when she shared her testimony with me and how she had accepted Christ. She would relate things about her struggles with her breathing, but she would also tell about the ways the Lord had strengthened her and was holding her up to cope.

"Another love in her life was her family. She loved to share about her daughters' accomplishments and how much she loved them and Jim. Mildred was a special woman who is truly missed."

Teri White

Teri is the wife of Bob White, Vice-President for Development and Operations, The Master's Seminary. Bob and Teri came to the seminary after selling out a Volvo car dealership in Santa Rosa, CA. They were hungry for God's Word, and when Bob came to my Bible interpretation or prayer classes, almost invariably Teri came with him just to sit, drink in gulps of truth, and grow. The Whites host, each Spring, a faculty dinner in their home, "The Western White House." It is difficult to imagine anybody ever reflecting more bright cheer on her face than is Teri's constant glow. She writes:

"I remember all the times you, Jim, prayed for us by name and I also heard of your prayer earlier, for Bob when his first wife was dying [of cancer]. I have such high regard for you as a man of prayer and a man who loved his dear Mildred so deeply.

"When I met this larger than life woman I was so enamored with her faithfulness to love you and serve you and God's people through her care in prayer. When I called to have lunch with Mildred she was so kind to find a date only later to have to postpone our time together due to illness. But she persevered and further on we were able to have lunch near your home [at Polly's Pie Shop, Whittier]. She walked in so distinguished, yet humble, pulling her oxygen tank.

"I was with Missy Mehringer, Pam Snider, and Delores Michaelson. We did a lot of laughing and I think Mildred was just excited for the Christian fellowship, thankful that we would drive so far to spend time with her. But we were the recipients of her many years of faithfulness to the Lord. I also remember when I used to attend chapels with Bob and your classes you would speak so highly and reverently about your beloved. You said that when you were so tired she would stroke your forehead and pray for you. I learned a lot about devotion to my husband in this.

"Even if Mildred wasn't able to attend church she was faithful to pray for the saints. From one who knew her for just a short time, I learned much from her life."

Pam Snider

Pam is the wife of Dr. Andy Snider, Associate Professor of Theology, a former student of TMS in my classes. This lady is "Musical Pam," a whiz of talent on the piano. One of her albums has often floated its melodies through the home for Mildred and me.

"I got to know Mildred late in her life as some of us faculty wives would visit in her home. Three characteristics about her spring to my mind. First was her air of dignity. She would meet me at the door, femininely dressed in a skirt and blouse, a sweater if necessary, and the appropriate accessories. Whether short of breath or not, she exuded an energy and zest for whatever God would bring in her day. She was a true lady in every sense. The second quality is her endearing personality. She was interested from the 'get-go' in my life, my family, my interests, as if nothing else in the world was as important. She also would always have the latest updates and pictures to share about her family and ministry, and seemed so excited to tell of her joy in them.

"Mildred and I both enjoyed a chuckle in finding out that we like to name inanimate objects. I quickly felt a kindred spirit when she told me her oxygen tank's name was 'Isabelle.' I, too, have names for certain personal objects. It helps to make the mundane more unique. This characteristic showed me Mildred's ability to find something funny in what could be an often long and tedious journey through suffering and its pain. She taught me that laughter is better than tears, and that we have much to laugh about.

"A third thing is this. Our spirits were even more united when I found out that the favorite place for both of us is Scotland. For her it was from having been there and seeing experientially what it was like; but for me it was through imagining its beauty and simplicity through pictures. We realized we had a link to the simplicity of that country after finding out that Mildred lived all her pre-teen years near the same town [Schultzville, New York] where I grew up. How small our world. She had gone to church, before me, in the same building where I went to Vacation Bible School!

"The natural terrain in that New York area, as well as the stone walls in the wooded areas and the covered bridges, have real similarities between the two countries. It was amazing that the Lord would allow our paths to cross, however briefly, to be touched and changed.

"I will always be grateful for the opportunity to meet a loving wife, faithful mother, and devoted grandmother. She loved people and the simple things of life, like good food, sweet fellowship, and the gift of laughter. I saw in Mildred a deep and abiding love for her husband, and full support of his ministry at whatever sacrifice it meant she could lay on the altar. That was the biggest encouragement for me since I also desire for the Lord to use my husband in the most effective way. Having older women pacesetting this example is so rare in our culture today. Mildred was faithful to this task in her home and the ministry she shared with Jim.

"We need more Mildreds in our lives to spur us on to fulfill the godly roles God intended us to pursue."

30

Ladies' Tributes from my Family

MOTHER ROSSCUP WENT TO glory in 1997 at an age just shy of 86. She told me time and time again such things as: "Mildred is a precious daughter"; "When I first saw Mildred I thought, 'she's one of the most beautiful women I've ever seen'"; "I love to be with Mildred; she makes me feel so much at home"; "I can talk my problems over with her."

But other memories come from Rosscup sisters, a niece Lalani, and a cousin, Diane Medico, who was Diane Fraley, one of five children born into my mother's family as a daughter of Uncle Bill and Aunt Emma. These people farmed in Hanford, CA and loved the Lord dearly. Diane when a student at Biola College stayed with us a semester along with her friend, Becky White. My sister Ethel taught school for several years. Lalani is Ethel's daughter and a long-time Wycliffe Bible Translators missionary to Indonesia, now in a missions teaching stint and doctoral studies at Biola University.

Tributes from our two daughters appear later in Chapter 32.

Ethel Rose Rosscup Wood

Ethel married Larry Wood, from the same Arizona home town, Buckeye. This couple now serve God in a fervent church prayer ministry in their retirement. Larry's father was a minister and a farmer, and his older brother Jerry a missionary to Brazil, though now retired and teaching a Bible class in Boulder City, NV. Ethel's memories follow.

"Mildred was both a friend and a sister to me. When I was a teenager, she gave me advice about living on the college campus [Arizona State], and even helped me find my first room mate. I was so grateful to her. She told me what I needed to take from home and what the dorm would furnish. She had bought a new iron, so she gave me her old one, which was still excellent. I used that iron for years.

"Our children [three for Ethel, two for Mildred] were born on alternate years, so Mildred shared maternity clothes, and then our little girls traded dresses.

"Mildred taught me a lot of things. Jim and Mildred settled in southern California shortly before Larry and I moved from Arizona. Mildred helped me learn how to drive in the heavier traffic. She assured me that navigating the busy freeways would become easy in a short time. From her I learned how to plan and execute a dinner party. She showed me how to knit and took me to a shop where she gave me pointers on how to select the right yarn. She encouraged me in so many ways. And she was the one I always could talk to about how I was feeling. The Lord steeped her in a deep, godly, homey wisdom.

"Our two families along with the Waughans [my sister Betty, who died in 2007, and husband Glen] celebrated the holidays, birthdays, graduations, and some summer afternoons together when our children were growing up. Mildred often was ill, but she did her utmost to make each time a happy one for all. My son Jerry remembers the parsnips, rutabagas, and mince meat pies she brought one Christmas when her father William joined us. These dishes were Dad Currey's favorites, as in the Curreys' New York garden, and her kindness pleased him as well as all of us.

"Lalani, Dianne, Glen, Carolyn, and Jerry played well together. So from babies to adults, they have had a real fondness for each other. I remember one Fourth of July at the California Angels' baseball park. We tailgated in the parking lot, enjoyed a game, then a fireworks display. Then another year we gathered in a hotel parking area to watch the Disneyland fireworks extravaganza. I remember a vacation in a cabin Jim and Mildred invited us to at Big Bear in the mountains, and the fabulous time boating, fishing, visiting a zoo, and playing games. Mildred always brought an air of happiness.

"She was kind and generous. I recall when Larry and I acquired single beds for our children. Before I could purchase sheets, Mildred appeared with some of her extra ones to share with us.

"Sometimes Mildred and Jim would rent a room of their home to college students. In each case, Mildred would make an extra effort to change the room to make the student comfortable. When our sister Catherine, a Biola student, stayed with them, Mildred meticulously painted flowers in the faded wall paper with Catherine's favorite color, yellow. Lalani remembers the days she stayed in that room as the best of her Biola time. She has said that the times she spent talking with Aunt Mildred were her most memorable. Many others stayed in that room at various times, and for each Mildred devoted the same attention in kindness to fit each person's tastes.

"Kindness was evident too in her other ways. Several of the plants in our yard were her gifts to me. The Shasta Daisies, Bird of Paradise, and Dahlias came from her flower beds. She shared what she had rather than throwing them away. She delighted in serving coffee or tea, using her pretty china cups and saucers to make her guests feel special. Usually she had dainty cookies to serve as well. She kept up this habit even when she was tethered to her oxygen tank. Serving others seemed to light a candle of happiness in her heart.

"Mildred loved and enjoyed her daughters. She played special games with them. One that I recall was a pretend mystery story that they would make up while waiting for a meal in a restaurant. There was a special language that the three of them spoke. She also spoke this language to her kitty cats.

"She especially loved and enjoyed her grandsons. Every time we spoke, she had a cute story to tell about how wonderful Zachary and Benjamin were. She so much enjoyed being a part of their lives" [she lived until Zach was 13 and Ben 12].

Mary Ellen Rosscup Edwards

This sister married Jim Edwards, who was a U.S. Phantom Jet pilot flying fateful missions over Cambodia and Vietnam, and later a commercial pilot for American Airlines. When Jim was stationed in Juneau, Alaska, Mary Ellen became one of a select group of beautiful models. These bright Christians, Jim and Mary Ellen, have been very hospitable in opening their home to family reunions on a plot of farm land that Jim's family previously worked. Mary Ellen has retired from a long career as a public school teacher, and written an informative book on customs in Saudi Arabia. This title, *Veiled Honor*, was published by Father's Press (Sept., 2009). She was with Jim when he spent two years in Saudi Arabia training Saudi pilots.

Mary Ellen shares these memories.

"'She's from New York!' To this Arizona farm girl who lived outside a small country town, those words about my brother Jim bringing Mildred Currey to our home for her first visit represented a new, unknown world. It was one of sophistication. education and glamour.

"My brother Jim wanted to bring her from Arizona State to his family circle to meet his parents and siblings. I feared that she would surely be shocked into dismay by our shabby old farm house, one that sat on a dirt yard near animal corrals, milking stalls, haystacks, farm equipment, and an old car no longer in use. The pump, situated just beyond the immediate yard, provided necessary water for the family, and the absence of indoor plumbing was glaring.

"Our mother set about cleaning, making the home presentable for our guest who would come for the evening with our oldest brother, our 'John Boy' as in the Walton's TV program, first in our family to go to college. But there was little we could do to hide the old, mismatched furniture, the windows bare of curtains, and the uncarpeted concrete floors. We could only hope that somehow, incredibly, this lady would not notice and feel she was at some shabby outpost.

"Mildred quickly relieved us of our fears. She charmed us all. Never did she indicate that anything about our home was disappointing. She sat on a bench at the wooden dining table, a table long enough to accommodate, at times, ten children and our parents. She showed keen appreciation in enjoying the meal in her honor. I marked her every move, struck with awe, knowing that from this gracious and gentle college girl from New York I could learn much. And so it was.

"Mildred would later sit at the same table and prepare beautifully hand-scripted wedding invitations. She would accept tea in chipped cups as graciously as if she were spending the afternoon with England's Queen. She laughed at simple jokes and pretended not at all to be aware of gaffes. Always considerate of the feelings and needs of others, she never belittled anything, complained, or expected preferential treatment for herself. This touched me, because her health was often on the frightful edge of the desperate.

"As the years passed I realized that Mildred was a Christian first, a wife, mother, and grandmother, a lady to the core, and always a good sport. She was a woman whose glowing godly character was born of deep conviction that, we learned, had nothing to do with being from New York, and much to do with commitment to Christ. Her life impacted many, and I was one who benefited from knowing this lovely woman, who lived her life so well.

"In her years of delicate health and increasing breathing perils, crowds posed very real threats to Mildred. But ours was an over-sized family, and we enjoyed reunions, gatherings of three and four generations of Rosscups. Most reunions were in the summers when school was out. But temperatures soared, exacerbating Mildred's physical battles to cope. On one occasion the rest of us were in the back yard by the pool, and Jim and Mildred in a bedroom as she was engaged in a most scary battle to get her breath. Soon after that, Jim rushed her to the Sky Harbor Airport in Phoenix, put her on a plane to fly home, and phoned friends back there to ask that they meet her at the Los Angeles Airport. He then drove himself and their daughters home to California.

"Always a good sport, Mildred never missed a reunion. She arrived with a smile and obvious eagerness. She gave an affectionate name, 'Isabelle,' to her small oxygen tank with a fine dash of humor that shined a brightness over her problem. Though she was unable to run in relay races or impromptu baseball games, she enthusiastically cheered for her grandsons. She engaged in spirited conversations and laughed at corny jokes. We felt deeply touched by her courage, her gracious carriage, and her enthusiastic spirit.

"My sister in law knew and lived 'true grit' even better than John Wayne who starred in the movie by that name. When she faced exhaustion and had to take time out for her oxygen machine, she quietly and without fanfare retreated to her motel room for respite. Upon return to the reunion, her parking space was likely filled, but she never requested assistance no matter how inconvenienced. Once we realized that she was being forced to walk needlessly, my husband Jim was quick to save a 'Mildred Parking Place' for her. She was incredulous. For it was not in her nature to ask for or expect preferential treatment.

"Mildred at all times was supportive of her husband, my brother. She honored how much his family meant to him. She had embraced his family as lovingly as if she had been born into it. She was our dear sister, a family member whose sweet spirit and enthusiasm for life inspired several generations. Family reunions will continue in Mildred's absence. But they will never be the same without this lovely lady."

Joyce Rosscup Potter

Joyce married Craig Potter of Phoenix, a gardening and landscape expert, and has been active in the Scottsdale Bible Church. One of her two daughters, Erika, is now waiting for full support to go with Christar Missions to serve in Turkey. Joyce agrees with Ethel's and Mary Ellen's tributes, and chuckles at another remembrance:

"Mildred was a lot of fun. She seemed, at times, to be a tease, to get a mischievous smirk on her face and a twinkle in her eye, and come out with something funny. She was a hit with all of us."

Lalani Wood

"Mildred was my aunt, and one of my favorite persons. I first met her, I think, when I was five. Jim and Mildred visited us on one of their trips from his seminary studies.

"A short time after that, both my father and my uncle Jim obtained jobs in the Los Angeles area. So the lives of both families began to intertwine. Somewhere between my second and fourth grades, Aunt Mildred fell into one of her critically ill times. As a child, I was intensely frightened that we would lose her. I sat in the hospital waiting room while my parents visited. Our parents would make arrangements so that we children also could sneak a peak into the room. I remember later lying on my bed at night praying for God to heal my aunt. I did this every night until she was released from the hospital. That was my first experience with intercessory prayer.

"From my child's perspective, Mildred recovered. I now know that she was very frequently facing intense battles. Of course, most of my memories involve playing with my cousins Dianne and Carolyn. The five of us cousins liked to create playhouses and stage made-up plays. We loved to 'sock skate' on the bedroom's hard, slick floor.

"My aunt was a part of most of my most treasured holiday memories. The Rosscup family often joined us in my early years for Thanksgiving and Christmas dinners. Mildred brought special dishes that were a delight but which we almost never had otherwise. Those included a vegetable called rutabaga and a pie called mincemeat. I always wondered how she was able to make chopped meat taste like a fruit! Later as an adult my ignorance was dispelled; mincemeat was a fruit.

"From that point on, my aunt became one of the best role models of a patient, gracious, and hospitable hostess. Through the years, her illness kept her from church most of the time. And she missed the majority of the other social activities. Still, I never once saw her downcast. I myself would have gone crazy from so much struggle and solitude. I would have lamented the loss of a cherished teaching career, which she had to bear. But Mildred never acted slighted. I was always amazed that she seemed completely content, submitting to the lot God had entrusted to her, and resting on Him [Phil. 4:11-12].

"I attended college at Biola. One of the reasons, among many, was the school's proximity to my aunt and uncle, only four miles. Every Wednesday evening they had me over for an early dinner, then Uncle Jim took me to the prayer meeting at their church. This weekly escape from my dorm meant so much. The chance to talk with Aunt Mildred was one of the brightest parts.

"She was an avid knitter. For some reason, my sweaters always developed small holes. Aunt Mildred was the only one who knew how to fix the holes in ways that did not show. One year, she made me a sweater and cap which I still have. I loved the color. Just this past winter while on leave from Indonesia, I pulled the sweater out of the trunk. It is still as nice as when it was new. I look forward to flying into the arms of Mildred when God calls me home too, to be with Him."

Diane Fraley Medico

"I often think of Mildred and the things she taught Becky and me. She loved to give us dating advice. Some of it was quite humorous, and some very serious. On the funny side I recall a time when I expected a young man who had asked me out on a date, and I was not certain how I should dress. Was I too casual, or too dressed up? So Mildred showed Becky and me a little secret. We went out near Jim's study, in those early years a 'cracker box' converted from a part of the garage. There we waited in the dark for my date to walk up the driveway. Peering out through the crack between the garage door and post, we had a good view of his approach. When we saw my date, we all knew I was dressed just fine.

"Another memory is of Mildred sitting Becky and me down and asking how we would feel about being pastors' wives. We both just sort of shrugged and said it would be okay. Mildred then reminded us that we were at a Bible university, and many of the young men were there as their first step toward being church leaders. We still thought it was okay. Then she asked how we thought the life of being a pastor's wife would be. She told us that unless we were willing to let everyone in the congregation view us as if in a 'fishbowl' we should not even consider it. She also pointed out that some people with good intentions or not would judge the way we disciplined our children, how we dressed, etc.

"She also made us aware that a pastor is on call 24 hours a day, very much like some medical doctors. We could easily be awakened in the middle of the night and have to go to somebody in need, or we might be planning a dinner or other engagement and our husband be called away. She gave us some very pertinent questions to ask ourselves. What she ended up telling us was that if we decided to marry someone going into the pastorate God would bless us beyond measure, but He would entrust tough times too.

"I bet she even gave that same counsel to her daughters, Dianne and Carolyn. Very good advice. Even though I did not marry a pastor, I have thought of her very words when I, too, was tempted to 'judge' our own pastor's wife."

31

Ladies' Tributes in the Church

MILDRED'S ILLNESS KEPT HER from church or Sunday School except on rare occasions. However, her breathing varied. Sometimes, though <u>never</u> really what people normally enjoy, it was temporarily eased enough to allow attendance. She even taught a children's Sunday School class for a couple of years. In another span she was president for two years of the Women's Missionary Fellowship that met once a month.

When, in her later years, she occasionally breathed well enough to go to a service, along with her went her wheeled oxygen tank friend, "Isabelle."

Ladies of the WMF at Calvary Baptist Church, Whittier, CA relate the impact Mildred had on their lives. We have been members in that fellowship since 1972.

Jody Cooper

Jody and her husband Leon were long-time missionaries in Brazil. After this they led Campus Crusade for Christ "Athletes in Action" teams to play and witness in several countries for a number of tours. Since then, Jody succeeded Mildred as president of the WMF for a couple of years.

"Dear 'Slugger Millie.' Did I hear right? During the Memorial Service for you several folk were referring to you as 'Slugger Millie'! I was more than amazed. Of all the things we shared during our frequent 'tea parties', however did you miss revealing this? [Mildred never paraded her accomplishments, and she wanted to be called "Mildred," not "Millie"]. Yet the more I pictured you standing ready as the pitcher let go with a fast ball, the more the name seemed to fit! My friend, my very special friend,

'Slugger Millie' standing at the ready with God's help to handle whatever He allowed life to send whirling her way. I always left your house encouraged and lighted with a smile.

"Your friendship meant worlds to me, and I wish I'd told you so. Never did you have a complaint. You accepted your health limitations with peace and trust, showing by your life that there truly is what the song says, '**joy in serving Jesus.**'

"What a terrific WMF president you made! Under you our group revived, got busy, developed vision, and found ways to serve, in one way by praying with much more fervor and faith for our missionaries. Later, as your health forced you to take more rest, you stepped down. Did you get any more rest? Well, you now have entered into your rest [Rev. 14:13]. But when you were no longer our leader, the most beautiful and timely monthly invitations to our WMF meetings began to appear in your so-called rest time. Looking back, I realize we should have kept a scrapbook. You must have spent hours over these wonders, finding just the right pictures and creative themes. But missions was always high on your list to keep informed about and absorb your prayers.

"There were just so many special qualities to be admired in you. You were a **giver**. If WMF needed a garage to store items in for 'Hope Again' Ministries, 'use my garage.' Or, 'you like the flowers in my yard? Here, take a cutting home.' At least half of our WMF ladies now have your prize flowers growing in their yards! If there was a family outing, 'come by my house first.' You gave us a send-off with a double sized fruit cobbler! And then, your **compassion**. Thank you for the hugs, love, and prayers that lifted me through the last months of our daughter Jamie's heart-breaking, losing battle with breast cancer.

"The blessing of knowing you has been immeasurable. I'll never forget you, 'Slugger Millie.'"

Terry Ortner

This lady is the wife of Dean Ortner, an electronics whiz who years ago succeeded the famous Irwin Moon and George Speak in leading Moody Bible College's "Sermons from Science" ministry. The Ortners, living in Whittier, have traveled to several countries where Dean has staged his mind-boggling shows, doing incredible things and giving the gospel, leading hundreds to Christ. When Moody a few years ago decided to discontinue this ministry, the Ortners came up with their own version for the same kind of outreach, "Wonders of Science." They are keeping up the far-flung efforts. They have often been in my Bible classes in the church. Terry writes:

"Enduring joy, an infectious smile, peace that passes all understanding, radiance, great wisdom, a fitting word, and a prayer warrior. These words describe Mildred Rosscup to me.

"My earliest memory of Mildred was at a Calvary Baptist Church dinner. I had one older teen and one entering those years. My husband was often gone and I was left to deal with the attitudes. I confessed my despair to Mildred, and she smiled and in a calm voice assured me that in a few years things would be better. She was right, of course, but just at that moment I needed her calm wisdom from experience. It helped me get through those years with hope and greater joy.

"I especially loved it when Mildred had a breathing break-through to attend the WMF. She added such a positive spirit and sparkle, but her praying gripped me the most. It was evident that her prayers came from one who spent much time in secret with the Lord [Matt. 6:6: "go into your inner room . . . pray"]. They exhibited her deep faith and revealed her understanding that our battle is not against flesh and blood, but against the unseen forces of spiritual wickedness in heavenly places. She prayed all-out with such a serious spirit, and God used her to help make prayer a holy occupation in my life. Thank you, Lord, for Mildred!"

The "holy occupation" drew some of its inculcation from one of Mildred's ABI books on the spiritual life, A. P. Gibbs' *Worship, the Christian's Highest Occupation*. And it found impetus from Andrew Murray's famous book, *With Christ in the School of Prayer,* but most of all from letting the Word dwell richly in her (Col. 3:16).

Beve Mengel

Beve and her husband Verdon have often opened their home in the hills of Whittier to host couples' get-togethers. Verdon was an electrician for General Petroleum, and as a young man one of the nation's top blazing softball pitchers, rarely losing. He also sang in the 1950's to the 1970's in a traveling Christian quartet, "The Calvarymen." Beve was married to another member of that quartet, Bill, who went to be with the Lord, as Verdon's wife Martha also did. Later, Verdon and Beve married.

"What a blessing for us to share what Mildred's life meant as seen through our eyes! I know that many will share all she did for WMF although her health kept her from coming to some of the meetings. She was there in spirit.

"Mildred was so skilled on the computer, and did much to make attractive, winsome things to plug our meetings. We saw her as a quiet testimony of God's sufficient grace [2 Cor. 3:5; 12:9], His strength, and courage through Jesus Christ. Mildred and I had many phone conversations on life and our grand kids.

"Joey Long is not here to share what Mildred meant to her [Joey was mother of Randy, who married our younger daughter, Carolyn]. Joey and Mildred talked almost daily as Mildred inspired Joey during her struggle with cancer. God blessed

Mildred and Joey with the same grandchildren. And how these ladies loved to glory in all the cute stories about the boys. Joey would call me and rejoice about how much Mildred was a blessing to her.

"How wonderful to know that my daughter, my first husband, Verdon's wife Martha, and Joey and Mildred, are all waiting to welcome us in glory. They now walk safe and free of pain, and we shall all be together some day. I believe soon."

Barbara Hill

Barbara followed Mildred and Jody Cooper as president of the WMF and has served for several years. She is a nurse, and wife of Steven Hill, an outstanding musician who serves in his specialty at the Whittier Christian Schools.

"Unfortunately, sometimes in church we miss knowing someone because we have a tendency to stick to our own age group, or those with whom we are the most familiar. Though I have belonged to Calvary Baptist for about 15 years, and known of Mildred, it was not until I started attending WMF that my eyes were opened to what a very special person she was.

"Recently, I was looking for someone's phone number from WMF and reached into my bag and pulled out the directory for 2007–08. Mildred had designed the cover and put together the several pages, with information that took hours of phoning to collect. Our theme that year was 'Great is Thy Faithfulness.' The officers had wondered how Mildred was going to be able to come up with a design for a cover expressing our theme. Well, of course, she did—with pictures of 'summer, winter, springtime, and harvest.' She consistently was resourceful to do this for all of our announcements, directories, and special projects.

"Take the announcements for our very first evening tea. I hate to admit it, but I was a little bit envious of her abilities to use the computer so skillfully. Her computer provided her with a wonderful means of communicating with family and friends, and especially glorifying God with her talents [1 Cor. 10:31; Col. 3:17, 23].

"Mildred grew the most beautiful dahlias. One year she was dividing the bulbs and asked me if I wanted some. I had never planted bulbs, but wanted some of those beautiful flowers. After she gave them to me I researched on the internet about planting them. I was very worried that I wouldn't get it right, that the bulbs would not flower. I actually fretted over this for a while. Finally, I decided, 'I'm going to plant those bulbs. If they don't bloom, at least I can say I tried.' When I saw my first bloom, larger than a dessert plate, I was so excited. We were leaving on vacation. I thought to myself, 'I will miss the whole blooming cycle.' Little did I know that those dahlias would bloom through September. Neighbors would come by and comment on their beauty. I took a picture so that Mildred could see how nice they were. This summer has been my fifth season with the flowers. They are just one reminder of Mildred.

"Two wonderfully vivid memories of Mildred are of her at a tea with the ladies from WMF, dressed in hats and gloves and boas. I have a great picture of her. Then, the second memory is of her arriving on her mechanical cart at Bev Bangs' house for a WMF luncheon [about one-half mile from our home]. We were all thrilled to see her. [Mildred never knew it, but I guessed the length of the meeting, drove to a spot not far from the Bangs home, and was there to make sure Mildred would get home all right. When I saw her head toward home on the cart at about 4 mph, I slowly followed at a distance, then joined her in our driveway].

"I admired Mildred beyond words—her positive attitude, her reliance on God, her exceptional knowledge of the Bible, her talents, her sense of humor. I asked her to pray for my son and daughter. I trusted that she would honor that request. Mildred represented to me the most beautiful of all women, those with the 'unfading beauty of a gentle and quiet spirit, which is of great worth in God's sight.' I cannot tell you how many times I think of her. I miss her dearly. While writing this, I have been thinking of the hymn, 'Face to Face,' and the words, 'when with rapture I behold Him, Jesus Christ who died for me.'"

Doris Peterson

Doris for many years has been one of the most active servants in the church. Her husband Joel died suddenly back in the 1970's, and she finished raising a son and two daughters. Her son, Glen, finished at Denver Seminary, and has led in different Christian ministries. Her daughter Audrey was one of our daughter Dianne's closest friends during grade school and high school.

"My first memory of really getting acquainted with Mildred was after Audrey and Dianne started in the Pioneer Girls Club at Calvary. I had known her by just seeing her in church with her dear family. I knew she had a health problem, but when I took her the material to make a uniform for Dianne, I would not have noticed any infirmity. She just got busy with the sewing and had it done in no time at all.

"Also when I would visit with her in her home she was so gracious and always talked about how much she loved and appreciated her Jim and her girls Dianne and Carolyn. She was a testimony of how a wife should support her husband.

"You both were so supportive to me after I lost my husband, Joel, in 1973. Helping with transportation to Camp Cherith was such a boost. That meant so much to me. Mildred was always cheerful and outgoing, including everyone in her group of friends. I never felt like a fifth wheel as some treat single people in this world of couples.

"After I retired [from being a nursing executive] I saw how much she had been doing for the WMF, printing the directories, praying, and baking treats. These are just a touch, a small sampling. She was never complaining even when she became dependent on her companion, the oxygen tank.

"I will continue to miss Mildred as a dear friend and a model of the Proverbs 31 woman. Her testimony is as in verse 10b, 'her price is far above rubies.'"

Bev Bangs

Bev has been very active in women's Bible studies, and for several years led the prayer time during WMF meetings.

"It is a real joy to be able to recall thoughts of someone so special as Mildred Rosscup. Thinking of her brings the warmth of a smile to my day. She was so aglow and loving to everyone who knew her. She treated everybody and every thing with such gentleness—people, animals, flowers. She always was willing to help anyone with a problem, particularly with spiritual matters. And how she knew her Bible! Her know-ledge made her answers deeply moving.

"I loved Mildred's sense of humor, the way she could tease, yet make one feel really good. One day she invited me over to share some tea. She poured my cup, then stepped away to the sink. As I reached to pick up my cup, I was startled, yet pleasantly. There, suddenly forming, was a picture of a butterfly on the cup. It hadn't been there before. I turned and looked quickly at Mildred, and she just stood there with a mischievous smile on her face. She had fooled me! It was a special cup that delightfully out the colors when the hot drink was poured into it."

Oleta Jones

This dear lady, now nearly 94, went through the painful death of her husband back in the 1970's. She is an example of the kind of woman Paul writes about in 1 Timothy 5:5, who, being widowed, continues in prayers to God. She has a ministry of phoning people to see how they are, and fostering prayers of care.

"The earliest thing I recall about Mildred is when I was teaching the fourth grade girls in Sunday School. One of Mildred's daughters was in the class, and Mildred surprised me by coming in to sit and visit. I felt like asking for her input as I did not feel adequate. But I went on with my class. She seemed so interested and friendly. I quickly felt reassured.

"Looking back, I remember how precious her input became to me and others in our missionary efforts. She acted as president for two years. I was vice-president or program director a number of years, so we would meet with her to chat together about our needs and aims for the year. As time went by and she became increasingly home bound, even in this she became the pivotal person for our monthly notices. All that she did was so top notch, so professional. I always looked forward to see the sharp product she would come up with for each annual directory: for 2006-07, Philippians 2:4; for 2007-08, Hebrews 10:23; for 2008-09, just before her home-going, Matthew 5:16.

"I know that others helped to bring information together, and Mildred would be first to point that out. She always served without fanfare, and heaped credit on others.

"One year some of the ladies met at my home for prayer. Mildred was among these. I was impressed by her reminding us of answers. I think that is the exciting thing about prayer. She helped me to see that, and it increased in me an expectant faith in the Lord. In these later years when I hesitantly phoned her, knowing of her oxygen shortage, it was such a joy. She was so up front about her condition, yet never complaining. So I was at ease, even lifted by her words of information, comfort, and blessings. She always was practical, in every day language, with no put-ons. And she was happy in the Lord. It always was an elixir, infusing new courage in my heart.

"I think the one thing I should say is simply this: I loved Mildred. Her family was incredibly fortunate to have her."

That has to be an under statement!

Lorraine Smotherman

Jim and Lorraine have been long-time Wycliffe missionaries to Peru, and for many years assigned in the States, living in Whittier. Their daughters Dee and Kay were friends of our daughters. Dee with her husband Mike Sylvester serves in the Campus Crusade ministry at USC, while Kay and her husband James Chambers lead in "Come to Him Ministry" that provides shelter, clothing, and witness to lead down and out people to the Savior and help them get established. Jim, myself when there, and another church leader, Stan Foss, have for years left the Sunday morning service just before the pastor gets up to preach, to go into a private room. We spend the hour calling on God for His blessed working. It is an "Aaron and Hur Group" (Exod. 17:8-13).

Mildred's and Lorraine's birthdays were at the same time. So for years they have gone out together for lunch to celebrate their special day, the fourth of February.

"It is almost birthday time when I write. And even though I love writing about Mildred, I am sad at our loss. She lives in my heart as a precious friend. May God strengthen you and see you [Jim] through her birthday month with happy memories and anticipation of a grand reunion.

"Happy birthday, Mildred. I have always felt honored to share a day with you. I looked forward to our annual lunch out, usually at Polly's Pie Shop. We had a great time exchanging cards and laughs. You usually thought our lunch should conclude with pie for two reasons. One, we were at Polly's where they specialize in pies, and two, it was a day to celebrate. In the last few years, 'Isabelle' [the portable oxygen tank] accompanied us. 'Isabelle' was never spoken of in an unkind manner, but rather in the way that only Mildred could, with humor and dignity. Dignity is a word that comes to mind when I think of Mildred.

"Mildred took her responsibilities seriously. She prepared our directory. She put so much thought into the design for the cover. It always coordinated with our theme for each year. She also faithfully prepared the colorful, fitting invitation leaflets that we passed out each month before meetings coming up. What cleverness she invested to make these provocative. For instance, when Kay Chambers [Lorraine's younger daughter] was to be our guest speaker, Mildred put the picture of a box of 'Special K' cereal on the cover!

"To me, Mildred embodied the verse in Philippians 4 which states, 'for I have learned to be content whatever the circumstances.' Her physical limitations were never the focus of attention, rather she concentrated on the person she was with. Her bodily problems never were in the way of praying with a needy friend, or helping one to solve a problem. Her delightful humor always shined through. I can hear her chuckle now.

"I miss you, Mildred. The birthday time won't be the same without you. You live on in my heart as an admired and precious friend. Thank you for sharing your life with me."

Jackie Jenkins

Jackie spent several decades in Japan as a missionary, and for several years has been retired, yet serving vitally in an area Japanese fellowship as well as coming to WMF meetings at Calvary Baptist. Frequently she would phone and arrange to bring lunch so that Mildred and she could fellowship over food, and chat and pray together. She has lived her life all-out as a faithful witness of God. She is one of the most high quality ladies in her walk with the Lord that have ever graced our lives.

"For you, Jim, Mildred's home-going brings rejoicing and grieving, all mixed together. What a lovely thing you are doing, writing a book of memories about Mildred for your family and others. Mildred was a precious part of my life, and the lunch/sharing/prayer times with her were special gifts from the Lord.

"Mildred is the one I ran to for prayer help when there was a special need. I came home from Japan in November, 1990. I knew Mildred before that, but it was through the WMF that I began to have one-on-one times with her. After a meeting, sometimes she and I would be assigned to update the directory or do some other task. That led to lunch, good conversation, and prayer for WMF, the church, missionaries, and mutual friends. And as we got better acquainted, we prayed for each other's needs, such as health, families, and other concerns.

"When I first returned from the field, people had lots of suggestions on how I ought to use my time in serving the Lord. But it seemed like the Lord was saying, 'Wait, I will show you.' I did know that I was to help my mother, for my father had died. I worked for two of SEND International's West Coast representatives, and they gave me Tuesday mornings off from the office to help with the English as a second language classes at the Evangelical Free Church in Fullerton. A lot of Japanese ladies came. Then I found the Vine Japanese Church, and still am serving there. Besides the work with the Japanese people, Bible classes in English for Japanese ladies opened up.

"Mildred had such a warm, unfailing interest in the people from the church and Bible classes. She quickly absorbed their stories, and at each prayer time probed me about them. 'How is it coming with the lady whose husband is thinking about becoming a Christian?' He did. 'The woman who brings her disruptive child to the class?' That child eventually grew up. 'The lady with the poor health and mental problems?' She was born again, and Mildred rejoiced in this before she went to heaven. Mildred prayed and followed up with interest, encouragement, and more prayer. It gives me great joy to think about the time that is coming when Mildred and many of these people she prayed for will meet in heaven at Jesus' feet. There won't be any language barrier, or problem about remembering names such as Toshiko, Ien Iida, Nagisa, Mari, Mr. Tamamachi, the Uenos, Shinobu, etc. [cf. 1 Thess. 2:19-20].

"Mildred's cheerfulness and attitude centered in others will always be an ex-ample and driving motivation to me. Illness, weakness, pain, inconvenience, loss of the freedoms good health could have opened up for her—I knew these were all problems, but they were not the center of attention. They were just some challenges to be worked around to get at the things we wanted to talk and pray about. No disparaging words. Not even explaining, until I would ask. Good humor, faith's optimism in God's good purposes, jokes about the oxygen tank and tubing, and the scooter.

"When Mildred had two broken toes, which the doctor couldn't do much about, I saw another example of her attitude. My niece, Dennise, worked at the 'Runner's Zone' in uptown Whittier. She knows a lot about how the right shoe can help almost any foot problem, and she advised me to take Mildred in to describe her problem and see if the store owner could fit her. But we were warned—one cannot be fussy about what the shoe looks like or the color. In a given year, the various manufacturers make shoes to correct certain problems, but there is no choice of color, etc.

"So, Mildred and I went. The owner tried several pairs on her, having her walk around the store, followed by Dennise, who observed how each shoe affected the metatarsal arch and the broken toes, and Mildred's gait. It hurt, of course, and very soon she was tired, but she did not complain. When everyone agreed on a certain shoe, white with yellow designs, Mildred accepted the decision in good cheer, with nary a word about yellow not being her color, or not going with the rest of her wardrobe. No vanity there, just being thankful that the shoes relieved some of the pain. And she wore the shoes faithfully. I thank God that from now on she will walk with a glorious liberty!"

Ila Barnhart

Ila has faithfully sent cards for our birthdays, anniversaries, and other special occasions. She did not attend WMF, but has been a steady attending member of the church, and we have prayed for and benefited from the continual prayers of Ila and her husband Dick.

"I met Mildred while she was a Sunday School teacher. I saw her gentle spirit and love for the children. She taught God's Word from her heart. I loved listening to her as I helped in her class room.

"She was an encourager with a sunny countenance and a great spice of humor. She had a delightful, artistic talent of which I have seen several examples in her 'Thank You' and birthday cards. She was someone that you felt really cared when she asked, 'How are you?' and listened intently while you told her. She was the kind of Christian woman I try to pattern my life after. I miss her more than words can convey."

Marcia Chartier

Marcia and her husband Barry, a fireman and later part of a crime investigation team, were long-time members of the church with us. They hosted lively couples' parties in their home. Marcia says:

"We rejoice at Mildred's 'home going.' She was a real heroine who sought to put others at ease, making such a serious illness appear to be nothing more than a little inconvenience. What a spirit with a heart to match!"

32

Ladies' Tributes at the Memorial Service

April 19, 2008

THREE LADIES SHARE MEMORIES from many years with Mildred. The first two are our daughters Dianne and Carolyn. Then one of Mildred's dearest, most considerate, long-time friends, Kathy Edwards, gives her tribute. Other words of esteem, such as by Ethel Wood and Jody Cooper who, with the ladies here, spoke in the Memorial Service, would fit in this chapter as well. But these also go well in memories by family and local church ladies, where they appear (cf. Chapters 30-31).

Dianne Rosscup Gutierrez (the elder daughter)

Dianne married Caleb Gutierrez in 1982. He works at Chevron Oil Company, and she decided not to teach in a Christian grade school but in a public school. She felt that there she could help pupils who, often, have no spiritual input. She has freedom at times to offer this in love.

"Mom always made our birthdays special.

"I always asked for spaghetti when I was young, and then Hungarian goulash when I became older. When I turned 16, Mom was very ill but she asked a friend, Lorraine Smotherman, to go and get my first lipstick. It was a shade that went with my very favorite color, lavender.

"For my wedding, Mom made my dress, my sister Carolyn's dress, and her own dress. She also devoted many hours experimenting with pomegranate juice so that she could make certain the punch tasted good and was lavender. She even planted sterling silver roses to try to have lavender roses for my wedding. They didn't bloom in time for the event, but she picked some and put them in a vase for my 25th anniversary.

"She never felt a task done for someone else to be too difficult or painstaking. She understood the self-sacrificing and truly considerate spirit of celebration. She was there when I was an adult. For example, when my car battery was dead on the first day of teaching school on a new grade level, Mom asked a friend for help, and brought me her car.

"When two of Caleb's and my three cats died and one was left alone, I asked Mom to come and keep the distraught cat company while we were gone to work, and she did. And when our house was to be uninhabitable due to remodeling, Mom and Dad invited us to stay with them. Then, when our home was still not finished a year later, Mom told us she and Dad would be with us until the end. She lived the self-sacrificial life of being there for someone. She stood out as a good and faithful servant. I could never repay her for all that she joyfully did for me. I only could do a few favors here and there, sometimes give her small gifts, and appreciate her. I could never even come close to repaying her for being faithful and denying herself to be there for me so many times and in so many ways.

"God frequently showed His faithful love for me through my Mom. He Himself had given me a self-sacrificial gift—salvation—that I could never repay. I have asked Him for things that I could not ask of anybody else. He has been and always will be with me, even though I cannot earn this and don't deserve it. I can only receive it and be grateful."

Carolyn Rosscup Long (the younger daughter)

Our younger daughter married Randall Winslow Long in 1986. She became a computer whiz at Biola University, and has worked at Hughes Air-craft, Fleetwood Enterprises with their highway recreational vehicles, and now at a Christian credit union. She is the mother of two sons, Zachary, now 14, and Benjamin, 13.

"Mom amazed me. She was an amazing person. Her talents varied from doing the taxes to fixing the toaster to designing cards! When I was young, she led me to know Jesus, and I prayed with her to receive Him. Mom was very considerate and giving. I think of a day in elementary school when I was frantic as I walked with a friend to school, because I had forgotten to bring some very important homework. During class, my teacher brought it to me, saying that Mom had delivered it to the school!

"She knew what I needed. Sometimes we would spend hours playing 'Monopoly'—my Mom, my sister, and I. We called Mom 'Money Bags' when she was winning.

"I will always cherish my wedding dress, which Mom carefully designed and sewed herself. When Randy and I started a home and family of our own, she gave me a love of roses and the garden, and taught me how to prune and where to plant.

After I married I prayed often, even though Mom's health wasn't the best, 'Lord, please let her and Dad live to <u>know</u> and <u>love my children</u>.' Thank the Lord, He abundantly answered that prayer!

"Together, Mom and I made the nursery bedding for my boys' rooms. Even this week, the night before she passed, I made a phone call to her for some sewing advice. I'm thankful I did. That was the last time I talked to her!

"Mom strove to be <u>active</u> even though her health worked against that desire. We couldn't keep her down. She insisted on walking up and down the street to watch her grandsons 'Trick or Treat,' toting her oxygen with her. She played Mastermind with my son Zach, and was an avid attender of Ben's Little League games, pom poms and all. Just a week ago, she was at the ball park. She loved to hear Zach play the piano and to be at his recitals.

"She was an amazing Mom and Grammy, and now, I'm sure, she is amazed by Jesus as she meets Him face to face."

Kathy Edwards (a dear friend)

This godly lady in her youth first visited along with her husband Stan to hear me teach in a Sunday School Bible class of Calvary Baptist, Whittier, in 1973. Kathy and Mildred soon found their hearts closely clasped in Christian love. God gave them a precious, mutually supportive friendship bond. Kathy often invited us to join her and Stan for meals, and they were guests in our home.

Even when this couple moved to Gresham, OR, an outskirt of Portland (1977–1988), Kathy kept writing letters to Mildred or calling her on the phone. The two ladies' high esteem for one another continued when the Edwards moved to Tucson in 1988. On drives to see her elderly parents in Springville, CA near Porterville, she and often Stan and three of their five sons stopped to be guests in our home. These were times God delightfully blessed. And we visited them in their Tucson desert home with the same exhilaration in the strong sense of Christ's presence as Lord of all.

To behold Mildred and Kathy so engrossed in the living room, relishing such fulfillment, peaked my joy. Here are Kathy's words.

"It was my privilege to be one of Mildred's friends for the past 35 years. She was a rare and a good friend, and such a lot of fun. We laughed so much together. Our talks were often pick-me-ups. She never criticized me, but had a gentle spirit in pointing out some other perspective I was missing. She encouraged me when I needed a lift, and allowed me to encourage her. If I was struggling she let me struggle until God was finished with His work to grow me. She rejoiced with me when I rejoiced, and wept with me when I wept.

"Mildred delighted in the things others could do that she was not able to do because of her health limitations. She was humble, adventurous, determined, practical, a no-nonsense person, who loved beauty and was not afraid to try anything. She had learned to embrace suffering, endure with patience, and accept with joy. She was considerate and generous. Once when I was ill, I heard heavy breathing and wheezing in my house, and by the time I made it to the living room Mildred had been there, left dinner for my family, and was on her way out. I felt a little like King David when three of his mighty men broke through obstacles, enemy lines, to bring him a cup of water from the well at Bethlehem.

"Our family moved from Southern California to Gresham, Oregon after four years [1977], and we kept up our friendship in so many ways. We talked about our family and friends, our day to day lives, our hopes, our frustrations, our ideas, our issues, God, heaven, the millennium, and Jesus coming back for us.

"On Sunday, just two days before we lost Mildred, she and I had a long talk discussing our dark world and our hope. I mentioned that some of our friends do not believe there will be a millennium after Jesus comes. Mildred was aghast, 'No, no, they are not going to rob me of my millennium!' Was Mildred perfect? No. She and I often grieved. We grew weary with our sin, and our longing to be like Jesus, complete. Now Mildred's salvation is so much more complete.

"When you called that Tuesday, Jim, to tell me 'we lost Mildred today,' I went into a time of weeping for you all and I wept for myself. But in a very short time God brought comforting thoughts to me. Number one, I had often asked God that when her time came He would take my friend gently, and He reminded me that before my prayers He had already anticipated this, and at His chosen time had fulfilled it.

"Second, I recall Mildred telling me years ago that when she was hospitalized just before I met her [1973] she was being scheduled to be discharged as an invalid for her remaining days on this earth. But God had come to her in some real impression during the night and given her the confidence that she was going to raise her daughters. She began improving the next day and did finish raising her girls, even saw them years into their marriages!

"Third, she had told me more than on one occasion how much she appreciated and loved her grandmother [Theda Currey, wife of George Currey], who was a wonderful woman. And just a couple of years ago she confided to me that she had always hoped to live long enough to be a grandmother to her grandchildren. When they were very young, she had thought, in her illness, that her time had come and gone. But God gave her 13 years to be a grandmother to her grandson Zachary, and 12 to Benjamin.

"When the phone call came of God taking Mildred home, at that moment on Tuesday in my imagination, and I have a vivid one, I saw her with her quiet reserve gazing upon the Lord Jesus with His scars. She was worshipping Him unencumbered. And once again, she was thanking Him for exceeding great and precious promises He had made good, and for allowing her the privilege of being Jim's wife and believing in him, and for being Dianne's and Carolyn's mother and believing in them, and for being Caleb's and Randy's mother in law and believing in them, and for being Zachary's and Benjamin's grandmother and believing in them. You were her treasures. Every letter, every phone call, and every visit she talked about you.

"Her passing into glory has left a great hole in my life, yet not nearly what she left in your lives. I am thrilled I knew Mildred, and I am glad I know the living God who is capable of the seemingly impossible, not only to make us His children and walk us through the dark days of pain and grief, but to take us into His glorious light.

"One more thing delights me about Mildred. I realize she does not yet have her glorified body. She will at the rapture. But, somehow in my mind's eye, I see her breathing great, delicious gulps of air. She is doing this with no pain, no wheezing, no cough, no congestion, no machine—and I am glad!"

33

Giving Thanks in All Things

POURING OUT THANKS IN all things is God's will for His children (1 Thess. 5:17). It is fitting to come before our Savior with praise. For as His faithful Word also says, "Great is the Lord, and greatly to be praised" (Ps. 48:1; 96:4; 145:3). To exult with adoration to Him "is pleasant and praise is becoming" (147:1).

God's blessings that have enriched Mildred's and my life inspire many offerings of gratitude. Andre Crouch's song, "My Tribute," captures the proper focus.

> How can I say thanks for the things You have done for me?
> Things so undeserved, yet You gave to prove Your love for me. . . .
> The voices of a million angels could not express my gratitude,
> All that I am and ever hope to be, I owe it all to You.
> To God be the glory, to God be the glory, to God be the glory,
> For the things He has done.
> With His blood He has saved me, with His power He has raised me,
> To God be the glory, for the things He has done.
> Just let me live my life; let it be pleasing, Lord, to You,
> And if I gain any praise, let it go to Calvary"
> (in *Hymns for the Family of God*. Nashville: Paragon Associates, Inc., 1976, pp. 365-66).

What gifts from God stir the celebrations of our hearts to exalt Him? How could I remember all the things of life? A brief list offers examples among multiplied thousands of the venues. A complete account is for me impossible, and besides it would fill many books.

1. He gave Mildred her first birth and also a second birth, and did these for me as well.

2. He gave Mildred Christian parents who truly followed Him, and granted her a home where daily she heard of Christ and saw His transforming

power lived out.

3. He helped her family through very difficult hardships, such as a hurricane's destruction of their barn in 1937, and a fire's devastation of another barn in 1949, a fire out of which God even took to heaven their beloved pastor.

4. He gave Mildred a father who cared enough to take her to piano and organ lessons when she was a teenager. She became a woman of music.

5. He helped her through about 20 hospital stays to assist her breathing.

6. He enabled her thousands of times to draw her breath when her lungs and air channels had seemingly impossible "roadblocks." He gave her courage to fight the battle to breathe when she faced these severely frightening times. He braced and comforted me as I stood by deeply concerned, and said "yes" to my prayers to free her by giving her breakthroughs.

7. He gave her parents who saw that Christian reading material was a rich treasury in the home.

8. He led Mildred all the way across the United States, from New York to Tucson, turned her face to Phoenix, on to Tempe, then led her into the same church and college class to help us meet and marry. How I got into a class that featured Shakespeare must have been by His providence, for that was not my natural, uncultured taste, though I came soon to value it keenly.

9. He led Mildred to a very good Bible school where leaders exemplified godliness and vision for sacrificial service (Rom. 12:1), the Arizona Bible Institute. Out of that school would go dozens of great servants to live Christ, win souls in many lands, and be people of prayer.

10. He gave her a sharp mind to be adept in studies, and facility in almost everything she attempted. He made her a quick learner.

11. He gave her souls saved in her witness in the New York churches, Arizona children's groups, missions labors in Montana, Whittier, CA Sunday School, on our block, and leading our daughters to the Lord.

12. He opened doors for Mildred to devote excellent service as a secretary to the president at ABI, and later at the offices of Dallas Seminary.

13. He rescued my own family from desperate depths of poverty and suffering in a "Grapes of Wrath" exodus from Oklahoma to Arizona.

14. He gave me and my siblings a father and a mother who loved us and provided diligently for us. The father came into my life after my blood father heartlessly walked out on the family and "left us in the lurch."

15. He gave me marvelous opportunities as a young boy to cultivate avid reading skills and do well in school.

16. He gave me one of the finest animal friends a boy or girl ever had, the quarter horse of blazing speed, "Molly."

17. He taught me, via my parents, a hard work ethic, rising a great while before dawn, laboring long with "true grit," and standing up to pressure. Later He would motivate me according to Psalm 5:3, "In the morning, O Lord, Thou will hear my voice; In the morning I will order my prayer to Thee and eagerly watch," as was Jesus' example in Mark 1:35.

18. He sent a Christian couple of vision to invite me to Sunday School and church, which soon led on to my salvation.

19. He gave me a first Sunday School teacher, a carpenter, who was sold out to Him and made things of God live to touch hearts in an upper room at the church.

20. He saved my mother, father, and most of my siblings as years went by.

21. He gave me a love for writing, and opened doors to hone writing skills. This was in newspaper jobs in my town, at college, in seminary, and on a Campus Crusade magazine. All these opportunities would help me later to write books, journal articles, and about 50 book-length syllabi for teaching the riches of His Word. Students would take these manuals throughout the earth to commit God's Word in turn to others (2 Tim. 2:2-3).

22. He gave me positions of leadership in high school and college to prepare me to be up front before people.

23. He led Mildred and me to be in the same church youth group at college where He would nourish our hearts in the same vision.

24. He gave me the forwardness to get to know Mildred, win her friendship, and later her hand in marriage—one of the greatest blessings in my life.

25. He provided jobs during college to pay my way, and help us on dates.

26. He gave me venues to learn to witness during college via Campus Crusade for Christ's leadership. Several students professed faith.

27. He gave me acceptance into Dallas Theological Seminary at a time when faculty were there in great days of the school's growth, and helped me do well enough to get into the doctoral program later and have His blessing in success.

28. He led me to a fine job as a sports writer to begin seminary and later again during the doctorate program.

29. He shaped me for teaching by the skills and godly examples of giants in the Word. Some were J. Dwight Pentecost, S. Lewis Johnson, Charles C. Ryrie, Howard Hendricks, Bruce Waltke, Haddon Robinson, and Stanley Toussaint (all in those days at Dallas), and I. Howard Marshall (The King's College, University of Aberdeen, Scotland). These men of precision led me to "cut it straight" in context, word study, grammar, historical background, manners and customs, and cross reference. In Howard Hendricks' case, the challenge came home to make it simple, motivating, and practical, though I am but a faint echo of his life-moving skill as a speaker. When I sat in Dr. Pentecost's Bible classes, I thought, "I never heard anybody show the Bible coming alive like he can do. Lord, help me be like 'Dr. P'."

30. Before my training, He gave Mildred in her Bible institute training one of His finest teachers and examples of godliness and passion to see souls saved, Dr. John Hubbard.

31. He gave Mildred and me safe drives on countless trips.

32. He saved our lives several times when we hung, as it were, over the "hair's breadth" precipice of death—in the freeze of the New Mexico highlands, when our car was suspended over a cliff in Charleston, West VA, also when treacherous Texas wind swept us into the wrong lane against oncoming traffic, later when I fell asleep at the wheel with a huge truck bearing down on me, and Mildred from collapsed lungs and hundreds of other death's

door breathing crises.

33. He kept Mildred, me, and our daughters free of burglary, safe in car accidents, and free from being victims of the preying and the violent.

34. He gave us great spiritual help in seminary trials so that we grew in Him, sank down deep spiritual roots, and counted the difficulties great open doors into learning better the life of trust.

35. He impressed others' hearts to give to assist us at many a crucial point, and taught us in turn to watch for and prize opportunities to give to those in need. We who freely received learned freely to give (Matt. 10:8).

36. He gave me the privilege of teaching collegians, seminarians, and business people in church classes while in seminary, and Mildred the ministry of prayer and skill on the piano that enhanced many classes.

37. He inclined Dr. Pentecost, supervisor of my seminary Master's thesis, to speak very highly of it and insistently urge me to come back for the doctorate.

38. His grace was upon me to do very well in the doctoral dissertation, the faculty's oral drilling, and the battery of long, exacting written exams.

39. He swung wide the door for a teaching ministry at Talbot Seminary. This lasted 22 years, and God gave Mildred and me "much fruit." He sent the invitation to Talbot "in the nick of time," for I already had a ticket to fly to a Bible college that sought me to join that faculty.

40. He gave us two daughters after a Dallas doctor told Mildred her precarious lung dilemma would never allow her to have children and live. As Stuart Hamblin's song says, "It is no secret what God can do."

41. He helped me lead athletes to Christ in Garland, TX while I worked as a sports editor, and in those days and since to impact hundreds of men and women in counseling.

42. He gave Mildred and me many wonderful and highly committed Christian friends from our seminary training days whom we have cherished all our lives.

43. He provided money to sustain us through the seminary Master's degree and later doctorate studies.

44. He gave Mildred an uncanny "knack" of putting together meals even when our cupboards seemed to have little besides the dishes.

45. He prospered me in Talbot teaching when my class load was double a normal assignment and the dean also called on me to speak in churches many Sundays, or I taught church Bible classes that required much preparation (couples, Church of the Open Door, Los Angeles; various classes during the years at Calvary Baptist, Whittier, and others).

46. He kept our daughters unspoiled in school from evils Satan cunningly used to deceive many young people to keep them in bondage.

47. He gave us good family devotions, heart bonding in love, respect for one another, and cherished memories.

48. He gave Mildred special strength at times to teach, even if for brief spans, in church Sunday School, and to be a woman of vision as a beloved, highly respected president of the Women's Missionary Fellowship.

49. He helped Mildred, even when not able to attend church or women's meetings, to sharpen her computer savvy. So she produced attractive leaflets for the WMF, notes to encourage, and other eye-catching materials. He fashioned her as a servant always, preparing her for an eternity when "His bondservants shall serve Him" (Rev. 22:4-5).

50. He gave me Mildred's patient tutelage to learn to use my computer.

51. He opened up happy vacation venues and good times of respite from trials severe for Mildred due to her breathing problems, and in a partner's empathy testings sometimes painful beyond description for me.

52. He saw me through long hours of study, pain of eye strain, and bone weariness in standing up to the rigors of responsibility to help others.

53. He provided the means for us to travel to Aberdeen, Scotland for me to sharpen myself via Ph. D studies in New Testament under one of the most respected British scholars, I. Howard Marshall.

54. He gave me the cordial favor of this leading New Testament scholar so that I could meet his exacting standards on my dissertation. He pleased Dr. Marshall so that he could okay each chapter without any delay.

55. He gave us dear friends in Scotland, and the grace to say "goodbye" when the tearful time came to leave and never see most of them again "'til we meet at Jesus' feet."

56. He supplied all we needed in Scotland (Phil. 4:19)—stamina for the long vigils, rides, assists in countless ways, protection of Mildred's health, spiritual refreshment with like-minded believers, etc.

57. He opened many privileges for me to speak in Scotland.

58. He sent many gifts of support even from unexpected sources when we were in Scotland. How faithful the supply of the God who opened a rock in the wilderness and sent waters gushing out.

59. He graced us by the richness of sitting under the preaching of a mighty man of the Word in Aberdeen's Gilcomston South Church of Scotland. He was our beloved William Still.

60. He opened up a special scholarship at Aberdeen once my supervisor felt my research met his high expectations.

61. He gave me the opportunity to attend what was then an "on fire" prayer meeting at Gilcomston South.

62. He gave us happy tours of Scotland, and an extended excursion to Shakespeare country and to London—joyous family memories.

63. He gave us precious friends in many countries. I have mentioned some of these earlier, and various lady friends of Mildred who wrote tributes to her in Chapters 28-32.

64. He bequeathed us the wealth of His Word, and His Spirit leading us to bear eternal "fruit." I am utterly convinced God will appraise Mildred's as greater than mine. Thanks be to God for sweet fellowship with many close by, and many who have gone to the ends of the earth to take the light of Christ and let His saving grace shine into hearts (2 Cor. 4:6).

65. He led our daughters to courtships and marriages with wonderfully fine men who are dear sons to us—Caleb, husband of Dianne, and Randy, husband of Carolyn. In these unions, He answered many a prayer.

66. He rewarded us with two grandsons, Zachary and Benjamin, in Carolyn's home that is built on the Rock. These lads were the joy of "Grammy" in frequent "baby-sitting," later "boy sitting," then Zachary's piano recitals and Benjamin's baseball games.

67. He gave Mildred the energy, when she enjoyed brief relief from harder breathing trials, to do kind things for others. Hers was a legacy of countless loving deeds (Eph. 6:8). This was whether in making sweaters, or giving away flowers, or writing cheering cards, or taking people places, or preparing food for people in need, or giving to boost people in the throes of difficult trials.

68. He gave Mildred numerous precious times ministering in her motherly care to Dianne and Carolyn. For example the three shared a tradition of happy shopping when a birthday came along, Mildred in her mechanical battery-run cart.

69. He has given our daughters, sons in law, and me, a mutually encouraging, very close heart bond since Mildred's home going.

70. He has supplied His sufficiency (2 Cor. 12:7-9) to the daughters, sons in law, grandsons, and me to cope with the indescribably difficult trial of losing Mildred, our greatest close-up example of Christ like life, our very dear one.

71. He gave Mildred a receptive heart for His Word, enlivening times in its treasures, and a ministry of serious prayer at God's throne for others.

72. He gave Mildred class, composure, charming ways, and finesse to walk with dignity in any situation or group, and be confident, cheerful, and at peace. How He did this with her breathing problems points to the incredible!

73. He gave her the ability to drive very safely. In latter years, when we went places, she almost always wanted to drive, so I had a "chauffeur." She liked the grip of the wheel, and it helped keep her mind off her struggle to

breathe. The portable oxygen tank sat behind her front seat, and a tube was a "life line" to where she sat.

74. He helped Mildred by always causing the oxygen company we had contacted ahead of longer trips to deliver a huge tank at lodgings where we were to stay. At times the company "kept us on pins and needles" by not showing up for hours. I became alarmed in her desperation for oxygen help, but the God who cares when our hearts are tried always brought the truck "in the nick of time" (Gen. 22:11-12; Heb. 4:16).

75. He graced me, to His praise, with a "true grit" patience to bear flexibly with the adjustments due to Mildred's illnesses and limited strength. I thank Him for concern, empathy, and sensitivity that came from His heart to help me to "take things in stride," be there at my loved one's side, "dig in," think of ways to be considerate, and do what I could to lighten her ordeals. Yes, the praise belongs to Him, and Him alone!

76. He gave Mildred a loving sweetness to be understanding toward me in my studies that were crucial to be ready for classes. He worked in her a true commitment to special urgencies of service. He seems to have prepared her by her own Bible institute rigors to grasp pressures and pleasantly offer her heart as a living sacrifice (Rom. 12:1). This blessed others for Christ's sake, with eternity's values in view. As one word, "others," could sum up the servant life of Jesus Christ, so it was a fitting banner over Mildred's.

77. He dealt to me a capacity He honed to devote detailed study to Bible passages so that I might explain them, and help on hard questions. In this, He enhanced the usefulness to give help to others in ministry.

78. He gave us a home where peace was a blessing (John 16:33; Phil. 4:7).

79. He provided, via Mildred's skill on organ and piano, frequent, lovely, and touching music that fragranced the home. The melodies often were catalysts to tone our hearts to draw nearer to God (Heb. 10:22).

80. He put in Mildred's servant heart joyous surprises to delight me in homecoming welcomes when I arrived back from trips.

81. He gave Mildred wisdom to counsel other ladies with practical help.

82. He helped me counsel hundreds who sought me out in person, via letter,

email, or in my office, or the study at home, on the phone, during trips, on walks, or other venues.

83. He gave Mildred a skill to be a hostess to bless guests and prepare for special parties, as for our wider family, students, ladies from the church or seminaries. She loved the "Old Country Rose" china that was my gift to her in Scotland, which we often enjoyed back in the States, and which Mildred bequeathed late in life to daughter Carolyn.

84. He helped us "tunnel through" or hurdle difficult times when something went wrong at home and I did not know how to fix it. He provided some "Johnny on the spot" who knew. We are grateful to Him and to those who came to our aid.

85. He gave us, in 1990, a large addition behind our home to be my study, adequate to house my three desks, three large files, the books, western paintings, mementos, and a big display board filled with cherished photos of students and their wives.

86. He gave us, in later years, many refreshing "patio breaks" tuning in to birds' songs, delighting in Mildred's flowers, and warming to fellowship of kindred hearts.

87. He enabled me to teach many series to church classes of various ages in Dallas, California, and Scotland. In these He gave us joys of seeing dear people change as the Spirit put His Word in them as the key to values.

88. He gave both of us innumerable privileges to counsel others in the church. Many visited our home over the years. On one occasion three young men I never had had as students phoned on a Sunday afternoon, in need of counsel for crucial decisions. Before they arrived I became very sick at my stomach. To God's praise He braced me to give counsel and stay "on an even keel" despite being so very miserable that it seemed like a miracle, not just Gary Cooper "High Noon" grit, to last through the session (Ps. 138:3).

89. He led people to give me books, or hand us gift cards to this or that, invite us to their homes, or take us to Angel games. Mildred liked to listen to Angel baseball, or watch the play on TV. In some degree this, meditating in the Bible, radio, music, work in her flower beds, or driving took her mind

off her hurting from the breathing struggles.

90. He always supplied so that we could pay our bills and have a good testimony (Phil. 4:19).

91. He gave Mildred a very sharp ability to keep careful records and stay on top of our business matters while ministering to many kept me busy.

92. He put it in Mildred's thoughts to be filing things constantly. After her going to heaven, I exulted in finding folders tucked away that I had not known about, a gold mine of letters, receipts, certificates, news clippings about family members, ABI history, things about both of us that she had treasured and kept, etc.

93. He gave us frequent blessed times in prayer when reports came of people's needs. Many were His answers, to the relief of others and praise to Him.

94. He gave us a happy courtship during college, and an exultant marriage in a friendship of between 53-54 years. Despite Mildred's precarious illness, we lived in the shadow of the Almighty (Ps. 91:1), abiding safely under His wings (v. 4), as people of very high privilege.

95. He put in our hearts the bright hope of being reunited in heaven and spending all eternity in fellowship with Him and all the redeemed.

96. He supplied many timely truths out of His Word to strengthen us for facing difficult trials and saying as the song says, "Jesus, I am resting, resting in the joy of what Thou art." Both of us went through several Bibles, and much in our Bibles went through us! Countless verses dealt their uplift, at different times, God helping when we needed Him most.

97. He gave us weekly a happy Friday night as "our night out."

98. He was rich in affording good times with our daughters when they were growing up—in devotional times, at church, on trips, excursions to zoos, animal farms, "goofy golf," frolics at parks, times at ice cream parlors, Disneyland, Knotts Berry Farm, tours through Scotland, etc.

99. He put in our hearts to find gifts for one another on birthdays, anniversaries, Christmas times, and other joyous days. We so often sought excuses to celebrate whatever sprang to mind.

100. He gave us blessings of uplift from the many cards that family and friends sent to cheer us on all sorts of special days.

101. He conferred on us surprise gifts. For example, a couple showed up at our door one night unexpectedly from out of state. They handed us a money gift they figured rightly was just enough to buy a filter system to purify the air as a help to Mildred's breathing. Many brought suppers, or Christmas candies, pictures, banners with Christian mottos, etc. We who received so much learned better to give from our own hearts.

102. He gave us the privilege of supporting several missionaries and other Christian workers. The money is His who gave it (1 Cor. 4:7), and we His stewards. We found that when we gave "hilariously" (2 Cor. 9:8), He never let us come up short, but prospered us with more—always. For He is El Shaddai, "the God who is enough" (Gen. 17:1). He also helped us deal with the sorrows of not having the money to give to many others in need. A tonic in this was that, for these, we could pray to the God of all supply, the God who answers (Jer. 33:3; Phil. 4:19)!

103. He gave us a long marriage, even though Mildred's perilous problems took her to the hospital many times. Our hearts very often feared whether she could survive. We were incredibly rich due to His delivering kindnesses. Oh, blessed God of the many rescues! How we praise you!

104. He kept us free of things that could hurt our lives, such as quarrels, drugs, bondage to strong drinks, indiscretion with the opposite sex, adultery, cursing, running up heavy credit card debts, getting carried away with cravings to have material things, reckless driving, getting into court squabbles, being victims of scams, having cancer, etc.

105. He gave me a child's ability to fall asleep easily when it was time at night and get my rest. In early days of teaching at Talbot, however, the double load made it impossible to take the time to prepare, yet get anything close to a normal span of sleep. God gave strength for the all-nighters and the nights with only two or three hours to rest. I thought of Paul's experiences (2 Cor. 6:4-10; 11:23-28), and realized my burdens were so very much lighter. I also thank Him for making me durable, tough, able to hold up to long vigils when necessary, and renewing my youth like the eagle's (Ps. 103:5).

106. He gave me vigorous health to be the "bread winner" and to do special

things that helped us, which Mildred's health did not allow. But I was often standing by in awe at astounding things God helped her do, and with her sweet spirit, even with her bodily strength so depleted.

107. He kept us optimistic by His cheering grace (John 16:33; Phil. 4:1-8).

108. He supplied furniture, in some cases as gifts. One example is the Dave and Bobbie Ifland family lavishing upon us baby beds and related items. Dave in earlier years ran a baby furniture business.

109. He prospered me in classes even when I did not know the answers to questions with which students surprised me. And he gave the humility to admit I did not know, and the wisdom to say I would study and get back to the person or the entire class for Christ's sake.

110. He crafted into my life in early years some ability in writing. This stood me in good stead on exams, papers, supervising theses, evaluating student papers, writing books and articles and letters, answering questions via email, etc. How faithful was His preparation before I ever could know for what God was outfitting me.

111. He supplied us with many different kinds of assists in our two-year doctoral stint in Scotland. One couple joyously insisted we use their car on trips. A man, Albert Rogers, volunteered to print copies of my dissertation as his gift. My supervisor cleared a scholarship for me. A lady drove Mildred to a food warehouse. Families came to take our daughters to parties with friends. On and on were God's blessings in watching over us.

112. He supplied countless other things we needed when we were so far from home in Scotland—such as putting it on hearts to write us letters of good cheer, and a friend taking care of our home in California.

113. He gave us the kindness of Philip and Iris Chan of Pasadena in their making the "Bethel" cabin at Big Bear available often as a haven for our family. The spacious getaway was a sweet respite from the pressing duties, answering phone calls, and the breathing battles.

114. He helped me get some books published—on *Abiding in Christ* (John 15), *Commentaries for Biblical Expositors,* and *An Exposition of Prayer in the Bible,* 5 vols.

115. He blessed me in getting three western cowboy novels I wrote published. This was the fruition of a western writing interest since the sixth grade. And he gave safety in special trips where I learned much local color about actual places of my novels so as to be accurate.

116. He gave me much enjoyment in leisure hours of reading fast-moving and gripping plots in Louis L'Amour's western novels.

117. He gave me, via a gift from my Friday "Lunch Bunch" buddies of La Mirada, CA, an all-day seminar hearing L'Amour at the University of Riverside campus. He also opened up a 45-minute chat with L'Amour at his invitation to his table (just three people) at a Holiday Inn Coffee Shop, and also nearly an hour with him at a Dalton Book Shop. He also moved L'Amour to write a cordial, full-page letter to me in reply to my sending him one of my novels and thanking him for what he had taught me about writing fast-moving, vivid westerns.

118. He gave me the privilege of writing a number of articles for *The Master's Seminary Journal*, and one for the *Grace Theological Journal*.

119. He enabled us to go to several Rosscup family reunions in California and Arizona. He strengthened Mildred in some degree to have the joy of joining in these.

120. When Mildred had breathing crises on trips, He always supplied safety when we needed to fly her home, and friends to meet her at the airports.

121. He gave us the boosts of many intercessors calling on God to help Mildred in her breathing and me in teaching. I made calls for prayer a regular thing in classes and in emails throughout the world, and many faculty families, students, alumni, and other friends went to the throne of grace for us. "S.O.S." calls have gone up for us in many lands.

122. He caused some of our appliances to have long lives, which saved us money.

123. He gave dear Mildred the love, taste, techniques, and good touches to keep a welcoming home, and even surges of strength to put up wall paper we enjoyed.

124. He placed gracious administrators over us in schools where we attended, or where I have taught.

125. He gave us faithful, cordial fellow faculty members and their wives as friends dear to our hearts.

126. He gave us many friends among students and alumni who continued to tell us—and now me—of their love. How precious would be the privilege of naming and rejoicing about each of these and, where married, their wives!

127. He led several men to be our faithful pastors in our local church—most notably Bob Warren (1954–57; 1972–1978), J. Vernon McGee (1966–1972); Ed Murphy (interim, 1979–1980), Richard Rigsby (mid-1980's), and John Ploog (1990–). And in Dallas we sat under the long-time faithful pastor, Harlin J. Roper at Scofield Memorial Church, and also heard soul-touching messages from Southland Keswick speakers there such as the expositor Stephen Olford of New York City. In days I sat in Dallas Seminary and Talbot Seminary chapels, I heard some of God's finest speakers, and this continues at The Master's Seminary. I have mentioned earlier our dear pastor in Scotland, Willie Still.

128. He has given us certain kind neighbors who have been of great help at times, and us the privilege of helping folk on our block.

129. He has kept our computers from crashing, and caused our printers to keep on keeping on.

130. He has caused our injuries or aches and pains to pass, or supplied sufficiency in them. For example, in Mildred's later years God kindly eased her through weaknesses of her foot bones, hip pain, and Shingles. In my own case, He supplied many sessions of therapy that eased horrific neck pain after a woman failed to stop and caused a five-car smash that included a harsh, stunning whack on my car.

131. He has helped our two daughters and their husbands walk with Him and maintain high moral standards.

132. He has kept our daughters' and sons in laws' jobs intact, and helped them show good expertise.

133. He has given our two grandsons fine success, Zachary (14) in playing the piano, and Benjamin (13) in nailing down first base in Little League seasons, as well as developing his guitar strumming.

134. He has kept me in seminary teaching, whether full-time for 40 years or part-time into the fifth year so far since 2005.

135. He has given me strong eyes for the enormous toll of reading that my work and the love of learning require. How gracious of God that He gave me a kindly optometrist my first year at Dallas Seminary to help my eyes when the heavy strain put me on the verge of being a "drop out."

136. He has given us many blessings in words from alumni about what our ministry to them has meant for their own Christian work (2 Tim. 2:1-2).

137. He has supplied sufficient grace to me and to our two daughters and their families to deal spiritually with the inexpressible pains we have felt on this earthly side since "one glad morning" Mildred "flew away" to heaven (Ps. 90:10).

138. He also has dealt Mildred and us joy because she is with the Lord, at liberty from heaving to breathe, and at perfect ease. This rest from her labors (Rev. 14:11-12) is "very much better" (Phil. 1:23-25).

139. He has given us the promise, so sure, that we shall see loved ones who know Him when we also get to heaven. The song is so true, "When we all get to heaven, what a day of rejoicing that will be!"

140. He has fulfilled His Word to us in countless ways these many years. Gratitude exults that He has only begun what flows into eternity.

141. He has kept our minds and hearts committed to His Word as being true, and given us ways of defending it before others.

142. He gave us reports beyond number from my former students about what God was doing through them for His glory in many countries.

143. He has given His "yes" answers to several thousand prayer requests, many of these Mildred's, and many annual vols. of recorded entries in my own day by day prayer journals.

144. He gave us precious pets, such as the Alaskan Samoyed white dog, "Mindy" for 13 years, and many cats that were especially Mildred's joys.

145. He always led us to good mechanics who saw that our cars kept running.

One was beloved Don Carr, a student at The Master's Seminary, who had switched from an auto racing career in which he held, for years, the world land speed record.

146. He gave us the privilege of friendships with some of His finest godly leaders.

147. He inclined different people in the family to keep files that have made possible the authenticity of this book. He also gave us other records as noted in the "Credits for this Tribute" at the outset.

148. He allowed me to outlive Mildred and have the training and passion to write this, as well as the good health.

149. His permitting of Mildred to go to heaven first shielded her from being left without my help should God have taken me first.

150. He worked in His providence to cause our daughter Dianne and her husband Caleb to live with us while rooms are being added to their home. So Dianne was at here the morning Mildred fell unconscious, found her not responding, and got her to the hospital when I was away on my part-time, one day a week stint of seminary teaching.

151. He led me to switch from full-time teaching to a part time schedule ahead of Mildred's death so that we could have more time together (2005–2008). The extra time has been a God-send for writing this account, and before it finishing the 5-vol. exposition on prayer.

152. He kept both of us on track believing His Word, and safe from any denial of His truth that victimizes many scholars. They arrogantly fancy now that they are wise, but God will show them to be some of the world's biggest fools.

153. He gave us a triumphant "Memorial Service" four days after Mildred's going to be with the Lord.

154. He blessed us with joys from the testimonies of many godly students and a number of faithful wives. Daniel Wong is one student. His family was persecuted in China. Police invaded their home and beat a brother so badly he died a short time later. The family came to the U.S. and Daniel to Talbot where he was known for praying three hours a day no matter what the

pressures, and was diligent in studies. Later, Daniel earned his doctorate in 1995 at Dallas Seminary, putting together the most complete work ever done on the "overcomer" in the Book of Revelation.

In a short time it was my privilege to recommend Daniel to The Master's College, where more than 70 applied for a position teaching Bible. The choice finally focused to this man of God. Just about every month Daniel has contacted me to see how he might pray in an "up to date" relevancy for Mildred and me. Now after her transfer to heaven, he intercedes for me.

This tribute is not yet finished. Let us here erect a sign that says:

Blessings To be Continued—for All Eternity
(Ps. 145:1-2; Eph. 2:4-6)!

The Final Tribute

Mildred's headstone, located in Rose Hills Cemetery, Whittier, CA.

"A Marker on Earth for One Who is in Heaven, Until We Meet at Jesus' Feet." – Jim Rosscup (2010)

Jim joined his beloved Mildred in heaven in 2020.

www.ingramcontent.com/pod-product-compliance
Lightning Source LLC
Chambersburg PA
CBHW070913120626
46546CB00001B/247